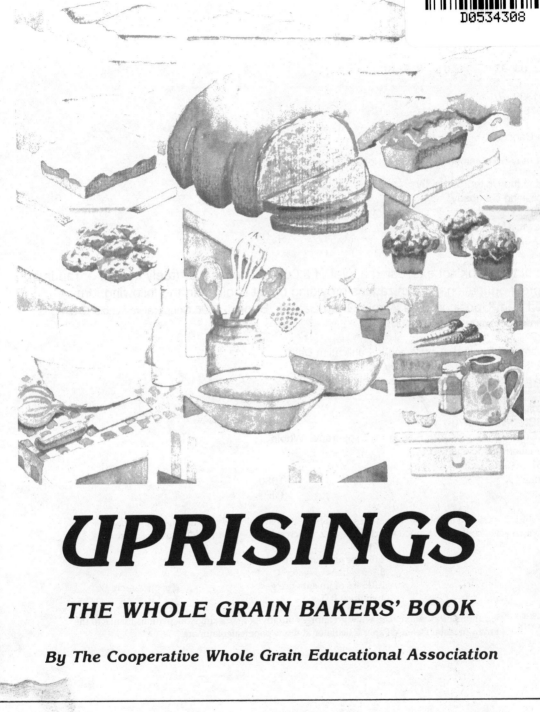

UPRISINGS

THE WHOLE GRAIN BAKERS' BOOK

By The Cooperative Whole Grain Educational Association

THE BOOK PUBLISHING COMPANY

SUMMERTOWN, TENNESSEE

Cover art by Karen Kerney

Design by Eleanor Dale Evans

First Edition Published 1983
Revised Edition ©1990 Cooperative Whole Grain Educational Association

11 10 09 08 07   5 6 7 8 9 10

ISBN 0-913990-70-1
ISBN13 978-0-913990-70-4

Printed in Canada

This book may be obtained through your local co-op or bookstore.

Published in the United States by
Book Publishing Company
PO Box 99
Summertown, TN 38483
1-888-260-8458

        Library of Congress Cataloging-in-Publication Data
Uprisings: the whole grain bakers' book/ edited by
Cooperative Whole Grain Education Association
            p. cm.
    includes index.
    ISBN 0-913990-70-1
    1.Cookery (cereals) 2. Baking. I Cooperative Whole
Grain Education Association (U.S.)
TX808.U67   1990
641.6'31-dc20   90-1030
                                     CIP

The Book Publishing Co. is a member of Green Press Initiative. We have elected to print this title on paper with
postconsumer recycled content and processed chlorine free, which saved the following natural resources:

                        23 trees
                        1,074 lbs of solid waste
                        8,365 gallons of water
                        2,015 lbs of greenhouse gases
                        16 million BTUs

BOOK
PUBLISHING   For more information visit: www.greenpressinitiative.org. Savings calculations thanks to the
COMPANY   Environmental Defense Paper Calculator at www.papercalculator.org

Foreword

Welcome to **Uprisings**, the whole grain bakers' book. **Uprisings** has been collectively compiled by experienced bakers from many small independent bakeries. It draws its inspiration from a number of uprisings—of grain, of bread, and of people. The most basic of these is the grain growing from the earth, nourished by the rain and sun. Wheat, rye, corn, barley, buckwheat, millet, rice—these are the fundamental ingredients of whole grain baked goods. Bakers, with a little help from yeast and other leaveners, create another uprising, as dough rises to produce fresh-baked loaves, filling our senses. The third uprising is the cooperative ethic of the bakeries we work in. There are no bosses, no employees. Instead, we all do the work together, sharing the responsibilities and the rewards. Our businesses put priority on serving the needs of the community, not on making profits for a select few.

In this revised edition of **Uprisings** you may find new information and new recipes as well as many old favorites. A conscious choice has been made to focus specifically on collectively run bakeries, therefore some bakeries which were present in the last edition have been omitted here. The whole grain, collective movement has evolved and changed as every living organism changes. We see a refreshing new focus on healthy living. New information on organics and bioregionalism have been a source of change in our ingredients, and we look forward to even more growth.

We think it's a great loss that so many of us are unfamiliar with these uprisings. Few people enjoy the delights of eating fresh whole grain bread, let alone the experience of making it themselves. It's also a loss that so few people have the satisfaction of helping to run their own workplace, doing interesting work that meets real needs. Cooperative whole grain bakeries are part of a rising tide of people taking more responsibility for what goes on in their lives. We want more and more of us to regain power over our food, our work, our health and well-being—in short, our personal, social, and economic existence. To achieve this, we heartily encourage these and other kinds of uprisings in all areas of our lives.

Cooperative Whole Grain Educational Association

The CWGEA was organized in the United States in 1978 to bring our far-flung members closer together. Incorporated in 1983 as a non-profit corporation exclusively for educational and charitable purposes, its Articles of Incorporation are these:

1. To provide education for members, including regular newsletters and conferences.
2. To foster good health by supporting nutritional awareness through education, including conducting nutritional education in public schools and other institutions.
3. To support international harmony among our members through education and meetings.
4. To insure that no part of the net earnings of the Corporation shall inure to the benefit of any member or individual.
5. To insure that this association is open to all people regardless of race, color, creed, sex, age or national origin.

The CWGEA has begun building networks to make information, resources, and raw materials available to cooperatively run whole grain bakeries across North America. Regional coordinators have been set up, and a newsletter is published. Every summer, a conference is organized by members, with workshops, guest instructors, recipe exchanges, and extensive informal discussions. Members travel great distances for the week-long gathering in a park location, to share, to enjoy, and to be recharged with collective energy.

The CWGEA (originally entitled the Whole Grain Collective Bakers International) has had an international perspective from the start, with contacts in Canada, South America and Europe. We feel it's especially important to share across national boundaries, increasing our knowledge of techniques and of grains other than wheat, and bringing to all people the consciousness of whole foods, self-reliance, and working cooperatively. Our food system now functions globally, and hence it is important that an awareness of its nature and of the alternatives be spread across the world.

CWGEA
c/o Amazing Grains
901 Mississippi
Lawrence, KS 66044

How Uprisings Was Put Together

Uprisings I

During the course of the CWGEA conference in the summer of 1980, the various representatives concluded that the ideas and energies of the association needed a direction. This new direction culminated in the production of a cookbook, reflecting the cooperative effort to collect recipes from members of the organization.

It took over two years and countless volunteer hours of baking and taste-testing to bring **Uprising I** to the point of publication. Some recipes were selected for innovativeness, some for special dietary consideration, some for the simply luscious flavor they provided. It was a long and arduous process, but the final result was a baking book dedicated to whole grain baking that would be easily accomplished in anyone's home.

Bakeries that submitted final recipes lent a homespun flavor to the book by supplying the publisher with handwritten and illustrated texts. Working collectively, diverse bakeries from all parts of the country contributed their specific recipes and philosophies. The whole was greater than the sum of its parts because of the unity of purpose and goals shared by the member bakeries of the CWGEA.

Uprising II

A second edition followed, along with a new publisher, in 1985. Changes were few, a new cover being the most evident.

Uprising III

Then came the summer of 1989 and the annual CWGEA conference. The second publisher had informed the CWGEA that it was about to discontinue distribution of **Uprisings**. The publishing rights were up for grabs. The associated bakeries took the opportunity to obtain those rights and subsequently find another publisher. This done, a new edition, the third, was planned.

This book is the fruit of that planning, nurtured with many hours of work and many helping hands. The precepts of the original book have not been changed. Whole grain recipes contributed by collectively run bakeries from around the country have been compiled to bring the reader tried and tested methods and ingredients.

All of us who helped create this baking book wish all of those who use it the best results and hearty enjoyment of those results. We hope these recipes inspire you to innovate and create on your own. If you ever wish to contact us, whether to discuss a specific recipe or to start another whole grain bakery, please do so.

Above all, happy baking.

Taste Real Bread Again!

Contents

8

Introduction–What's In Uprisings

The focus of **Uprisings** is three-fold: presenting whole grain recipes, discussing the use of ingredients used in these recipes, and providing information on cooperative work places. In these pages you'll find over two hundred recipes, created by past and present bakers in eighteen whole grain bakeries. Many of these recipes represent the bakeries' most popular and inspired products, made lovingly time and time again to satisfy hungry customers; they come recommended to you by steadfast bands of bakery connoisseurs across the country. Every recipe in **Uprisings** has been reduced to homesize batches. To be sure the scaling-down process worked, each recipe has been made by a professional baker and taste-tested by a group who rated it, rejecting and retesting when necessary. Most of the comments with the recipes were taken from volunteer tasters.

For several reasons, our recipes are especially good for making at home. Because the bakeries are generally small, with few machines, techniques developed in them are easily transferable to home kitchens. The structure of the bakeries encourages experimentation and innovation, so you'll find many new and creative ideas. Our bakeries always have to ask the question, "Can we make this bread or cookie relatively easily, often, and cheaply, and have it come out good most of the time?" So simplicity and consistency are very important, and that's also good for home bakers.

The baking here isn't hard. Most "goodie" recipes can be boiled down to: mix wet ingredients; mix dry ingredients; combine them; bake. Even bread, despite rumors to the contrary, is neither difficult nor complicated. By following a few simple steps, we help along an ancient process which continues to yield that wonderful reward for bakers and friends—fresh, hot bread! Almost all of us working in bakeries were at one time intimidated by the mysteries of that unknown—making bread. We continue to learn more about bread each time we bake, and we have found the rewards are well worth the time and patience spent experimenting with doughs. Baking can be very basic and simple, an art we can all participate in.

Suggestions on how to bake, and what tools and ingredients to use, are here to help you if you need it. You'll also find discussions of the reasons for using whole grains, and of the benefits of working cooperatively. The last few pages of the cookbook contain a reference and resource section which can be quite useful in investigating further into baking and the politics of food. These topics are linked to many important issues discussed later in the book. Our concern about these issues keeps our work stimulating and rewarding.

Recipes are grouped according to their bakery of origin and preceded by an introduction written by the local bakers—often a simple account of the bakery, sometimes a poem, sometimes a polemic. Whenever possible, bread labels and bakery logos are used as illustrations. For easy reference, there is a comprehensive alphabetical index at the end, as well as listings of recipes by type of baked good, special dietary characteristic, and major ingredients.

We present recipes bakery by bakery to give a feel for the character and integrity of each one, for each is very different. If you find yourself drawn to the individuality of a particular bakery, consult the map and list of bakery addresses on pgs. 62-3. so you can stop by if you're in the area. Most bakeries welcome people to come visit and learn about whole grain baking. The chances are they'll be baking your favorite bread or cookie, as well as other inspired creations that couldn't be squeezed into **Uprisings**. Our bakeries rely on the interest and support of people who prefer fresh, nutritious food produced by workers who care about each other, their products and their communities.

Member bakeries in the CWGEA share in the belief that education is the tool and means of changing the world toward a more positive and healthy lifestyle. We recognize not only the importance of offering whole grain baked goods to our community, but also the importance of educating people and empowering them to make a positive change in their lives and health.

Whole Grains–It's Living

There are many reasons for preferring whole grains, and whole foods in general, to white flour and other processed foods. There's how the food tastes, what it does to you, what it implies about the food distribution system, and what it says about the state of the "food industry"—its practices, priorities, and philosophy. The absence of whole grains in most of our readily available food is a grim illustration of the decline in the quality of our diet, and hence the quality of our lives.

Whole Grains–
Some Basic Information

Most of this discussion focuses on wheat, since wheat is far and away the dominant grain in our lives. Much of what is said, however, can be applied to other grains. The wheat (or rye, or rice) berry is the fruit of the mature plant, and contains the seed of a new plant. When the dry berries are ground, whole wheat flour, light brown and grainy, is produced. This is what we use in our bakeries and in **Uprisings**.

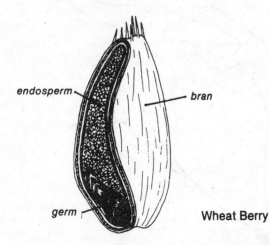

endosperm — bran

germ — Wheat Berry

Refining the ground berries into white flour involves sifting out the denser, darker particle to obtain a whiter, more powdery and silky-textured product. What gets removed during refining are the bran and the germ of the wheat kernel. The bran, the outer layers of the wheat berry, contains carbohydrates, proteins, vitamins, minerals—especially iron—and fiber. The germ contains a high concentration of vitamin E, B vitamins, iron and other minerals, polyunsaturated fats, proteins, fiber and carbohydrates. The germ is actually the embryo of the new life that would grow if the seed were germinated, and, appropriately, the nutritional riches are concentrated here.

What is left in white flour is ground-up endosperm, predominantly starch, with a modest amount of protein in the form of gluten and cellulose walls. The endosperm is a high carbohydrate food supply for the growing germ at the beginning of its life, and is low in nutrients. Therefore, white flour is devoid of **over half** the nutrients available in the wheat berry. A comparison of the nutritional content of whole wheat and white flour reveals dramatic reductions in all vital elements.

Not only are these losses measurable numerically as depletion of nutrients, they also register as loss of flavor. As anyone who has savored its rich nuttiness will attest, whole wheat can stand on its own and doesn't have to be "doctored" (with sugar, salt and other flavors) to ensure a full-bodied taste. Like other whole foods, in contrast to their refined versions, whole wheat satisfies both our nutritional needs and our taste buds.

Whole Grains and Health

The removal of most nutrients and almost all fiber from grains creates a severely imbalanced product, which taxes the body during digestion and assimilation. Nutrients from both the bran and germ are needed by the body in order to metabolize carbohydrate contained in the endosperm. When the pulverized endosperm is eaten alone, nutrients must be pulled from the body tissues as metabolism proceeds. This also occurs when other refined carbohydrates, such as white rice and white sugar, are eaten. They drain, rather than nourish, our bodies.

Composition of Various Wheat Products, *per 100 grams, edible portion*

	Calories	Protein g	Fat g	Carbohydrate g	Fiber g	Ash g	Calcium mg	Phosphorus mg	Iron mg	Sodium mg	Potassium mg	Thiamine mg	Riboflavin mg	Niacin mg
WHOLE WHEAT FLOUR	333	13.3	2.0	71.0	2.3	1.7	41	372	3.3	3	370	.55	.12	4.3
WHITE FLOUR (UNENRICHED)	365	11.8	1.1	74.7	.3	.4	16	95	.9	2	95	.08	.06	1.0
WHEAT GERM	363	26.6	10.9	46.7	2.5	4.3	72	1118	9.4	3	827	2.01	.68	4.2
WHEAT BRAN	213	16.0	4.6	61.9	9.1	6.0	119	1276	14.9	9	1121	.72	.35	21.0

Source: USDA, *Handbook of the Nutritional Contents of Foods*, Table 1.
The figures given are for hard whole wheat flour, unenriched white bread flour, and crude, commercially milled wheat germ and bran

What is more, without natural fiber, refined foods clog the intestines. Remember what great play-glue white flour and water make? Refined grains interfere with functioning of the colon, particularly peristaltic action which keeps everything moving right along and propels wastes from the body. The intestinal muscles literally can't get a grip on the gummy paste, and some of it remains to coat and clog the surface and minute folds of the colon. It takes about thirty hours for whole grain bread to move through the intestine, while it takes approximately eighty hours to digest white bread.

White flour and white flour products, in constipating the bowels, are responsible for much ill health. Stagnation of wastes in the digestive tract leads to development of unhealthy microorganisms that cause discomfort and disease. In particular, carcinogenic secretions can develop; hence the strong connection between refined carbohydrate intake and cancers of the colon and rectum, now leading killers among the "diseases of civilization." Moreover, many experts believe that changes in intestinal rhythm have a direct effect on blood flow, which can lead to varicose veins, hemorrhoids, pulmonary embolism, coronaries and so on—all again related to a diet of white bread and other refined foods.

Changes in the American diet during this century have been directly linked to changing patterns of disease. A rise in major degenerative diseases has been directly related to a decrease in complex carbohydrate consumption and increases in fat and refined sugar intake. Whole grains and whole grain products used to be the major source of calories and protein in the American diet—almost 40% of each in 1910. Today's consumption of grains is less than half what it was then. More importantly, almost all of the grain eaten in the United States today, including our flours, breads and cereals, is heavily refined—a sharp contrast to earlier in our history. There is no longer any doubt that such rapid changes in eating patterns are directly related to dramatic increases in the incidence of chronic degenerative diseases. We have reached the point where the majority of Americans (including a significant proportion of young people) are afflicted with chronic disease. Similar dietary trends in other advanced countries are rapidly producing a similar deterioration in their population's health. We are literally eating ourselves to death.

Our Diet-Wholeness is Natural

As we've become more and more "civilized," we've forgotten that we are indeed living organisms like the other species on this planet. A comparison of our physiological make-up with that of other animals shows we all share similar growth patterns. We also share similar needs for elements in our diets to ensure proper health, physical maintenance, and energy supply. Animals, other than humans and their domestic pets, live on a range of unadulterated whole foods, each species having its appropriate diet and eating only what it needs. Animals usually live six times the length of their age of maturity, and die from any of five to ten diseases. Human beings, on the other hand, consider anything we can create from our environment—**anything**—fine for shoveling down our throats. And we live only three to four times our age of maturity, much of that time being spent gradually dying from over two hundred and fifty diseases. We're rapidly inventing new illnesses to die from, too, at a speed that parallels the degeneration of our food supply.

Whole foods are natural. We are natural beings, though we seem so far from it in our modern way of life. Our digestive system— almost identical to that of our close relatives, the vegetarian apes— has changed little over thousands of generations. We still need a diet as close to natural as possible, or else we invite inevitable impairment of our wellbeing—physical, mental, and spiritual.

Nature isn't just "the rest of the world" (we've already heard too much about "Man and Nature," especially about "Man's Dominion Over Nature"). Nature is the aggregate of all living things, on this planet and beyond. Like it or not, the human species (and that includes both sexes) is a part of nature. And we are at our strongest and happiest when our lives harmonize and are in balance with the natural world. In nature, balance is the prevailing aim of all energy. Human beings have lost sight of the ways to achieve both inner and outer balance, and have forgotten its rewards. But we can rediscover both. We need to start by tuning in to our physical selves and surroundings, becoming aware of all the distress we cause by imbalances in our diet and style of living, and the abuse of our environment. We should recognize the benefits of exercise and good food, work that is pleasurable and unstressful, loving relationships, and responsible management of the environment. By doing this, we will be able to discover our real needs, and satisfy them by drawing responsibly from natural resources, respecting their integrity and the overall balance of which they, and we, are a part. Only then do we know the feeling of being integrated with the living world, and that brings rewards which are hard to imagine until we experience them.

Bread and Survival

Connect with bread. Feel it and get to know it. It's interesting—you can't exactly predict what it will do next. Bread dough grows, overflows, flattens, and comes creeping back again. It's fun to handle. Without fail, children enjoy working with bread dough—they know a good time when they see it! It's uniquely satisfying to wrap your fingers around some dough and get into it with your wrists, shoulders, back, and mind.

Breadmaking is typical of those activities which are basic, pleasurable, and a part of doing things for yourself. It combines physical and mental activity in a task that connects you to living things and yields a useful end-product. What more satisfying work could there be? It used to be that life consisted of such purposeful and harmonious activities, providing one's needs through one's own creativity. For many people, mostly outside the "developed world," it still does. It is a more natural and truly civilized way of living your life. Let us re-experience the enjoyment of practicing these useful and rewarding survival skills, and regain confidence in our own resourcefulness and respect for the bounty of nature.

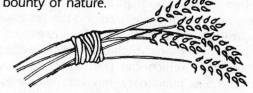

How We Got to This Point–
A Short History of Bread

For centuries, grain has been regarded as the staff of life. Prehistoric people collected wild grains and ate them just as they found them. With the coming of agriculture to the Fertile Crescent about 9,000 years ago, people began to experiment with the grains they harvested, roasting them over a fire or mixing them with water to form a porridge. A thicker paste, formed into cakes and dried in the sun, became the first loaves. Bread of this kind has been found preserved in Stone Age settlements. Baking the loaves on hot stones was the next step in history.

No one knows for certain who was the first to learn the secrets of fermenting dough—the Chinese or the Egyptians—but well-preserved loaves have been discovered in pyramids dating back 5,000 years. The Chinese style was to steam the bread, much as they do today, but it was the Egyptians who developed and perfected the craft of breadbaking. Their bakers used the yeast produced in brewing beer to ferment and leaven bread doughs, and breweries and bakeries came to be located side by side. It was a mystery to them how fermentation worked; they merely observed that when they baked fermented bread, something different happened. The necessity of baking this bread evenly and in quantity led to the invention of the first ovens. These were made with bricks of Nile clay, and resembled beehives.

Around 600 B.C., Phoenician sailors carried the Egyptian ideas and developments to Greece where they were refined into an art. The Greeks created many kinds of bread, and their bakers were considered important enough to stand for election as senators. The Greeks in turn passed on their taste for bread to the Romans.

The Romans developed breadmaking still further, with the invention of rotary milling stones. An upper stone revolved on a stationary lower stone as grain was fed through the axle. The resulting flour, made from barley, rye, millet, or wheat—all 100% whole grain—was leavened with brewer's barm, kneaded mechanically, and baked in clay ovens. At the time of Christ, Rome had an average of one mill-bakery for every 2,000 inhabitants.

Originally, milling and baking were twin arts practiced by the same person. The advent of water-mills, and later, windmills, led to the formation of two distinct crafts, and by 1,000 A.D. baking and milling were completely separated. Because people's lives depended on bread, the people who controlled its production were extremely powerful. Bakers and millers were among the richest people in any town.

For centuries, stone-ground whole grain flour formed the basis of the bread of both rich and poor. The bread of the poor was coarse, heavy, and brown. The bread of the rich was lighter and more refined, due to sifting techniques in which the ground meal was "bolted" through a silk cloth to remove the coarsest particles. White bread became a status symbol—the whiter the flour, the richer the household. Because of this, bakers used slaked lime, alum, and chalk to whiten flour until well into the eighteenth century—which at least tells us that additives for the sake of profits are not new!

In the 1870s, the invention of a new roller-milling process for flour put white bread within the reach of everybody, rich and poor alike. Roller mills crack the grains between sets of increasingly fine-grooved metal rollers, blowing off the particles of bran and germ in the process. By the end of the century, however, it was evident that people were suffering from this nutritionally deficient flour, and governments began to require the addition of some nutrients in synthetic form, to "enrich" or "fortify" the stripped white flour.

Today's bread market is dominated by the factory-made, wrapped, sliced loaf, the sad result of many years of research by technologists in the food industry. It is designed to have a perfect, light-textured, white crumb, excellent keeping qualities, and the right shape for toasters and sandwiches and stacking on supermarket shelves. To achieve this miracle of chemical engineering, forty to sixty additives are usually put into commercial loaves; over seven hundred chemicals may be used in baked goods. These include bleaching and improving agents, raising agents, enzyme active preparations, yeast stimulators, preservatives, emulsifiers, stabilizers, anti-oxidants, coloring agents, acids and dilutents. Some of the additives, such as lecithin (an anti-oxidant obtained from soybeans), caramel (a coloring for brown bread, made from burnt white sugar), and chalk (a dilutent for other additives), are "natural" substances. The remainder are chemicals, many of which have not been adequately tested, either alone or in combination. Some are believed dangerous, such BHT (Butylated Hydroxitoluene, an anti-oxidant), which was banned in Sweden and Australia in 1962 after tests showed considerable toxic effects. Quantities of sugar and salt are also added to today's commercial loaf, in an attempt to give the denuded and chemicalized product a semblance of taste to the desensitized palate of the typical processed food eater. The majority of additives to bread **do not have to be listed on the label**. You really have no way to find out what you're eating when you consume commercial white bread.

The same warnings must also be made about one of the recent trends in the baking industry— mass-produced "whole wheat" bread. The labels of such breads may reveal an even greater variety of sugars and additives than white breads, and frequently do not list everything contained in the product. Listing white flour as "wheat flour" is a common deception; only 100% whole wheat flour may be called "whole wheat." To avoid being misled and misfed, the clear alternative is to make your own bread, using simple and wholesome recipes like those in **Uprisings**, or to buy bread produced by conscientious, small, whole grain bakeries.

What's Happened in the "Food Industry"

At Home...

The fate of flour and bread is typical of the way things have been going in the food industry. In America, people now eat more processed than unprocessed food: 75% of Americans' food comes from factories, not farms. At an accelerating pace, products are becoming more refined and adulterated with chemical substances put in to enable cheap, large-scale mechanized production, long-distance shipping, and unnatural endurance capacity (otherwise known "shelf-life").

One reason for this trend is that the food industry is increasingly dominated and controlled by a small number of giant companies, themselves part of multinational corporations. These companies—it seems almost unnecessary to add—are guided solely by the profit motive, and there is much more profit in processed foods than there is in the unprocessed. Today's food chemists and technologists are meeting this purely economic challenge, in a market saturated with unneeded products, by concentrating on the development of totally artificial "non-foods." Another major development in this onslaught is increasing "vertical integration," in which a corporation controls the entire process of research, growing, transportation, processing, packaging, distribution, and even sale of a given product. By controlling each part of the process, more money is made and greater power is gained over the consumer.

In agriculture, there is a strong emphasis on larger and larger farms, high energy consumption, and manipulation of plant genetics. The biologically weakened, insect-prone hybrid strains require the artificial stimulation of chemical fertilizers (made from natural gas and petrochemicals) and frequent dousing with inorganic pesticides. The very basis of agriculture, the seed industry, has recently undergone many changes, with huge conglomerates that manufacture these pesticides and chemical fertilizers swallowing up independent seed companies. This trend, along with legislative and judicial decisions affecting the patenting of life forms, makes it possible to impose the domination of hybrid seeds, which cannot reliably reproduce themselves. In other words, the farmer and the gardener in practice **must buy new seeds each year**. This frightening control over the production of food is being vigorously pursued in both Europe and America, and if this trend continues, diversity may indeed disappear.

Organic growing, which is nothing more than the way farming used to be done before chemicals were introduced, recognizes the importance of

building the soil, rather than meddling with natural balances. There are many reasons to choose organically grown food, and our bakeries put a priority on using organic flour and other naturally grown ingredients whenever possible. For one thing, organic farming yields crops that are better in flavor and higher in all nutrients than commercially produced crops. (Chemical fertilization drastically reduces the optimum nutritional values of grains, especially vitamins, trace elements, and protein, while excess carbohydrate—starch and cellulose—develops instead.) For another, organic crops are free of poisonous chemicals, many of which have been used specifically to kill some form of life, which are used on commercial crops. What's more, the miserable end-product of agribusiness, when harvested, is often just at the beginning of a long, polluted journey to somebody's supermarket cart. Once it is taken from the ground, the industry really gets to work on it— heating, pulverizing, deodorizing, homogenizing, hydrogenating, and adding any number of the 3,000 food additives now in use.

With the food industry using over a billion pounds of chemicals a year, it's not surprising that the average American consumes five to ten pounds of additives yearly. Most of these have been inadequately tested or not tested at at all. It may seem like only a little per product, but five pounds is a lot of alien chemicals in an organism not equipped to cope with them. Furthermore, each year, this average eater consumes fifteen pounds of salt and one hundred and thirty pounds of sugar and other refined sweeteners. Salt and sugar may not be commonly thought of as "additives," but they are highly refined end-products, devoid of nutrition and damaging to health. They are added to give the illusion of taste to a devitalized product, and to satisfy the salt and sugar addictions that are started by our earliest consumption of baby foods and children's snacks.

Finally, as if all this weren't enough, buying commercial foods helps finance a massive propaganda campaign. Over $4 billion a year is spent on advertising by food manufacturers striving to gain the competitive edge over the other 10,000 products in the supermarket. Over $400 million worth of television ads are aimed each year at young children, and in one year a child sees about 10,000 ads for "food"—mostly candy, beverages, and cereals, loaded with sugar and artificial ingredients.

...And Abroad

The food situation on the home front is part of a depressing global picture. The West's—and in particular America's—high-meat, high- technology diet and methods of agriculture are responsible for hunger, disease, and social injustice among many of the world's populations. (This is thoroughly documented in *Diet for a Small Planet*, *Food First*, and other publications of the Institute for Food and Development Policy). The massive and unequal consumption of resources by America's food industry has been brought to people's attention in recent years by figures such as:

- Each American citizen consumes, on the average, 2000 pounds of grain yearly, compared to 400 pounds per person in poor countries (Americans consume most of theirs indirectly as meat and dairy products).
- One pound of steer sold as edible meat represents sixteen pounds of soy and grains—an energy wastage of more than 90%. Over 50% of the total harvested acreage in the U.S. (including 90% or more of corn, oats, barley, sorghum, and soybeans) is fed to livestock.
- In 1910, the American food system consumed less energy (in calories) than it produced as food calories; by 1970, it used nine calories of energy to produce each single calorie of food.
- For every unit of energy expended in on-farm production, three more units are used in processing and distributing thousands of food products.

Meanwhile, Western agribusiness has had a disastrous effect on the economies and political conditions in many Third World countries (see *Food First* for details of this role). It has disrupted local ecologies and created hunger in poorer nations by imposing a single export crop economy in the place of the diversified agriculture which previously grew the local food supply. In some places, a completely unfamiliar luxury crop, such as strawberries or asparagus, may be introduced, while in others, the numerous local varieties of a traditional crop are supplanted by a weak hybrid strain necessitating the use of chemical fertilizers and pesticides (including very toxic ones banned in the U.S. such as DDT). Gassing, bleaching, dyeing, spraying, and other chemical treatments follow harvesting, in order to store, preserve, and transport the crop. Most of this is done with complete disregard for workers' safety.

There are many aspects of the world food situation that we don't even touch on here. One, for example, is the domination of wheat in world grain consumption, a development encouraged by the big wheat brokers of North America to enlarge their market and their power. Increasingly, too, food manufacturers are boosting sales and profits by marketing their most processed products abroad.

Our global responsibility comes home to us in baking because there are several common ingredients produced only by agribusiness in Third World countries. Many bakeries have raised the question of whether or not to continue using products such as cashews, coconut, and bananas, all of which are treated with chemicals by native workers who have no protection from these questionable substances. As a matter of course, many of our bakeries have never used coffee, cocoa, and refined sugar—prime products of multinational agribusiness. We never recommend the use of these non-foods. As for the use of Third World crops in your own baking, you'll have to make those decisions yourself.

Whole Grains-For Life

Looking at the question of whole grains versus processed foods leads us to many issues, as we've seen in the preceding sections. Proceeding from taste, to health, to harmony with the environment, we finally reach national and global levels of concern and responsibility. As we begin to see our present food system for what it really is, it becomes more and more of a pleasure to detach from it. At the most basic level, despite a lifetime of conditioning about the great taste and superiority of processed, packaged foods such as white bread, an increasing number of people are realizing that the darn stuff doesn't even taste good or, somehow, make you feel too well.

Because of all this, many of us are gradually disengaging from the "big business" food industry. In its place, we are linking up with local networks of conscientious organic farmers, small independent mills, and suppliers such as cooperative warehouses and stores. These regional networks have begun to mesh across larger areas, even nationally, through coops and organizations like the Cooperative Whole Grain Educational Association. As this alternative system stresses involving and serving people rather than exploiting and making money from them, we begin to lose that feeling of being the powerless consumer dangling at the end of a long chain which exists only to make a profit for all of its links.

Because the issue of nutrition is inextricably tied to the economic and political aspects of whole grains, choosing whole grains is in itself a political statement. It is a rejection of the prevailing system of supplying food to make money, regardless of the damage to people and to the earth. Moreover, it is an assertion of concern for health and well-being, and of our place in society and nature. Let us recognize that we are living parts of an organic whole, and begin to be conscious of our responsibility to ourselves, to other people, and to the natural forces that are the driving energy of our world.

Cooperation–It's Working

Many people aren't at all sure what a cooperative is—it's not surprising in our competitive society that there are widespread misconceptions about doing things collectively. Yet cooperatives are a part of our history, spanning many areas of economic endeavor that include agriculture, housing, production, finance, and the distribution of goods and services. In recent years, cooperatives—enterprises organized and operated for mutual benefit—have enjoyed renewed interest. Coop food stores can now be found in most population centers and in many rural areas as well; they are usually open to everyone, whether or not a member.

Collectives, another term for cooperative enterprises or the people working in them, can vary considerably. Certainly there are many differences among our bakeries. But there are common principles we all share as collectives, and these are basic to their success and to the satisfaction of working in them.

Collectives as an Alternative

Most small businesses have an owner whose primary goal is personal profit. This owner hires people to work for wages. Everyone employed has a supervisor or boss, and that person probably has someone above them—and so on and so on, the complexity of the hierarchy depending on the size of the operation. The owner gets to shoulder both the burdens and the benefits of ownership, taking on the headaches and decision-making as well as taking home the extra money made by paying less in total expenses (rent, wages, ingredients, etc.) than comes in from sales—the profit.

In contrast, a typical collective has these features:

- All the work is shared among the people operating the business.
- No-one is anyone else's boss.
- Decisions in the running of the business are made by the whole group, by consensus decision-making. Problems or issues are worked on until a decision is made to which everyone can give their consent.
- In general, collective members are familiar with all, or most, aspects of the work and participate in them in varying degrees. Some collectives do rely more heavily on separation of tasks and specialization by workers, usually citing reasons of convenience and efficiency. But most collectives hold non-specialization as an ideal and all tasks are shared, sometimes being rotated over periods of months.

These characteristics offer benefits for both the enterprise and the individuals in it. For the business, it means increased versatility as well as freedom from purely managerial costs—since everyone who works also manages. For the individual, this all-round competence and total involvement helps remove the feeling of being alienated from your work, of being limited, exploited, or just plain bored by having to do it. Working cooperatively with others and learning to be responsible to them and to yourself is an empowering experience. It's fun, too; people working a group can accomplish tremendous things. There are few things as pleasant or satisfying as solving a problem or completing a task—together. We think everyone should have the opportunity to work this way, instead of the present system of working in competition with people, afraid of your supervisor's power, and frequently taking out your frustrations on the people under you. This only seems to create anxiety, bad feelings, and poor work.

In collectives, one priority is to act in such a way that you are working as harmoniously as possible with other people, providing and receiving support, encouragement, constructive feedback, and kindness. This involves being conscious of how you relate to people so you can be both more honest and more constructive. Because of this emphasis on understanding your own behavior and dynamics between people, working in a collective is usually very stimulating towards personal growth and change. It's hard to stagnate with constant opportunities to evaluate, learn, and innovate in areas of both practical concern and personal dynamics. Thus it's exciting and meaningful work.

The economic differences between collective and capitalist businesses are another big part of what makes working in a collective worthwhile. The main goals of a collective are generally to provide a needed community service and to treat its workers fairly and equally. Business decisions are made based on whether or not a certain product or service is socially beneficial, not on its ability to increase profits for an individual owner. Hence, the phrase "Food for people, not for profit" has been the slogan of the food coop movement for decades. This ideal is shared by the bakeries in this book. All the money earned goes back into the business— to pay the workers and cover costs. If a "not-for-profit" business finds itself generating a consistent surplus it can choose to lower prices, improve employee wages and benefits, or begin providing new services to its community.

Since the intent of cooperatives and collectives is not to generate profit for a few people, being involved in one feels different from being in a regular business. We find it very enlightening to stop viewing people in terms of the money you can make from them. The nature of your work begins to feel different and your relationships with your fellow workers and with your customers change. You realize how strongly such things influence how you feel about yourself and the way you live.

The Success of Collectives

Working in a collective is not always easy. In the distinctively hostile environment of the competitive business system, survival of a cooperative enterprise is often a struggle. Some collective bakers have gone without pay when the business needed it, particularly when trying to get a new bakery off the ground. But other rewards were compensation enough at such times.

Above all, we want people to know that coops and collectives **work**. Most of our bakeries are successful businesses of several years' duration. Our bakers are both paid and happy! And we wouldn't trade the challenges and joys of working collectively for anything. Collectives are effective, responsible businesses and exciting, humane workplaces. Although we are surrounded in our present society by traditionally competitive institutions and beliefs, we are quite sure that the future belongs to people working together. Cooperative, collective workplaces will be the nuclei of future communities in a society that brings respect, fulfillment, and peace to all.

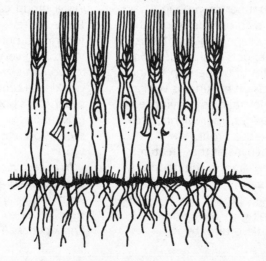

Bread and Nutrition

Nutrition is undoubtedly one of today's "hot" topics. Concern about the effects of what we eat is a major part of the growing interest in health that is evident these days. Dietary theories are iterated by the hundreds, ranging from the conventional approach of the four basic food groups to more esoteric macrobiotic diets and beyond. Diet regimens of many kinds flood our bookstores, each claiming discovery of the secrets of weight loss and optimal nutrition. Countless millions of people substitute margarine for butter, stuff their sandwiches with sprouts, snack on carob-yogurt chews and gobble vitamin supplements. In this complicated melange of conflicting claims and ideas, where does one turn for responsible information and advice?

The questions regarding nutrition asked by most people are basic ones; what are the nutritional requirements for good health?; how can these needs be met?; and what difference does it make anyway? In attempting to answer these questions, modern nutritional science has painstakingly searched for, discovered, and classified many of the individual components. Thus, most modern writings on nutrition concentrate on identifying and defining the nature of proteins, fats, carbohydrates, vitamins, and minerals, and describing the individual role of each in nutrition. Further, science continues to test and document the effects of various diets on the incidence of disease and life expectancy.

Today we have increased concern and awareness regarding nutrition and health. This concern, however, sometimes takes on a narrow scope. Nutrition and health "experts" seem to rapidly pass from one cure-all food to the next. Unfortunately the overall picture is sometimes missed. In **Uprisings**, we have tried to present a holistic picture of healthy foods and a whole diet of which whole grain baking is a part. We can benefit from bran, for example, by eating whole grains. Economically, whole grains make sense too. Utilizing only a part of the grain drives the price up due to increased demand as we saw with the oat bran craze. Good nutrition and health is not a fad, it is an ongoing lifestyle, one to which we are all entitled.

Initially, however, we should understand that nutrition, much like modern medicine, is an infant science. The elementary facts we accept as gospel now were unknown well into the twentieth century; for example, the molecular structures of vitamins A, B-1, and C were not discovered until the 1930s, the word "vitamin" having been coined only two decades previously. The effect on the body of food and its individual components is by no means fully understood, much less set in stone. Facts remain to be discovered, theories to be tested and re-evaluated, delicate relationships and interactions to be explored. In all probability, what we don't know about nutrition will prove even more important than what we do now know.

Good examples of the type of knowledge presently provided through modern nutritional research are the Recommended Daily Allowances (RDAs) of some individual components of our food supply. The tendency of most people—whether expert or layperson— is to accept these figures as an absolute standard or goal and to be satisfied if their diet meets these requirements. But this blind faith gives potentially dangerous credence to a scientific approach which is fraught with weakness. Among other problems, the RDAs are generalized estimates based on averages; hence the entire range of individual variation, whether among people or for the same person in different circumstances, is not taken into account. Moreover, as continual updating of the figures shows, they reflect only the current state of nutritional knowledge, which is widely acknowledged to be partial and fragmented.

Further, the RDAs only make sense if we know how much of each nutrient is present in our daily food intake. But the tables giving the nutrients in common foods (another achievement of modern nutritional science) have huge weaknesses of their own. They are only averages of the nutrients found in a limited number of laboratory samples of a particular food. In reality, there is enormous variation in the nutrient content of different samples of the same foodstuff. Such factors as climate, type of soil, and agricultural methods have a major impact on nutrient content. (For example, the nutrient tables credit broccoli as a good source of iron. But if the soil where your broccoli was grown is deficient in iron, your broccoli may be similarly lacking.) Another source of variation lies in the length and kind of storage and/or processing. The effect of cooking creates a further gray area (many tables give figures only for raw foods). Nutrient content depends on the method and length of cooking, as well as the amount of heat applied. But significant changes do occur, and all of them for the worse. Finally, whether from acquired allergy, genetic limitation, or general state of health, your body may not assimilate a nutrient as well from one food as it can from another. Inevitably, then, individual variation in response to food undermines the attempt to "eat by numbers."

If we match the RDAs against our food intake and discover a deficiency, many of us are tempted to take a food supplement. But are synthesized vitamins the exact nutritional equivalents of the vitamins consumed in whole foods? Remember how little we really know, scientifically, about nutrition. And remember too that the RDAs are for the most part only the amounts necessary to prevent clinically identifiable disease. But the difference between the amount needed to prevent disease and the amount required for optimal health may be significant.

Nonetheless, despite the shortcomings of the scientific approach to nutrition, it is becoming increasingly evident that numerous scientific advances are pointing to a larger picture concerning our health and what we eat. This larger picture is also suggested by a common-sense appraisal and understanding of who and what we are, and where we have come from. Let's examine a few fundamental concepts.

First and foremost, we know that whether one favors the creationist or evolutionary explanation of our origins, the human species has been molded by evolution. Each person is the product of a complicated genetic code, passed to us by our parents from a long series of ancestors stretching back for thousands of generations. And in turn, this genetic code was (and continues to be) determined by the environmental conditions humans faced; the climate they lived in, the lifestyle they adopted, the dangers they faced, and the food they ate.

There is no question that for the vast majority of human history, our species lived a simple, energetic life and ate a simple diet. When hunger was felt, food was eaten until the hunger was satisfied; if there was no hunger, the human didn't eat. And what was eaten was usually freshly picked or caught. "Refining," "processing," "pasteurization," and "preservatives" were unknown concepts, and even simple cooking was a relatively new development. The human existence was an active, sometimes strenuous one; great distances might be traveled in search of food, and humans were, by nature, endurance athletes.

As could be expected, the human body adapted to dealing with and thriving on this type of diet and lifestyle. Some members of the species tolerated these conditions poorly, and failed to survive. Others succeeded, and produced offspring with similar genetic characteristics. After eons of this natural selection process, the human being entered the modern era (defined as the last two or three thousand years) firmly tied by evolution to this ancient and relatively constant diet and vigorous lifestyle.

In the modern era, however, and particularly in the last century, we have greatly altered the environment in which we must exist. Today we deal with physical and psychological stresses never encountered by early humans: environmental pollutants, pressures in the modern workplace, the pursuit of material wealth, the threat of nuclear annihilation, a sedentary lifestyle, and perhaps most importantly, a diet which is highly processed, refined, and chemically altered.

The modern human eats too much food, and too much of the wrong kind of food. The results of this unplanned experiment are becoming obvious: our bodies, having evolved to thrive on an entirely different diet, are breaking down in vast and increasing numbers. Research tells us that the plagues of modern society are a creation of our present lifestyle. Our high fat diet directly affects the rate of heart disease, our low fiber diet and environmental pollutants (including food additives) produce huge increases in human cancers, our diet replete with highly refined foods is directly related to the incidence of diabetes, and our sedentary ways lead to obesity and severe stress on a body begging for exercise. We are simply asking ourselves to do the impossible; the process of evolution does not produce such rapid changes.

So what are we to eat? Fortunately, it's not as difficult as it might seem. By understanding our origins and paying attention to our needs, we find that we thrive on a simple diet of fresh, whole foods, grown in naturally composted, nutrient-rich soils. If we treat our bodies to a nourishing, organically raised, whole foods diet and really pay heed to our reaction to this diet, the chances are good that we will be getting just what we need.

How do processed foods fit into this picture? Of course, the term "processing" has an extremely broad meaning, encompassing lightly-handled foods like frozen blueberries to items more appropriate to a science fiction novel (Question: What product contains sugar, dextrose, cornstarch, modified cornstarch, salt, calcium carageenan, plysorbate 60, artificial flavor, natural flavor, artificial color, including FD&C Yellow? Answer: Banana Cream Jell-O-Pudding! Question: Where are the bananas? Or the cream, for that matter?) Some processing may in fact be unavoidable in our modern, complex society. But the question of high technology food processing (heating, refining, preservatives, coloring, long storage, strange chemical combinations, and so on) and its effects on our health is one we cannot afford to overlook.

Here the broader evolutionary perspective helps us understand the facts. From time immemorial, the diet of humans had no processed food of any kind.

Only fresh, whole foods were eaten, and eaten immediately after harvest. Our bodies are simply not prepared to deal with the radically different diet of the last few decades—hence the epidemics of degenerative diseases. And this observation is reinforced by health statistics from the few modern-day societies which still eat a simple, non-processed diet; the people in them are virtually free of these diseases. Even more telling, when such "primitive" people are transplanted to the "civilized" world and adopt a modern diet, they too become prey to heart disease, cancer, and other "diseases of progress."

The present controversies over salt and refined sugar relate closely to the question of processing food and its impact on mental and physical health. If one's diet consists entirely of fresh, whole foods, one's daily intake of sodium chloride will usually average between 500 and 1000 milligrams, and that amount is of course what our bodies are adapted to accept. However, the average American, eating a diet replete with processed foods, consumes twelve to thirty times this needed amount. The results are entirely predictable: massive overload on the system, and an epidemic of hypertension (high blood pressure).

Refined sugar is a highly processed, nutrient-free substance, consisting entirely of simple carbohydrates. The average American eats 130 pounds of the stuff each year. This amounts to over 600 calories per day—or 20% to 35% of the total diet. Our human ancestors did in fact eat substantial amounts of simple carbohydrates—in the form of fruit. But the simple carbohydrates in raw, whole fruit come complete with all sorts of vitamins, minerals, enzymes, and fiber (as well as any yet undiscovered essentials), and our adapting bodies need all of these nutrients along with the carbohydrate. That's one of the subtle and insidious dangers of refined sweeteners; the body has to find all of these nutrients somewhere to help assimilate such massive doses of sugar. If these nutrients do not come with the food being eaten—and they decidedly do not with refined sugar—the body must provide them itself from its tissues. This constant sacrifice by the body is a severe strain upon its health—for those sacrificed nutrients are needed elsewhere for crucial body functions.

Another example of our diets evolving faster than our bodies is evidenced by an examination of fat consumption. Forty percent of the total calories in the average American's diet comes from fat, and this is primarily saturated fat from animal sources. This represents an enormous increase in dietary fat during the last 150 years, and is three to four times more than the amount of fat consumed by our ancestors. The results, documented by decades of increasingly compelling research, are epidemics of heart disease, obesity, and cancers of the breast and digestive system. (A further implication of our society's "steak religion" is the vastly increased consumption of protein, along with the belief that we need huge amounts to function; overconsumption of protein has been linked to many maladies, especially cancer and kidney failure.) We urge a drastic revision in America's dietary habits: less total fat, less saturated fat, less salt, more complex carbohydrates.

Again, considering our origins and evolutionary history helps us find the answer. The diets of our ancestors were comprised of fruits, vegetables, nuts and seeds—all fresh— and occasionally the flesh of fish and wild animals. Almost all fruits and vegetables have little or no fat. Nuts and seeds are generally high in fats, but these are largely unsaturated; moreover, because each nut was solidly encased in a frustratingly hard-to-open casing, levels of consumption were naturally controlled. And even though the wild animals that may have been consumed did have saturated fat (all animal fat is saturated), there were at least two limiting factors: (1) wild animals have considerably less fat than the sedentary feedlot beasts of the modern era; and (2) chasing an antelope with a stone axe did not guarantee meat at every meal. Moreover, the highly active life both burned more calories and helped eliminate waste products from the body at a much higher rate than our typical low-energy existences.

Once we begin to see our place in the natural scheme of things, we can begin to choose and act more wisely. We don't have to become neander-

thals again to respect and re-assume many of the practices that have assured our health and vigor throughout our evolutionary development. We can orient our diet toward whole, raw, and fresh foods, growing our own where possible, and growing it organically. We can decrease our level of food consumption overall and adopt a more active lifestyle—do more things ourselves, enjoy being energetic, and adopt a regular program of vigorous exercise, such as walking, running, cycling, swimming. We should educate ourselves about the modern food industry, understanding the possible effects of certain processes and additives. We must avoid processed foods whenever we can (and we usually can), or at least scrutinize the labels if we can't. We must listen to our bodies, and eat the foods that we really demand, rather than habitually eating those products urged upon us by the ubiquitous advertisements of the corporate food industry. In other words, we can personally take charge of our own diets and lifestyles, and make them as simple and "time-honored" as possible.

It is in doing this that we will discover our greatest resource in the move towards optimal nutrition and greatest health—ourselves. It can be argued that just as science does not give the whole picture, neither does slavishly following the rules of the past. Our ancestors were highly diversified, over time and space, and we cannot determine with precision what is the biologically perfect human diet from studying their ways. Moreover, evolution is not a thing of the past! It is an integral and ongoing process of life itself. Our own lives are themselves experiments in newness. Hence it is primarily through taking charge and experiencing our lives that we can best learn what is right for us. Our greatest source of knowledge about what we should eat and how we should live is, therefore, personal experience.

Our society has taught us to depend upon experts and outside sources of information for the truth about even the most personal and intimate parts of our lives, such as how we feel physically, mentally, and emotionally. Ethnic patterns in our eating habits result in desiring and consuming foods which put a strain on our systems and ulti-

mately lead to breakdowns. Nonetheless, it's true that we (our bodies/our minds) can discover and prefer what is best for us. We can make this highly functional sense come through more and more clearly as we take steps to improve our diet and lifestyle, so that after a while we can begin to rely on our regained nutritional instinct.

This process of rediscovery isn't an instant one, though. We won't be able to trust our instinct about what is best for us for some time at least, since we've confused things with a lot of habits and addictions that give false promptings of our desires and dislikes. We have to work on understanding and facing these promptings, part of which involves undoing a lifetime of programming about what we should and should not eat. Nutritional information and awareness of our species' history help us eat wisely while we're developing a reliable and accurate inner nutritional sense.

While both modern science and human evolution point to the appropriateness of a simple, fresh, whole foods diet, the real test—what will most deeply convince us—is how it feels. No matter how persuasive the arguments, we humans demand the ultimate proof of personal experience. And even though at first when we "listen to our bodies," we may not hear much, increasingly the channels will clear and new awarenesses set in. With increased sensitivity and unity of body, mind, and spirit, the deleterious or beneficial effects of consuming a given food will be quite apparent to us. Health comes to be felt as something considerably greater than mere absence of disease, and the new experiences of feeling really good promote us to choose more and more those foods and behaviors that add to our well-being and new-found vitality. But—don't take our word for it! This is an experience that is within the power of each one of us to realize. Take control of your life—it is your unique opportunity to affect the conditions of your own existence and, however minutely, contribute to the exciting evolution of the human species, and of all life.

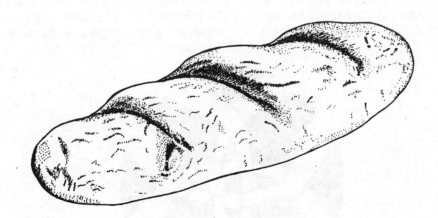

Bread and the Healthy Diet

Where does bread fit into this picture? Is it part of the problem, and therefore to be avoided? Or is it part of the solution, and therefore to be encouraged? The answer is "it depends"—depends on what goes into that bread.

The modern commercial loaf is in many ways an almost perfect mirror image of our present dietary problems. It is made primarily from highly-refined wheat flour, denuded of the nutrient-rich bran and germ. It is frequently doused with quantities of both salt and sugar (the latter coming under a wide variety of names: sucrose, dextrose, glucose, fructose, maltose, brown sugar, corn syrup). It is replete with chemical extenders, conditioners, emulsifiers, preservatives, flavoring and coloring agents. It frequently contains significant amounts of saturated fats—in the form of lard, palm oil, or coconut oil. And if we slather each slice with salty butter to give it a semblance of taste, the nutritional disaster is complete.

On the other hand, the home-baked, whole grain loaf can be a real nutritional plus. A simple loaf made from freshly ground whole wheat flour, yeast, and water contains plenty of vitamins and minerals, no added sugar or salt, lots of complex carbohydrates and protein, and no chemicals or saturated fats. And when you are doing the baking, you can control the quality and type of ingredients that go into the loaf. For a sweeter loaf, you can add honey, malt syrup, or fruit instead of refined sugar. For a sharper taste, you can add herbs instead of salt. For a moist rich crumb, you can add cold-pressed safflower oil instead of lard. And to extend the loaf's keeping qualities, you can add a tablespoon of vinegar instead of BHT.

The simple whole grain loaf was in fact a part of the diet of our evolutionary forerunners, at least in their later stages. But you must keep bread in its proper perspective. As bakers, we are well aware of some less positive aspects of consuming baked goods—especially in excess! Bread and other baked goods are definitely a heavy. A baked treat—even whole grain and natural—is often a complex blend of ground or semi-"refined" ingredients (flour, oils, nut butters, molasses, for example). Moreover, the baking process requires extended exposure to high heat, and we know that heat destroys many vital elements in foods. For these reasons, the primary dietary emphasis should still be on fresh, raw, whole foods. Even more importantly, though, our ancestors ate a wide variety of foods, and a diet based largely on bread would miss that necessary range and diversity. Maintain a sense of balance, and be attentive to your body's real needs. Enjoy home-baked bread made from fresh, whole ingredients—but enjoy it in moderation.

Organics–An Important Source

Until a few years ago, the word "organic" was one of the most misused and misunderstood terms in the food industry. Marketers of natural foods, or "health" foods, used the word to convey many different meanings....or no particular meaning at all. However, this is changing rapidly as millions of Americans are learning about the value of organically grown food.

Though standards vary somewhat, "organic" generally describes a method of farming that avoids the use of artificial pesticides, fertilizers and other petrochemical inputs. Concern over the dangers of chemical contamination of our soil and water, as well as the food we eat, has become a major social issue in this country. Many people are shunning produce and other items grown with pesticides and fertilizers. Exposure to these petrochemicals has been clearly linked to a higher incidence of cancer, birth defects and other health problems. This translates into a serious health risk for farm workers, people living in agricultural areas and consumers.

As more and more people find the products of big agribusiness unacceptable, those who care about safe food and the environment must respond with an alternative. Fortunately, there is a small but committed group of farmers across the country who have been growing organically for many years, and an increasing number of others who have begun to turn to chemical-free alternatives. Many sectors of the food industry are putting a greater emphasis on organics. The bakeries in this book, along with food coops, are leaders in bringing safe food to concerned consumers. At the 1989 whole grain bakers' conference, members of the CWGEA stated more strongly than ever their commitment to supporting organic farmers and to producing goods made from organic ingredients.

We see supporting organic agriculture as being important in two ways. First, it goes hand-in-hand with our commitment to whole grains in terms of eating healthy food. Second, it is an essential part of sound environmental policy. We owe it to future generations to provide them with farmland capable of growing food. Chemical-based agriculture is depleting our soil and contaminating our water. However, there is great hope in the regenerative ability of organic farming.

It is true that organic food can be more expensive and more difficult to find. Still, we must be willing to make this choice in our homes and in our businesses. Shop at your local food coop or farmers' market. Inquire at the grocery store about the possibility of carrying organic foods. If you work in a food business, encourage the use of organic products. Doing these things takes a little extra time and energy, but we hope you'll agree that saving our nation's farmland is well worth it!

Foods For Whole Grain Baking

Understanding the variety and properties of ingredients, and choosing them carefully, is basic to successful baking. Using poor quality ingredients or combining the wrong proportions will give the baker disappointing results. In this chapter, we provide a review of the foods used most often in baking.

A good general guideline is to buy your ingredients as "whole" and fresh as possible, obtaining organically grown products if you can. If possible, buy whole grain flours which have been stone-ground. Look for unfiltered, uncooked honey and unrefined, unbleached oils. Keep whole grain flours, oils, seeds, and nuts refrigerated in sealed containers to preserve freshness, and use them within a short period of time.

In making bread, there are actually only two ingredients which are absolutely essential—grain and liquid. Historically, bread began as a simple, unleavened loaf. Roughly ground grain was mixed with water, shaped, and baked in the sun. Try making it this simply sometime.

Grains

Many kinds of grains are used in baking throughout the world. The North American perspective is inevitably wheat-centered, and thus we tend to see other grains as additions to wheat bread rather than the central grain in the loaf. However, there is a wide variety of grains, ranging from the more subtle oat, millet, and rice to the uniquely-flavored buckwheat, sorghum, barley, and corn. All of these grains, and others even less familiar to us, have been, and still are, staple foods in other civilizations and cultures.

Grains are seeds and can be used in many different ways: whole, sprouted, cooked, roughly milled or cracked, rolled into flakes, or ground into meal or flour. Grains are highly nutritious, being excellent sources of protein, carbohydrates, fats, vitamins, minerals, trace elements, and fiber. Loss of nutrients occurs when grains are refined in any way, so make sure the grain products you are buying are 100% whole.

Grains have several key functions in bread. The complex carbohydrate in all grains provides food for the yeast organisms (whether added by the baker, or incorporated from the air), allowing them to grow and multiply rapidly. In growing, yeast converts sugars and oxygen into carbon dioxide and alcohol, the first of which causes the bread to rise and the latter contributing to the bread's flavor.

The flours of some grains contain gluten, a protein consisting of *gliadin* and *glutenin*. When bread dough is kneaded, these two stick together to form an elastic network which traps the carbon dioxide released by the yeast. This causes the bread both to rise and to keep its shape during baking. Wheat is highest in gluten; rye and triticale contain less (mostly the stickier gliadin). Oats and barley contain a little, and other grains none; thus only small amounts should be used in combination with mostly wheat flour if you want your bread to rise well.

Gluten, especially wheat gluten, causes adverse (or "allergic") reactions in some people. However, many of these people can tolerate other grains, including rye, and even wheat if it has been sprouted. Essene bread is a very ancient bread, made only of sprouted grains (usually wheat), ground, shaped, and then baked at low temperatures. If you are "allergic" to wheat flour, you might try essene bread instead.

Grains in all their different forms provide an exciting variety of tastes and textures in bread. Without demeaning basic whole wheat bread, the same loaf undergoes remarkable changes of flavor and texture when stone-ground cornmeal is added (or try some cracked wheat, oats, barley flakes, cooked rice, sprouted wheat, or whole millet). Multi-grain blends of flours can be extremely delicious. Grain flours other than wheat can work very well in muffins, cakes, and cookies, while oats and other flakes provide the basis for granolas, bars, and many cookies. To guide you in your choice of grains for baking, we offer the following review of whole grain terminology.

Amaranth

Although not widely used in our culture at present, this ancient grain is expected to become more available in the near future. It is exceptionally high in protein, especially the rarer lysine and sulfur-containing amino acids. Amaranth was cultivated on this continent thousands of years ago, and was a staple in Aztec culture before its eradication by Cortez. Reportedly, the small grains can be popped and used in cereal or confections, while amaranth flour can be added to whole wheat to enhance the flavor and nutrition.

Barley

Extremely hardy, barley flourishes from the Arctic Circle to subtropical climates. It is believed to have been the first grain cultivated by humans, and is still today a dietary staple in many parts of the world. Barley has been largely forgotten in the West, however, where most of the crop is fed to livestock. Sprouted barley is used to make malt and beer.

Most of the barley commonly available is "pearled," which means it has been refined to remove the bran and the germ, and hence much of the flavor and nutrition. Try to find natural brown barley, which has only been hulled. Grind it yourself into fresh flour, or buy it ready-ground. Adding this mild-flavored, low-gluten flour in small amounts to a yeasted wheat bread (lightly pretoasting it, if you like) gives a moist, sweet, cake-like texture. Barley flour in combination with whole wheat flour creates a delicious, chewy unyeasted loaf. Used alone in cookies, barley flour yields a tasty, light-colored, slightly pasty product. Cooked barley and rolled barley flakes can also be added to bread.

Berry

The berry is the whole grain, before it is hulled, cracked, milled, or processed in any way. It contains bran, germ, and endosperm (see diagram, pg. 12). Buy berries to sprout, or to grind into flour yourself for maximum freshness. Soaked, cooked, or sprouted berries give a nice chewy texture to yeasted breads.

Bran

Usually, we associate this term with the partially ground husk of the wheat berry, and any product just called "bran" is almost certainly wheat. However, the term properly refers to the husk layers surrounding any grain. These layers have some protein, vitamins and minerals, and lots of fiber, all of which are lost when milled grains are refined. Adding extra bran to your breads (and goodies) makes them high in fiber and darkly-flecked, although bran is naturally present, of course, in whole grain flours. Warm bran muffins are unrivaled for breakfast!

Buckwheat

Probably first cultivated in ancient China, it was spread to Europe by migrating tribes. A refined version of buckwheat flour was farinha, which became a staple around the Mediterranean. "Farina" today is usually degermed wheat. Buckwheat is still an important foodstuff in Eastern Europe and Russia, where the groats are roasted and cooked as a gruel, called kasha.

Buckwheat in the United States is mostly fed to animals, or plowed under as green manure. However, buckwheat flour and groats (hulled whole berries) are available, and may be used in baking. Fresh flour can be ground from groats in a blender. Buckwheat has a nutritional value similar to wheat, and is outstandingly high in lysine.

Buckwheat has a distinct and unusual flavor, which can easily dominate a bread. Experiment with it judiciously to see if you like the taste. Try adding some cooked groats or substitute ½ cup buckwheat flour in a two-loaf batch of whole wheat bread. It will come out somewhat heavier and more fully-flavored. A terrific unyeasted bread can be made using cooked buckwheat and buckwheat flour, with some whole wheat added for gluten.

Corn

A grain which probably originated in Mexico, corn was first cultivated by the earliest inhabitants of North and South America. Literally hundreds of varieties exist, many grown only in isolated South American communities. Corn is very nutritious, and is the only grain high in carotene, which produces vitamin A.

Yellow cornmeal is most commonly used in baking, giving a crumbly, slightly crunchy sweetness and golden color to whole wheat products. It makes a nice addition to yeasted breads, and is delicious in corn muffins and quick breads. Since cornmeal is often "degermed," make sure you are buying whole cornmeal, preferably stone-ground. Cornmeal is also used to dust the baking sheet to prevent sticking of round loaves, pita bread, or pizza. Dried whole kernels of corn can be cooked till soft and added to yeasted bread for a chewy surprise, or cooked, ground, and shaped into patties to bake a popular Venezuelan staple called *arepas*.

Cracked Grains

Whole grains are broken into several rough pieces by coarse milling to produce cracked grains. Cracked wheat, the most common, gives a nice texture when added in small amounts to whole wheat bread.

Endosperm

The starchy inner part of the cereal grain, the endosperm contains carbohydrates and occasionally, as in wheat, some protein. It is low in vitamins and minerals, and entirely lacking in fiber. White flour is made up of ground endosperm alone.

Germ

An inner part of the grain berry, containing the embryo of the new plant, the germ is naturally high in food value. Wheat germ is most commonly available (see "Wheat" on pg. 34), and makes a rich, flavorful addition to breads, muffins and cookies.

Meal

Meal usually refers to coarsely ground flour. But in England and Australia, for example, "wholemeal" flour means "whole wheat" flour. The addition of some meal to bread gives it a grainier texture.

Millet

One of the most ancient of grains, millet was a staple in China long before rice. Millet flour is much used in Africa, and is the basis of the national bread of Ethiopia (injera), the flat cakes of India (roti), and is a staple of the Hunzas. It has a very high quality protein (though it lacks gluten), is particularly high in minerals, and is said to be the most digestible of grains.

The tiny, delicately-flavored grains have usually been hulled before reaching the stores. You can grind these into flour in a blender, and use in baked goods for a light crunchiness and sweet richness of flavor. Toasting it first enhances the sweet, nut-like taste. One-half cup in a two-loaf batch of whole wheat is a good rule of thumb. Small quantities of whole, uncooked millet add a gentle crunch and an attractive, white-flecked appearance to breads. You can also cook the grains and use a little in bread for a moist sweetness. And a successful wheatless cookie can be based on cooked millet (see Peanut Minus Cookies in the Index).

Oats

A relative newcomer among cultivated grains, oats were apparently first used extensively by the Roman Empire. Oats grow worldwide, flourishing in climates that are too cold for wheat.

Oats are available in several forms: whole groats, generally hulled; thick-cut and regular rolled oats (sometimes misleadingly called oatmeal), which are made by rolling whole groats; instant rolled oats (made by cutting the whole groats into pieces, precooking the pieces, and then rolling them super-thin); steel-cut oats (groats cut lengthwise with

sharp blades); and oat flour (groats or rolled oats ground to a fine meal). You can grind your own flour in a blender.

Oats make a delicious and nutritious addition to baked goods, and because they contain a natural anti-oxidant, they extend the keeping quality of breads. Oat flour contributes a moist sweetness to bread; use about one cup of the low-gluten oat flour to four cups of whole wheat. Cooked oats in bread produce a sticky dough and a moist, sweet loaf. Rolled oats appear as pale flecks and make the bread chewy; they'll absorb some water during kneading and rising, so make the dough a little wetter than usual.

Rolled oats produce a nice flavor and great chewy texture in cookies, and are the mainstay of bar crusts. They also make excellent cereals, whether left raw, as in muesli, or mixed with other ingredients and baked, as in granola.

Rice

Rice is an oriental grain that has been grown in India and China for over 4,000 years. Its cultivation was not adopted in Europe until the 15th century. Today, rice is the staple food for over one half of the world's population.

In its whole state, as brown rice, this grain is very nutritious and high in B vitamins. Refinement into white rice by removal of the bran and germ greatly depletes the flavor, texture, and food value. Rice can add an exciting variety of tastes and textures to your baked goods. A couple of points about buying rice; firstly, it is susceptible to many field diseases, so commercial rice products are high in pesticide residues. Buy organically grown brown rice if at all possible. And secondly, the rice flour that is most commonly available is made from white rice, with the same nutritional deficiencies, so look for brown rice flour, or grind your own from whole brown rice.

Sample the sweet graininess of brown rice flour in your recipes, pretoasting it lightly if you like. Breads with some rice flour tend to come out moist, dense, and smooth. It holds up well alone in a wheatless cake, creating a close but delicately-textured crumb and a subtle sweetness. A soft, close texture is obtained when rice flour is used alone in cookies; ground rice, coarser than flour, gives a soft sandiness when blended with whole wheat flour in shortbreads.

Cooked brown rice gives yeasted breads a moist, chewy character, and long-cooked rice gruel can be the basis for a delicious unyeasted bread. Coarsely ground rice grits add crunch. Rice polishings (the inner bran layers) are by-products of the refining process, and can be used like wheat bran or wheat germ in baked goods. They are, of course, high in fiber, as well as B vitamins, calcium, phosphorus, and potassium.

Rye

Another of the newcomers to the cultivated cereal family, rye was apparently first grown during the Roman Empire. Its moderate gluten content and distinctive hearty flavor have made it a staple bread flour in northern regions where wheat cannot subsist. Black rye bread, sweetened with molasses, is popular in Eastern Europe and Russia, sourdough rye and pumpernickel are German favorites, and a lighter rye bread, made with honey, and often, orange, is common in Scandinavia.

Rye is a soft grain, nutritionally very similar to wheat; it is high in minerals and B vitamins, particularly potassium and riboflavin. When buying flour, make sure you get the dark variety; "light" rye flour has had some of the bran removed. Whole rye berries can be readily ground into flour at home.

A yeasted loaf made entirely of rye flour will be fine-textured, moist and compact, with a unique, rich, slightly sour flavor. Rye flour produces a sticky dough, not as smooth as whole wheat dough. But if you avoid the temptation to keep adding flour, you can get a nice rise and reasonably light texture even in 100% rye bread.

Perhaps the most delicious "rye bread" is made from equal amounts of rye and whole wheat flour. This bread has a dark color, rich aroma, and distinctive rye taste, and is still buoyant and light-textured. Caraway seeds and molasses complement the flavor of rye, while a touch of anise is another

popular flavoring. Rye flour used alone can make a decent wheatless muffin, with currants as a nice addition. Rye meal can be added to whole wheat breads, too. Rolled rye flakes may be used in baked goods, though they are tougher than rolled oats. They are often combined in small quantities with oats in granolas and cereals. Finally, an unexpectedly delicious way to prepare rye is to sprout the whole berries, grind, shape, and bake the loaves at low temperatures; it produces a rich, dark, sweet essene bread.

Sorghum

A food staple in Africa and Asia, sorghum is third only to wheat and rice in worldwide consumption. It is a relative of millet and somewhat similar to corn nutritionally. Until recently, it was widely grown and eaten—especially the sweet syrup extract—in the southern United States. You may be able to find the grain at feed stores and elevators, and it is very inexpensive. Whole sorghum can be cooked or ground into flour (which is very low in gluten). This is a grain we haven't worked with much, but it is said to make a tasty addition to bread.

Triticale

A cross between wheat and rye, triticale is a monument to modern agricultural research. It reputedly combines some of the best qualities of each grain; the high-protein, high-gluten content of wheat and the high yield and ruggedness of rye. You can buy triticale as whole berries, rolled flakes, or flour. The grain has a subtle yet distinct flavor which many find delicious.

An excellent loaf of yeasted bread can be made using 100% triticale flour, but the technique is somewhat different. The gluten in triticale is quite soft and must be treated gently. Gentle rather than vigorous kneading, and allowing only one rising of the dough rather than two or three, preserves the elasticity of triticale gluten. However, we haven't worked extensively with a 100% triticale loaf, and the flour is usually combined with wheat to ensure strength and shape. Rolled triticale flakes can be added to breads, cookies, and granolas. Whole berries may be sprouted for essene bread, but the sprouts tend to spoil easily.

Wheat

Wheat is thought to have originated in the Middle East, possibly Turkey, and competes with barley for being the oldest cultivated grain. A hardy, rugged plant which grows almost anywhere if it has fertile ground and water, wheat has been a food staple of many ancient civilizations. Containing the highest amount of gluten of all grains, it is today widely considered in the Western world as being almost synonymous with bread.

Wheat is extremely nutritious, containing most of the elements needed for human nourishment. The whole grains are rich in magnesium, iron, phosphorus, vitamins B and E, carbohydrates, protein, and numerous trace minerals. (See pgs. 12-13 for diagram and more detail about the constituents of the wheat berry.) When the grains are ground, the natural fats begin to go rancid, so grind or buy your whole wheat flour as fresh as possible, use quickly, and refrigerate if necessary. Any wheat flours other than 100% whole wheat have been refined and therefore have fewer nutrients and less flavor. That includes "unbleached white flour," which though lacking chemical bleach and sometimes preservatives, is still devoid of the most nutritious parts of the grain: the bran and the germ.

Try to buy your whole wheat flour stoneground. Stone-grinding, as opposed to conventional high-speed milling, does not overheat the grain and cause serious deterioration in nutrients and flavor. Grinding your own berries is best of all, of course.

There are two distinct types of whole wheat flour used in baking, and it is important to understand their properties and uses.

Hard Whole Wheat Flour, or **Whole Wheat Bread Flour** should be used in breads, or the gluten network will not be fully formed and the bread won't rise well. Hard whole wheat flour is milled from hard red spring wheat or hard red winter wheat, both of which are high in gluten. It is desirable for bread flour to contain about 14-15% gluten. A flour significantly deficient in gluten may give you rather flat bread.

Whole Wheat Pastry Flour or **Soft Whole Wheat Flour** is usually used in cookies, cakes, muffins, piecrusts, and so on. It is much lower in gluten than hard whole wheat flour, and produces tender, finely-textured goodies. It is milled from soft winter wheat.

Additional points about the use of these two kinds of wheat are:

1. Hard whole wheat flour can be used in cookies, bars, and brownies, either alone or combined with pastry flour. The texture will be less fine and delicate. It's not recommended for cakes and muffins, though. If a "goodie" recipe doesn't specify whole wheat pastry flour, you can use either kind, bearing in mind the slight differences in your results.

2. Whole wheat pastry flour can be added to breads, but use plenty of hard whole wheat too, or the bread may turn out heavy and flat.

3. Some yeasted sweet rolls and desserts use all whole wheat pastry flour. The yeast will still produce a rise in the dough, but the texture will be more soft and cakey, rather than firm and elastic.

4. Sometimes a hard wheat crop may be too low in gluten to produce a well-risen yeasted bread. If you're really unable to get hold of flour with adequate gluten content, you may want to consider using additional gluten flour as a last resort (see pg. 35 for definition and caveats).

5. For sprouting whole berries to make essene bread, use hard whole wheat for a more cohesive texture. Pastry wheat sprouts produce a softer, more crumbly dough, and tend to spoil more quickly.

Other Wheat Products:

Cracked Wheat is whole wheat berries, usually the hard red variety, which have been coarsely cracked into small pieces. A small amount adds a crunchy texture to yeasted breads. Bulgur, which has been cooked and parched before cracking, can be used similarly.

Wheat Bran, the outer layers of the whole wheat berry, is a by-product of refining white flour. High in vitamins and minerals, it adds nutrition, texture, and fiber to baked goods. Remember, too, that whole wheat flour already contains its own bran.

Wheat Germ is another by-product of the refining process. It is the nutrient-rich embryo of the wheat plant, containing a high concentration of B vitamins, vitamin E, iron, and protein. Because of the high oil content (wheat germ is high in unsaturated fat), raw wheat germ goes rancid very easily. There is evidence that rancid foods draw nutrients from the body during digestion. If wheat germ hasn't been refrigerated and smells somewhat strong, it is probably rancid and not worth eating. Toasted wheat germ has a pleasant nutty taste and keeps somewhat longer than raw if refrigerated; however, the toasting destroys many of the nutrients. Wheat germ makes a healthful addition to breads and goodies, giving richness, fiber, and a nice flavor to baked goods.

Wheat Flours not explicitly labeled **100% whole wheat** have been processed to remove some or all of the bran and germ of the whole berry, thereby reducing the flavor, texture, and nutrition. In addition, most commercial flours have been treated with chemicals and preservatives. We do not recommend any refined flours. There is no need to use any white flour in baking to produce well-risen loaves and delicate cakes and pastries.

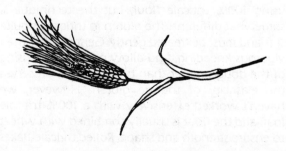

Gluten Flour, also called **High Gluten Flour** or just **Gluten**, is a highly refined mixture of white flour and additional gluten; gluten itself is refined from white flour. If you seem unable by any other means to make your bread rise, and know that the hard whole wheat flour you can obtain has a low natural gluten content, then you might consider adding gluten flour in very small amounts. This product, like all highly refined foods, is difficult to digest and many people suffer strong reactions to it. Our bakeries prefer not to use it and we don't recommend its use. It is occasionally added by a few bakeries, however, to boost a low-gluten whole wheat flour.

Liquids

Liquid is the other indispensable ingredient for bakers. Liquid combines the dry grains into a workable dough, allowing you to shape an endless variety of loaves and rolls (or in the case of essene bread, cause the grains to sprout and grow into a dough). Liquids serve as a vital catalyst in the leavening of baked goods, providing the moist environment in which bread yeasts can multiply and chemical leaveners react. Lastly, liquids can add flavor, nutrients, and texture to breads and baked goods.

Water

This is the common denominator and one indispensable element of all liquids. Water is all you ever really need in breadbaking—it's also the cheapest and most available. Many people in bakeries are concerned about the quality of municipal water, and look for more healthful alternatives.

Milk (see also "Dairy Products", pg. 41)

The use of milk in yeasted doughs adds flavor and protein, increases the browning, produces a softer, smoother crumb, and is somewhat more preservative than water. Whole milk is most often used in sweet, rich doughs, like tea rings or sweet rolls. The fat in whole dairy milk tends to coat the flour particles and somewhat inhibit the formation of gluten. For this reason, as well as to avoid saturated animal fats, many people prefer to use skim or non-fat milk.

Non-fat dry milk, either made liquid with water or added dry with adjustment in the liquid, is used in our bakeries to make a sweeter, richer bread that appeals to people trying to move away from white bread. Milk and milk powder give richness and cohesive texture to cakes, muffins, and cookies.

Buttermilk (See also "Dairy Products", pg. 41)

Buttermilk adds nutrients and a cheesy flavor to bread, plus a more finely textured dough and less fat than whole milk. Unfortunately the buttermilk of today is produced chemically, not naturally. Buttermilk powder has recently become available. Like other cultured products, such as yogurt (which can also be used in breads), buttermilk gives a delightfully rich tang to cakes and biscuits.

Fruit Juice (see also "Sweeteners", pg. 38)

It's nice to make your breads using warm fruit juice. Cider or the juice in which dried fruits have been soaked are most common. Fruit juices add nutrients as well as sweetness and distinctive flavor to baked goods; you can reduce or eliminate the concentrated sweetener in the recipe by using them.

Potato Water

Made from steeping raw grated potatoes, potato water is thought to aid the rising of dough by encouraging yeast activity. It also contributes nutrients and flavor.

Beer

Beer provides an interesting flavor, not unlike some sourdough breads. It is not widely used in the actual baking process.

Leaveners

Leaveners cause doughs and batters to rise, making them light and porous. There are really only two types, both producing carbon dioxide, but in different ways; the live variety (yeast, sourdough), which gives off gas as it lives and multiplies in the dough; and the chemical versions (baking powder, baking soda), which leaven through the reaction of acid and alkaline substances.

Yeast

Yeast is a microscopic fungus which reproduces rapidly by budding when provided with a warm, moist environment and carbohydrates to feed on. Enzymes break down carbohydrates into sugars which the yeast ferments into carbon dioxide (CO_2) and alcohol. The alcohol contributes to the flavor of the bread, while the CO_2 is trapped by the elastic network of gluten formed in the flour by kneading of the dough. As the yeast organisms continue to multiply, more CO_2 is formed and the dough rises.

It is important to keep these two by-products in balance. Too much yeast, or over-rising of the dough, results in excessive production of alcohol, and the finished loaf may well taste disagreeably "yeasty." (This may happen more quickly when the bread is unsalted.) Although you can eliminate a surplus of CO_2 by simply punching down the dough, the dough may have expanded beyond the elasticity of the gluten bonds. This would result in tearing of these bonds and a heavier, more coarsely-textured loaf.

Baking yeast (not to be confused with brewer's or nutritional yeast) comes to you alive, but inactive. Dry yeast is inactive because it lacks moisture. Fresh or cake yeast is inactive because it is kept cold. Yeast organisms need warmth to become active, but begin to die at about 120° F and are useless at 140° F. To activate dry yeast, dissolve in lukewarm liquid in the range of 95° F - to 115° F. Fresh yeast likes it cooler, 80° - 105° F. The liquid should feel slightly warm or neutral to the fingers, but not hot. Yeast will come alive, but more slowly, at cooler temperatures.

All of the recipes in this book use dry yeast, as do the majority of bakeries. Dry yeast can safely be stored for months in a sealed container in a cool, dry place. Fresh yeast should be refrigerated and used within one to two weeks. It can conveniently be frozen, in one batch blocks, for several months. Use immediately upon thawing.

The equivalent for using the two types of yeast is:

1 Tbl. dry yeast = 1 oz. fresh yeast

If you are uncertain of the quality or freshness of your yeast, you may want to test or "proof" it. For this method, see "Making the Sponge" in "How to Bake—Yeasted Breads." To activate yeast, it is not essential to use a simple carbohydrate—some form of sugar—since the organisms will come alive in warm water alone, and can break down the carbohydrate in flour to feed on. This process will take a little longer, though.

Sourdough

This leavener is actually just one special way of introducing yeast organisms into bread dough. It produces a distinctive sour taste, which can be delicious. A mixture of flour and liquid is left in a warm place to "ferment," during which time natural yeasts in the air and flour are trapped in the dough. This is the means by which all unyeasted breads rise. The sourdough "starter" is kept inactivated by refrigeration, like fresh yeast. It comes to life in a warm, moist environment, when left out to warm up to room temperature and then mixed with other ingredients. For details of how to make and use sourdough, see "How to Bake—Sourdough Breads" and recipes in the Index.

Baking Powder and Baking Soda

These chemical leaveners are commonly used in many types of baked goods. Their action relies on the chemical reaction of acid and alkali, which gives off carbon dioxide. **Baking soda**, sodium bicarbonate, is an alkali which reacts with acidic ingredients such as honey, vinegar, fruit juice, buttermilk, etc. **Baking powder** contains sodium bicarbonate and its own acid agent, as well as starch. It reacts

when moistened. Commercial baking powder usually contains calcium acid phosphate (as its acid ingredient) and cornstarch. For a better home-made blend, using cream of tartar (potassium bitartrate) and arrowroot powder, see "How to Bake—Substituting Ingredients." Be aware that baking soda is very high in sodium. By making your own baking powder, you eliminate some of that sodium and all of the toxic aluminum compounds that are frequently added to commercial brands.

Both baking powder and baking soda work quickly; in fact, they generally require a minimum of mixing and speedy dispatch into the oven, or they'll begin to puff up the batter prematurely. They successfully leaven flours with no gluten content, and thus open up a wide range of possibilities for quick breads, muffins, brownies, and cakes. Baking soda used alone produces a very tender crumb. They can also be used in cookies to give a more porous texture.

Sweeteners

All sweeteners are a form of sugar. Often confused, there are two very distinct definitions of the word "sugar." The **chemical** definition refers to all simple carbohydrates—including those found naturally in fruits and vegetables as well as those known as sweeteners, such as honey, maple syrup, and table sugar. Within this chemical definition, there are several named varieties of "sugar" based on chemical structure. Fructose, sucrose, maltose, and glucose are examples.

The **common** definition of sugar refers only to the refined products of the sugar cane or beet. This includes white (granulated) sugar, confectioner's (or powdered) sugar, brown sugar, and raw or turbinado sugar. We do not use or recommend **any** of these sugars. They are highly imbalanced products which are absorbed too rapidly into the bloodstream and put considerable strain on the body. The consumption of refined sugars has been shown to be responsible for many health problems. Other refined sugars to avoid are corn syrup and commercial fructose.

The major sweeteners used in whole grain baking are honey, malt, and molasses. As previously mentioned, sweeteners hasten the action of yeast and add sweetness and flavor to baked goods. Here we briefly review various sweeteners, but bear in mind that most sweeteners are almost totally lacking in food value other than calories. We're so fond of them because we've been raised on sugary foods. But reducing sweeteners in your baking will bring an appreciation of the flavorful sweetness in grains and other natural foods. In particular, remember that sweeteners are **not** essential to a successful loaf of bread, and many people find they prefer the full grainy flavor of unsweetened bread.

Honey

Many people ascribe a wide variety of health-giving properties to honey. Moreover, it is the sole source of nutrition for a very active and industrious animal—the bee—and as far as we know, white sugar alone will not sustain any form of life. So, although analysis indicates that honey has a similar chemical structure to white sugar, perhaps science does not yet know everything...! Always try and buy raw honey; the others have been pasteurized and this heating does no good for honey's nutritive benefits.

There are many different honeys, from light-colored and mild to dark, strong-flavored ones, such as buckwheat. Most of our baked goods call for a mild honey. Honey gives a nice golden color and a delicious aroma and flavor to whole wheat products. In its uncooked, undiluted, and unfiltered form, it seems to have a preservative effect. Honey has an acidic quality and thus can be used to catalyze baking soda.

Malt

Available in either powdered or very sticky liquid form, malt is made by sprouting wheat, barley, or corn, lightly toasting the sprouts, grinding them to a powder, and then filtering out the solids. Malt is 65% maltose and contains moderate amounts of minerals and vitamins. It is, perhaps, the best of all sweeteners and is preferred by a number of bakeries for its more subtle sweetness and greater nutrition. It works well in all kinds of baked goods.

One tip about using malt syrup: to avoid having sticky strands everywhere, coat your measuring cup or spoon with oil before dipping it into the malt.

Maple Syrup

This comes from the sap of the sugar maple tree, which is boiled to produce the very sweet, delicately-flavored, and expensive syrup. It is a simple sugar, about 60% sucrose, and many of the nutrients are destroyed in the refining process. Many of the larger producers use formaldehyde in the extraction of the sap (a practice permitted by the USDA), and add flavoring and antifoaming agents. Try to buy pure maple syrup, and keep it refrigerated to avoid fermenting.

Molasses

Most molasses is a by-product of the refinement of white sugar. In this process, the cane or beet is crushed and then flushed with water to extract a syrup (molasses). The degree of sweetness in different types of molasses is determined by the number of sugar crystals that are removed from the syrup in the refining process. Molasses contains vitamins and trace minerals like iron, calcium, zinc, copper, and chromium. Blackstrap molasses is the residue of the third and last extraction. It is about 35% sucrose and has the highest concentration of minerals—and also, unfortunately, of pesticides and residues of the refining process.

Molasses has a strong flavor, particularly suited to dark rye breads and gingery cakes and cookies. It is used sparingly, often in combination with malt or honey.

Fruits

Don't overlook fresh fruits, fruit juices, and dried fruits as sources of sweetness. They avoid the intensity of concentrated syrups and also contain other balancing nutrients and fiber. Juices, including water in which dried fruit has been soaked, are good liquids for sponging breads or binding cookies and muffins. Soaking raisins or dates is most common, while figs or apricots add a unique flavor. Well-soaked dried fruits can be blended, ground, or mashed into a paste or butter and then, for example, substituted for honey in a recipe. Dates give the smoothest butter and a very sweet, wonderfully rich flavor. They are high in natural sugar (about 70%) and rich in minerals and B vitamins. *Date sugar*, usually ground dried dates, is a dark, granulated sweetener sometimes used in cakes.

During the drying process, dates and other fruits are often treated with sulphuric acid. Apples, peaches, and apricots dried commercially are frequently bleached, and sorbic acid is usually added as a preservative. Try to obtain unsulphured, organic dried fruits if possible.

Among fresh fruits, mashed bananas, chopped apple, and applesauce give a moist richness to quickbreads, muffins, and cookies. Don't forget the appeal of a handful of blueberries, cranberries, cherries, or chopped peaches in cakes and muffins. Grated citrus rind and juice give a flavorful zing to doughs and batters; orange goes nicely in fruity breads, and lemon brings a fresh flavor to "goodie" recipes. Finally, fruits can be used to make cake fillings, frostings, and toppings; pureed soaked dried fruits, mashed bananas, or raspberries cooked to a gel with arrowroot are just some of the ways to give a wonderful fruity sweetness to a special cake or dessert.

Sorghum Molasses (or Sorghum Syrup)

Derived from the stalks of sorghum, a relative of millet, sorghum molasses was a staple sweetener in the Southern United States until sugar began to dominate the market. It contains mostly levulose sugar (fructose) found in certain fruits and honey and is quite high in minerals. It is milder than molasses, but can be substituted for it, or for malt, or used in combination with other sweeteners.

Rice Syrup

Made from rice, this is one of the mildest sweeteners, but rarely used in baking.

Refined Commercial Sweeteners

Raw or **Turbinado Sugar** is the light brown crystalline substance that is separated from molasses in the first step of the sugar refining process. It is a highly processed product, having gone through all but the final filtration of the refinement process. It contains 96% sucrose, and almost no nutrients—only calories.

White (Granulated) Sugar is produced by further refining turbinado sugar. After being washed and clarified with lime or phosphoric acid, the sugar is filtered through charcoal to whiten it and remove any calcium and magnesium salts. White sugar is 99.9% sucrose—it is nutrient-free, a veritable non-food.

Confectioner's (Powdered) Sugar is made by pulverizing white sugar into a powder.

Brown Sugar is simply granulated white sugar, colored with a small amount of molasses or burnt white sugar.

Corn Syrup, frequently seen on grocery shelves by the brand name "Karo," is nothing more than corn sugar in a liquid state. It is mostly glucose and is a highly refined, nutrient-empty product.

Fructose is a type of simple sugar, found naturally in most fruits and in honey. Commercially available fructose, however, is highly refined from corn and comes in liquid or white granulated form. It is the sweetest of all sugars, only a marginal improvement on regular white sugar, and a lot more expensive.

Salt

Salt has been used in breadbaking primarily for its taste and preservative qualities. It also slows and regulates yeast growth, and should not be added to doughs until the yeast has had a good start. Salt-free bread tends to rise faster and should be watched to avoid over-proofing and development of too yeasty a flavor. It may have a somewhat coarser texture than salted bread.

However, we want to stress that salt is not essential to breadbaking. You can make a great-tasting loaf without any salt, and yeast activity can easily be controlled by other methods. The addition of salt to cakes and cookies is just habitual and completely unnecessary. It can even be unpleasant when a soda taste is already present from baking soda or powder.

Salt is a ubiquitous taste that we encounter continually from birth. Almost all processed foods, from baby foods through pot pies and sweet snacks to soups and beverages, are loaded with salt. Our palates become habituated, and food without salt seems "tasteless." In fact, much salt (and sugar) is put into processed foods in order to conceal the fact that they have been completely denuded in taste! Meanwhile, modern science continues to uncover evidence that overuse of salt poses a serious health risk. So why eat it if you don't need it?

Many people aren't aware that commercial or table salt is refined by applying great pressure and temperatures to 1200° F, and then flash-cooling the salt solution. This strips away the many minerals and trace elements naturally present (though in minute quantities) in unrefined salt. The resulting crystals— 99.9° pure sodium chloride—are very small, with a tighter molecular bond than occurs during natural crystallization. According to several authorities, this makes refined salt not completely soluble and harder for our bodies to digest.

Moreover, a number of chemical substances are added to commercial salt: potassium iodide (supposedly as a health measure); dextrose (sugar) to keep the iodine from oxidizing; sodium bicarbonate to prevent the iodine turning the salt purple; sodium silico aluminate or magnesium carbonate to coat each crystal and prevent moisture absorption; silicon dioxide, yellow prussiate of soda (sodium ferrocyanide) and green ferric ammonium citrate—all permitted additives to promote free flow. Needless to say, none of these additives (including iodine) is necessary. So if you thought that—even if it was bad for you—at least salt was "pure," now you know! Just remember to say, "Pass the sodium ferrocyanide, please."

Commercial salt is generally made from inland salt deposits, originally left by oceans millions of years ago. Sea salt, available in coops and many groceries now, is richer in trace minerals than inland salt and our bakeries generally prefer it. The primary emphasis, however, is on using as little of this highly concentrated substance as possible—even when unrefined or "whole."

When you use whole grain and natural products, you will find your baked goods have a much more hearty and varied range of flavors than anything you ever bought at the supermarket. Enjoy these new and delightful tastes, and don't mask them with salt! All foods, including grains, naturally contain some sodium along with other minerals. If you feel initially that your bread is lacking in flavor, experiment with gradually reducing the salt, or use a substitute. Try any one or a combination of the almost endless variety of herbs and spices: basil, oregano, dill, thyme, tarragon, onion, garlic, caraway, poppy seeds, cumin, coriander, cinnamon, ginger, nutmeg, to name just a few. While making a transition to unsalted bread, some people use a more nutritious salty substance such as seaweed (powdered kelp, for example), nutritional yeast, or fermented soybean products like tamari and miso.

The recipes in **Uprisings** omit salt from cakes, cookies, muffins, granolas, and bars, since we have found its presence there to be unnecessary and even distasteful. In the bread recipes, two loaves rarely call for more than a teaspoon of salt. We encourage you to reduce or eliminate even this amount. Most of our bakeries offer salt-free breads, although the majority of loaves still contain it. Unyeasted breads work especially well without salt.

Fats and Oils

Fats and oils give richness, flavor, moistness, and calories to baked goods. They act as tenderizers in doughs by coating flour particles and inhibiting gluten formation. There are two main categories of fats: animal and vegetable. Animal fats include butter, egg yolks, cheeses, cream, and lard. They are very high in both saturated fat and cholesterol. Since all modern scientific research indicates that our diets are too high in these substances, many people avoid animal fats whenever possible. Environmental pollutants also concentrate in the fats of animals.

Vegetable fats include margarine, avocado, and many oils: olive, peanut, corn, safflower, sesame, sunflower, coconut, palm, and soybean, for example. Most of these are polyunsaturated fats, at least in their natural state. However, coconut and palm oils are high in saturated fats, and by hydrogenating any oil to make margarine or shortening, for example, the food processors turn them into saturated fats. You can cut out saturated fats by avoiding any fat that is solid at room temperature.

One serious problem with fats is their potential for rancidity. Any oil begins to oxidize, or go rancid, upon contact with air. Oxidation goes on even inside the body after oil has been consumed, and nutrients are taken from body tissues in order to try to digest and eliminate the undesired substances. In solid fats like butter or margarine, salt is often added to conceal the rancid taste and to act as a preservative. The process of oxidation in extracted oils can be slowed if they are kept tightly capped and refrigerated, but cannot be stopped altogether.

Common oil extraction methods involve heating and the addition of petroleum-based solvents. "Mechanically pressed" oils are superior since crushing is used instead of chemicals; these are sometimes referred to as "cold-pressed," although temperatures may reach 150° during processing. In addition, unrefined oils still contain nutrients, especially Vitamin E (an anti-oxidant which helps preserve the oil), lecithin, and some particles of germ. In contrast, refined oils have been bleached and deodorized, turning them pale and bland, and often disguising the fact that they are rancid.

The oil most commonly used in our bakeries is safflower, the oil highest in unsaturated fats. If a recipe just says "oil," it's probably safflower. Corn and soy oils are stronger flavored and are sometimes used in breads. Oil is usually put in bread recipes, but it can be omitted. It can often be

reduced in goodies, if you allow for the reduction of liquid. Oil works well in cookies, cakes, and pie crusts, although solid fats tend to produce a flakier dough. An oil gaining popularity among cookbook bakeries is canola oil. You might try experimenting with its light flavor in some of your baked goods.

Dairy Products

Dairy products add richness, texture, flavor, and nutrients to baked goods. Milk, the most common ingredient, produces a softer crumb and has a browning effect. It also retards staling better than water. However, with the exception of nonfat products (nonfat dry milk, nonfat yogurt, whey, and traditional buttermilk), dairy foods add lots of saturated fats and cholesterol to our diets. They also contain high levels of pesticide and pollutant residues, and additives such as hormones, which concentrate in the fat. Many people connected with our bakeries have come to feel that cow's milk, especially when pasteurized, may produce undesirable health effects (such as respiratory and digestive problems), so use dairy products with care.

Remember, too, that most cheeses are loaded with salt, though the unsalted versions are increasingly available. Dairy products are naturally high in sodium, so when using milk powder, many bakers reduce or cut out the salt. For other functions of milk and buttermilk in baked goods, see "Liquids" in this chapter. For suggestions on dairyless baking see "How to Bake—Substituting Ingredients." Despite our warnings, however, we can't pretend there's anything quite as rich and melt-in-the-mouth as a buttery cake or cream cheese frosting!

Eggs

Eggs contribute richness, nutrients, lightness, and a golden color to baked goods. The egg's protein coagulates during baking, adding to the structure of the crumb, while the lecithin serves as an emulsifier and the liquidity increases the moisture content. When beaten, eggs incorporate air and give batters a light airy texture. The whites alone can be beaten into a stiff, air-filled mass, and give a special lightness to cakes when folded in last of all ingredients. The yolks are very high in saturated fat and cholesterol, and give a thick richness to baked products.

Many people do not eat eggs because of the contaminants they may contain, their high fat content and the methods used in modern poultry production. Eggs can produce congestion and allergic reactions in many individuals. They are not essential in baking, since lightness and richness can be introduced by other means (see 'How to Bake—Substituting Ingredients). It is best to use eggs that are as fresh as possible, and at room temperature. Look for "free-range" and fertilized eggs for a more natural product.

Other Ingredients

Legumes

Beans, peas, lentils, and peanuts are legumes (or pulses), the fruits of leguminous plants. They have been eaten for thousands of years and today are food staples in many cultures; for example, lentils and chickpeas (garbanzo beans) in the Middle East and India, beans in the Americas, peanuts in Africa, and soybeans in the Far East. However, they are largely, and sadly, overlooked in the Western World.

Legumes are high in complex carbohydrates, vitamins, minerals, fiber, and protein (which complements the protein in grains). For the most part they are low in fat, and contain no cholesterol. Most of the nutrients are increased by sprouting.

Legumes can add flavor, texture, and nourishment to baked goods. Soybeans are most often used, generally as soy flour, which adds protein and helps bind in breads and goodies. Garbanzo flour can also be useful and makes an egg substitute. Soy oil, soy grits, and sometimes soy curd (tofu) are also used; tofu can be pureed into an egg substitute, or beaten smooth for frostings and cheesecakes. Peanuts and peanut butter are favorite baking ingredients, and make classic cookies. They can go rancid easily, however, and develop a toxic mold called aflatoxin, which survives roasting; check your source. Look for peanut butter without added oil, salt, sugar or stabilizers.

Nuts and Seeds

There is a large variety of nuts and seeds, including almonds, walnuts, pecans, cashews, filberts, or hazelnuts, Brazil nuts, coconut, sunflower seeds, sesame seeds, pumpkin seeds, poppy seeds, and caraway seeds, to name just a few. They can make very positive additions to the taste, texture, and nutrition of baked goods. Most are high in fat, though largely unsaturated, so use with discretion. Seeds and some nuts can be sprouted, or at least soaked, for greater digestibility.

Use nuts and seeds raw or toast them lightly for a stronger flavor. They can be ground into meal, toasted if you like, and added to baked goods for richness of texture, or first ground and then beaten at length, producing smooth nut butters. Nut butters made from almonds, pecans, walnuts, cashews, or sunflower seeds can make wondrously rich cookies and candies. For a dairyless frosting, cashews may be blended to a powder and mixed with liquid into a creamy paste. Nut and seed milks can replace dairy milk in recipes; simply soak almonds or cashews in water, strain, and blend with fresh water. You can filter out any solids if you prefer. Sunflower and sesame milk can be made the same way; the former is mild, while sesame milk has a strong, very rich flavor.

Coconut is usually finely shredded or in flakes, strips, or chips. It adds richness (it is high in saturated fats), flavor, and a pleasing texture to cakes, cookies, and candies. Shredded coconut can be lightly toasted before use. Fresh coconut can be used to produce vastly superior grated coconut, or coconut milk (blend grated flesh with water and strain), a very rich addition to cakes.

Nuts have the best flavor and food value when bought in the shell and shelled at home. In any case, refrigerate shelled nuts and don't buy them if they have a strong or rancid smell.

Sprouts

On all parts of this earth, seeds have been an object of reverence and awe throughout history. And well they should be, for a seed contains both the potential to become a plant and the elements necessary to sustain it through its early stages of life. Seeds are thus one of the richest foodstuffs for both humans and animals. But nutritious as the dry seeds are, their vitamin, fat, protein, and mineral content becomes even higher and more digestible when they are sprouted. Sprouts of all kinds are sufficient to sustain life, and are believed to have a cleansing and rejuvenating effect on our bodies.

Sprouts can make a great addition to breads, adding flavor, texture, crunch, and lots of nutrition. Wheat sprouts give a chewy sweetness to yeasted breads, and of course can be used alone in essene breads and goodies (see "How To Bake—Essene Bread"). Rye and other grains can be sprouted for this purpose. Other sprouts that go nicely in yeasted breads include alfalfa, mung, lentil, sunflower, and chickpea. Experiment and find your favorites. Buy organic seeds and sprout at home— it's easy, inexpensive, and fun!

Fruits and Vegetables

These can add a great variety of tastes, textures, sweetness, fiber, and nutrients to your baking. We talked about fruits in "Sweeteners," earlier in this chapter. They can be used fresh (in chunks, purees, sauces, or juices) and dried (whole, chopped, soaked, pureed, or ground). Soaking in apple cider or brandy adds a distinctive flavor to festive breads or cakes.

Vegetables can be incorporated into bread in chunks, grated, or pureed. Puree of winter squash will give you a delightfully golden loaf with a subtly delicious flavor and soft, moist texture. Mashed or grated potatoes add texture and flavor, and potato water is sometimes used to aid rising. Finely chopped or grated vegetables give wonderful flavor and aroma to breads; onion rolls are a classic, while a mixture of carrots, celery, onions, and green

pepper makes a delicious vegie bread. Tomatoes worked into your dough give a nice hint of color and fresh zesty flavor.

Kneading dough containing fresh fruits or vegetables will squeeze out juice and make it somewhat sticky. It is therefore easier to add them after some mixing, unless you want the flavors to permeate the bread. If so, be prepared to knead gently and perhaps add extra flour.

Herbs and Spices

These can add a wide variety of flavors, textures, and appearances to baked goods, and your lightly flecked dough will give off tantalizing aromas. Try one or two of your favorite herbs, but use discretion. Two herbs, each with a distinctive character, may taste odd when combined. Dried herbs are usually used, but try fresh for extra zip. Herbs are a good way to make a very flavorful bread in the absence of salt. Vegetables and Italian herbs added together to a loaf come out smelling like pizza!

Spices have their best flavor if used fresh; for instance, grind up cinnamon sticks, grate nutmeg or gingerroot, or lightly roast whole seeds and grind just before using. However, powdered spices will work fine. Use a little less of a spice if using fresh, as the flavor will be stronger. Keep herbs and spices in tightly capped containers to retain freshness.

Whole, Cracked, or Rolled Grains

Although we covered grains in some detail earlier in this chapter, it is worth noting here that grains in all forms make excellent additions to breads and goodies. If using the whole berries, presoak or sprout them. Cracked grains, grits, flakes, or meals add a nice variation of texture and taste.

Carob Powder

Carob powder or flour is ground from the carob pod or locust bean. It is believed to have been the staple of St. John the Baptist's diet in the wilderness—hence the name St. John's Bread, often applied to carob. Carob is a balanced product, naturally sweet, high in complex carbohydrates and nutrients, low in fat, and completely lacking in caffeine. These characteristics, along with its dark brown color and chocolatey flavor, have made it a popular replacement for cocoa products in baking. It can be used in small amounts for a subtle sweetness, or added generously for dark, aromatic products. The powder is available both raw and roasted, the latter being darker and perhaps more richly-flavored.

The ability to make carob chips using carob powder and a few other ingredients has given us a wide range of delicious chip cookies, just like the old days! Look for carob chips containing no additional sweetener, but be aware that they contain hydrogenated fats, such as palm oil, and sometimes milk powder.

Vinegar

Vinegar can be used for a variety of purposes in baking and derives from a variety of sources. Sugar vinegar comes from molasses, malt vinegar from grains or potatoes, wine vinegar from wine, and apple cider vinegar—most common in our bakeries—from apples. One tablespoon of vinegar in a loaf of bread is an effective preservative and mold retardant. In quick breads and cakes, vinegar's acidic quality reacts with baking soda to produce carbon dioxide and a very light texture.

Flavorings, Colorings, Trimmings

A few drops of flavoring essence or oil give great versatility to your baking. You can vary a basic butter cookie or cake recipe, for instance, by reaching for the vanilla, almond essence, orange or peppermint oil, to name a few. Vanilla essence finds its way into almost all "goodie" recipes—the flavor seems to complement others (it makes carob taste more chocolatey), and stands fragrantly on its own. Pure vanilla is made from beans (which you can buy and soak), and usually contains alcohol, which evaporates during baking. Even though expensive, it's vastly superior to synthetic vanillin, which is widely available. Look for flavorings labeled "natural." Even some of those we're not sure about, so buy and use them with awareness. With all the other good stuff going into your baking, it's worth keeping the dreadful artificial flavoring chemicals out of your kitchen.

Another chemical horror to avoid are the little bottles of coloring; artificial coloring agents are frequently carcinogenic. We've found several ways to color naturally for special occasion frostings, and there are probably many more plant-based dyes that haven't been explored. These natural juices tend to fade and separate after a period of time, so make and eat frostings quickly. Some suggestions:

> **red and pink:** beet juice (which will also produce a light pink in baked batters), hibiscus, concentrated red fruit juices
> **green:** parsley juice, any high chlorophyll juice (such as wheat grass)
> **orange:** carrot juice, orange juice
> **yellow:** turmeric (watch the quantity and flavor!), saffron
> **purple:** blueberry juice
> **brown:** carob powder

Let us know if you discover other safe and natural colorings.

Finally, for those finishing touches, avoid the bright-colored crystallized fruits and molded sugar decorations that are often used on cakes. Instead, create your own delightful patterns with fresh fruits, leaves, and flowers. These can be edible (mint leaves and violets are favorites), or can be removed before eating. For obvious reasons, these natural creations should be put together just before the big occasion.

HOW TO BAKE

This chapter contains suggestions on how to make bread and other baked goods. We want to do away with the mystique that surrounds baking; neither inborn talents nor lists of complicated directions are needed to bake well. Before you begin following your first bread recipe, it's better if you understand the simple processes that you initiate and help along when you bake. In the guidelines that follow, we describe what's happening in the dough as we set up methods. The more you bake, the more you will understand what's going on and why, and the results of your efforts will reflect your learning. That's why baking—bread, especially— is never simply repetitive. You learn something from how every batch behaves!

Nevertheless, don't feel too much trepidation about how doughs will act. There's actually a great deal of leeway in what you can do and still have things come out well. Experiment for yourself and your baking will get better still.

The methods described are ones that we have found to work well. The nature of our bakeries encourages the development of simple and straightforward, yet effective, techniques, and these are what we pass on to you. If your baking experience is limited, some practical advice will come in handy, while even the most seasoned baker may learn something from our approach. This isn't an exhaustive review of our techniques; for fancier stuff, consult a more "gourmet" bread book, and for any details you find lacking here, we recommend the **Tassajarah Bread Book** or **Laurel's Kitchen Bread Book** for their comprehensive instructions.

To eliminate a possible source of extreme frustration, make sure you have all the ingredients and equipment you'll need before beginning the baking process. Check the recipe, and then your supplies. It will be hard to make challah bread if you're out of eggs. In fact, it doesn't hurt to measure out your ingredients ahead of time. They're best at room temperature anyway. Make sure you have some extra flour for kneading, and oil or cornmeal to coat your pans or baking sheet. And check your equipment. Do you have what you need? Probably—you can get by with very little, as we'll see in the following section.

Useful Tools

You need only a few basic pieces of equipment to follow the recipes in **Uprisings**. Baking is an ancient method of preparing grains for eating and the tools have been mostly simple and functional. The criteria should be that the tool fit the task and feel comfortable in the hand. So be inventive.

Hands

Fortunately, the most essential tools most of us already possess. Hands get used a lot around our bakeries—to measure, mix, shape, scoop, test and taste. Although the baker's hands need to be, and will grow to be, strong and often calloused by the oven's heat, they need to remain gentle and sensitive. They must be able to lightly touch a baked good to test for readiness or caringly form a loaf. Take care of them.

Oven

The heat source for your baking is another important tool. Some baking can be done in the sun or over a fire or griddle, but you'll need an oven for most things. Learn the ways of your oven. Discover its hot and cold spots. While muffins and cupcakes prefer to "jump up" quickly in the hot part of the oven (usually the top shelf), most yeasted goods do well in a more moderate heat (middle perhaps). Borrowing or buying an oven thermometer lets you accurately test the oven. To avoid lopsided cakes, check the levelness of your oven. Unevenness can be remedied either by leveling the entire oven or simply sliding something non-combustible under one side of the baking pan to make it horizontal.

For a bread which has a thick hard crust, you may want to line the bottom of your oven with fire brick or quarry tile. Place a small pan of water in the oven to create steam. The brick retains heat and the steam creates a pleasant crisp crust.

Recently there has been a rebirth and interest in wood fired brick ovens. Though generally used commercially, some individuals are working to promote home sized, or small commmunity sized ovens using local materials as well as traditional brick and mortar. These ovens are regaining popularity for their unique style of bread baking, an added plus for a small group of people who want to further their bread baking skills.

Containers

Next, you'll need a few containers for mixing and baking (though you can mix doughs directly on a surface, by pouring wet ingredients into a well in the flour and mixing with your hands). Mixing containers should be non-porous, washable bowls or pots. A variety of sizes is useful for all-round baking, but you only need one large bowl for bread. As for baking containers, keep in mind that they must be ovenproof and non-toxic. Within those guidelines, be creative. Metal, tempered glass, ceramic and clay molds, pots, and pans are all suitable. A rectangular 4½" X 8½" pan gives you a standard 1½ pound loaf, but round pans and baking sheets will also do fine. Unusual containers for baking bread are empty metal cans and clean clay flower pots. It's best not to wash bread pans—let them get well-seasoned so the bread won't stick.

Utensils

A few simple tools can help you out in your baking. Measuring cups and spoons are useful to get proportions right. A sturdy long-handled wooden spoon (metal is OK) is good for mixing and beating batters and doughs. Also helpful, but even less essential, is a dough knife or scraper of some kind for cleaning encrusted dough from your kneading surface; a more flexible spatula or scraper to thoroughly empty a bowl or pan (you can make a semi-circular one by cutting a firm plastic lid in half); a brush for oiling pans or glazing dough, a sieve or sifter to keep lumps out of your dry ingredients; for cookies, a tablespoon, ice cream scoop or small cup for scooping batter, and a cookie press, jar lid or tumbler for pressing them down; and perhaps a rack for cooling your baked goods.

Kneading Surface

One final important tool is the kneading surface for your bread dough. Keep in mind that semi-porous surfaces, such as marble or oiled wood, are the most desirable. But any smooth, clean surface that does not flake or splinter will do. The remaining consideration regarding the work surface is that you arrange it to be at an appropriate height so you can knead comfortably while standing.

Finally, try to bring yourself—your time, thought, and caring—to your baking. We know so well, from our bakeries and kitchens that our creations can only be as good as the energy and love that we put into them. OK, we're ready to begin with ...

Yeasted Breads

Making the Sponge

The sponge is the batter containing liquid, yeast, sweetener (optional—see below), and some of the flour. When allowed to sit for a period of time, the sponge puffs up. The yeast organisms become very active and produce carbon dioxide, which stretches the gluten in the flour and causes the whole thing to rise. This way the gluten gets a good start in developing its muscle.

Two points about a sponge: first, **sweetener isn't necessary.** The yeast will feed on the starch in flour, which first must be converted into sugars by the action of enzymes. So an unsweetened sponge will take a little longer to rise.

Second, you may want to **"proof" or test your yeast** before making the sponge. This simple step checks that the yeast you are using is good—still alive and ready to activate.

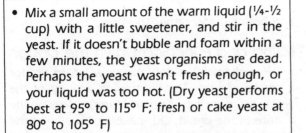

- Mix a small amount of the warm liquid (¼-½ cup) with a little sweetener, and stir in the yeast. If it doesn't bubble and foam within a few minutes, the yeast organisms are dead. Perhaps the yeast wasn't fresh enough, or your liquid was too hot. (Dry yeast performs best at 95° to 115° F; fresh or cake yeast at 80° to 105° F)

The sponge method, fully described in Tassajarah, is favored by most of our bakeries to produce good texture and rise. It can be omitted, however, as we discuss in the next section.

- Mix the warm liquid with the sweetener, if used, and stir in the yeast till it dissolves. Beat in a portion of the flour, producing a thick, gloppy batter.
- Stir the sponge vigorously with a whisk or wooden spoon for a few minutes (about 100 strokes). You want to remove any lumps and see the batter begin to develop a stretchy texture.
- Cover the bowl and let the sponge sit in a warmish place for 30 to 60 minutes, although less is alright. If your yeast proves to be alive, just add remaining liquid and sweetener and proceed with the sponge.

After being left for a while, the sponge will rise and develop a bulging, frothy top, somewhat reminiscent of geothermal bubbling mud pools. (If it doesn't, start again, proofing your yeast if you haven't already done so). Keep an eye on a rising sponge—cleaning up an overflow is no joke. You can beat or whisk a sponge that's getting too high, and cut it down to size, but it'll come up again. Don't beat it down too many times, though—this seems to exhaust the gluten.

Omitting the Sponge

As we said, some bakeries don't sponge their bread and it comes out fine. If you want to skip this step, just mix all the ingredients into a dough (starting with liquid, sweetener, and yeast) and begin kneading. But since the gluten hasn't had a workout already, be prepared to knead longer to develop a good elastic texture in the dough. If you're dubious about your yeast, it would be advisable to proof it first before mixing everything or you could waste a lot of food.

Mixing the Dough

The most important point about mixing the dough is to **leave some of the flour till the end** so you can adjust the amount. The absorbency of flour can vary a lot, so feel your way, incorporating it gradually.

- Into the frothing sponge, mix the remaining ingredients, reserving some of the flour. (It may be easier to add chunky ingredients, like nuts or fruits, after you have kneaded for a while.) Stir well with a wooden spoon and/or your hands.
- Add flour gradually, until the stirred dough begins to come away from the sides of the bowl and becomes a more compact mass. This tells you that you are ready to start the kneading process.

Kneading

At this stage, you want to give the dough a thorough massage to achieve a smooth, well-mixed texture and a springy elasticity. This is when you can really develop the gluten and you will feel the dough become more cohesive and bouncy under your hands. (For rolls and yeasted pastries, less kneading will produce a fluffy rather than elastic texture.)

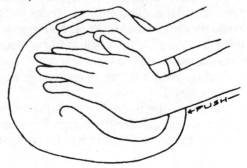

- Sprinkle your kneading surface with a dusting of flour and tip out a small extra mound of flour to one side. Pat your hands in this, repeating as often as necessary to avoid sticking.
- Turn out the dough from the bowl in a compact mass and begin to knead. Putting the base of your palms into the dough, push it down and away from you with a firm, rocking motion. This is not a time to be delicate; push with power, but don't be too rough or you'll tear the dough. Add flour if it seems too sloppy.
- After each push, rotate the dough a quarter turn, fold it in half towards you and repeat the process. Try to develop a good rhythm: push—rock—rotate—fold. Keep the flat surface of the dough down on your kneading surface and the folded surface on top.

You are finished kneading when the dough feels cohesive, smooth, and elastic. This usually takes about 8-10 minutes. Some useful indicators are:

1. The dough no longer feels sticky (see below for exceptions).
2. Little blisters appear just below the surface.
3. When pressed, the dough springs back.
4. When stroked, the dough feels cool and smooth, like your ear lobe. The surface is almost shiny.
5. A cherry-sized piece of dough can be stretched to approximately two inches square before tearing.

The dough may remain sticky while showing other indications of being well-kneaded when it contains any of the following: lots of eggs and butter; some cooked grains; juicy fruits and vegetables; or, most commonly, a fair amount of rye flour. In these cases, avoid adding more and more flour or you'll end up with a dense, unresponsive dough and heavy bread.

If your loaves are to be free-form (baked on a sheet, not in a pan), make the dough firm enough to retain its shape. You'll want it to be on the firm and bouncy side, rather than soft and stretchy.

Rising and Punching Down the Dough

The well-kneaded dough is now left to rise for a period of time. The continuing activity of the yeast will make it puff up and further develop the texture of the bread. Our bakeries usually let the dough rise twice before shaping into loaves. One rising is adequate, but the texture and lightness of the bread improves with additional risings.

- Oil your bowl lightly and place the kneaded dough in it, smooth side down. Rotate the dough in the bowl, then flip it over. A fine film of oil prevents the surface from crusting over. Cover the bowl with a damp cloth, towel, or apron, or place it in a large plastic bag.
- Set the bowl in a warm, draft-free place. You don't want it much hotter than 100° F; the dough will rise in a cooler place, but will take more time.
- Leave the dough alone until it has puffed up to approximately double its original bulk. This may take anywhere from 30 minutes to several hours, depending on the temperature and the density of the dough, but usually 45-60 minutes is about right. A good test: poke your finger about an inch into the dough. If a hole remains, the dough has risen sufficiently. If the hole slowly springs back, leave the dough to rise some more.
- When fully risen, punch down the dough by thrusting your fist into it repeatedly (this is great fun with 100 lbs. of bread dough!) You want to flatten most of the air out.
- If you are having a second rising in the bowl, cover again and let sit until nearly doubled. This will probably take 30-45 minutes. Punch down.

Now, with your once- or twice-risen dough, you are ready to shape the loaves and leave them for the final rising.

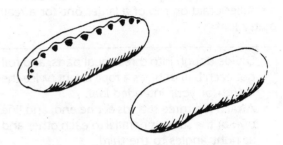

Shaping the Loaves

There are as many different ways to shape loaves as there are bakers! The two principal concerns are getting the air out of the dough and having a nice smooth top to your loaves as they fit snugly in the pans or sit handsomely on the baking sheet. Feel your way with these aims in mind. We describe some common methods below, in case you need help.

Regular-shaped Loaves

- Perform a kind of one-handed kneading, pushing with one hand while rotating and folding in the far edge of the dough with the other. Just do this briefly until you have a compact round-oval shape with the smooth surface on the bottom.
- Flatten this lightly to an oblong or round-cornered rectangle, about the length of your pan. (Or adjust your kneading to achieve this shape right away.)
- Pick up the edge of the dough nearest you and roll it up in a fairly tight roll.
- Pinch the dough together along the seam, then tuck in and tidy up the ends of the loaf. Gently roll the loaf on the seam a few times to perfect the shaping.
- Place smooth side up in an oiled bread pan.

Round Loaves

If this is to be a free-standing loaf, remember to have the dough firm enough to hold its shape without support.

- Briefly knead the dough, pulling in the farthest edge and rotating the dough until you have a compact round shape with the smooth surface on the bottom. Squeeze and pinch the folded-in edges together.
- Flip the dough over. Cup the left side of the dough with your left hand, and the right side with your right. Shuffle the dough around with your hands in a circular direction, shaping and perfecting a symmetrical round loaf.
- Place on an oiled or cornmeal-dusted baking sheet.

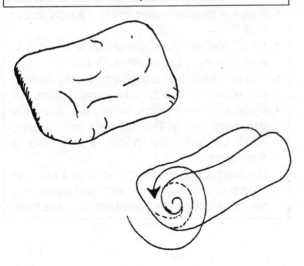

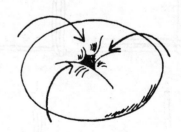

Braided Breads

These are very easy and look great. You can place a smaller braid on top of a larger one for a really pretty loaf.

- Divide dough into three equal parts, and roll out each ball until it's a rope about twice the length of your intended loaf.
- Attach the three strands at one end, and line two of the strands parallel to each other and at right angles to the third.
- Take the outer parallel strand, bring it over the other parallel strand, and place it parallel to the original single strand. (Don't cross the original single strand!) Repeat.
- Continue repeating the last step, always moving the outer parallel strand, until the dough has been used up.
- Pinch the three ends together to complete the loaf.
- Place in an oiled bread pan or on a dusted baking sheet.

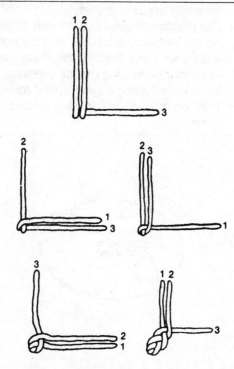

French-style Long Loaves (Baguettes)

Unless you have a long, thin, pan, remember again to make a firm-textured dough so it doesn't flatten too much on the baking sheet. Then merely adapt the regular loaf, shaping to produce a long loaf with somewhat tapering ends.

Rolls

The shapes of rolls are limited only by your imagination! Play with small mounds of dough and see what you can come up with. Rolls can be set on a baking sheet or in a muffin pan. A few suggestions:

- Shape a regular round roll like a mini round loaf.
- Divide roll into three round balls and tuck into a muffin pan, for cloverleaf rolls.
- Roll out the ball of dough into a long sausage shape, and tie knots, make spirals, twists, etc.
- Make a crescent roll by rolling out into a flat triangular shape. Roll up tight from a wide edge towards the point. Curve into a semi-circle.
- For bagels, either join the ends of a sausage shape, or make a round ball and push your thumbs through the center, shaping the hole.

Final Rising

After your loaf has been shaped, it must rise once more before baking. This is called "proofing" (or "proving") the bread. Bakeries use a warmed, humid cabinet—the proof box—for this step.

> - Place the bread pan or baking sheet with the shaped loaf on it in a warm, draft-free, and preferably humid spot. Cover with a damp cloth, or place in a plastic bag.
> - Let the loaf rise till it's about doubled in size— usually about 20-30 minutes. Allow less time for rolls.

At the end of this final rising, the loaf is ready to bake if it looks quite puffed up, with a kind of inflated tension to its surface. In a bread pan, the sides of the loaf will come up to the top of the pan while the center of the loaf's top will be an inch or two above the pan. A common test is to gently press the loaf with the tip of a finger. A soft impression that doesn't bounce back indicates that the bread won't rise much more and it's time to bake. A little resistance to your touch is alright, though— the bread needs a last bit of rising power when it first goes into the heat of the oven. If your loaf "overproofs" (gets overblown-looking and wrinkles or collapses), you can take it out of the pan and reshape it. Then let it rise again in the pan. If you don't reshape an overproofed loaf, the top will probably collapse in the oven, or you may get large air pockets in your final loaf.

Just prior to baking, some bakers like to make one or more shallow slashes on the top of the loaf with a sharp knife. This relieves surface tension and allows the loaf to rise in the oven without splitting; it also looks nice. This is most often done on free-form loaves. To glaze breads, brush lightly with milk or egg for a shiny crust, or spray or brush with water (and again in the oven) for a chewy crust. Brushing with oil *after* baking produces a soft crust.

Baking

The oven should be up to full heat when you put the bread in. Bread is usually baked at 350° F for 45 minutes, but some bakeries bake for 30-35 minutes at 400° F. The recipe will specify.

> - Gently put the loaf into a preheated oven (the middle shelf is often a good spot for moderate heat).
> - Check the loaf after the recommended baking time. It should be golden brown. Take it out of the pan; the bottom corners should be firm, not soft, and the loaf should sound hollow when solidly thunked with a finger or knuckle. If it doesn't feel and sound right, return the bread to the pan and the oven, and give it more time.
> - When you are satisfied that the bread is done, take it out of or off the pan right away and place it on a rack to cool.

Oven temperature gauges being notoriously unreliable, it's a good idea to keep an eye on your breads as they bake until you learn the characteristics of the oven. If a loaf darkens prematurely, place another pan over it, tent it with foil or parchment, or turn down the oven a little.

Storing the Bread

Bread keeps best in an airtight bag in a cool, well-ventilated spot. Make sure it is completely cooled before bagging it, or the moisture that builds up will give you wet bread that molds rapidly.

Keep bread in the refrigerator if you're keeping it for more than two or three days, especially in summer. Refrigeration retards molding, but the bread will become drier and less flavorful. A tablespoon of vinegar in a loaf acts as a preservative to some extent. Bread can be frozen, but loses texture and some taste. Use immediately after thawing and don't refreeze. Slicing the loaf before freezing allows you to thaw just the amount you want at any one time.

Slightly stale bread can be reheated satisfactorily in a 350° F oven for 10-15 minutes. You can heat even small amounts if wrapped in foil. Sprinkling the oven floor with drops of water or quickly brushing a loaf all over with water or milk, and then placing unwrapped in a hot oven for 10-15 minutes, really rejuvenates a loaf and gives it a nice crusty surface.

Old bread can be used in a number of ways: for breadcrumbs, soft or toasted; croutons; rusks or zwieback; French toast and garlic bread; or recycled in bread pudding recipes (see Index).

Slice bread with a serrated knife if possible. If you use a regular kitchen knife, make certain it is very sharp or it will tear the bread. If you're slicing a warm loaf, wash and dry the blade after every one or two slices; this prevents the blade from sticking to the bread and tearing it.

Sourdough Breads

Here in the United States, the special flavor of sourdough is commonly associated with San Francisco. However, sourdough is an ancient form of bread baking the world around. Sourdough cultures are handed down from one family to another, often spanning over a hundred years in places like Germany and Holland. Many European breads are sourdoughs, and we in the States are recognizing the beauty of sourdough once again.

What sets sourdough apart from other types of bread is the inclusion of a sourdough "starter," or culture, for leavening and taste-enhancing purposes. This starter is nothing more than a blend of water and flour which has been left to ferment, producing the distinctive sour taste.

- To make sourdough starter, combine ⅓ to ½ cup of any flour with 1 cup of water. Keep it in a warm place and stir daily for one week. Your starter is then ready for use.
- Keep the starter in the refrigerator when not in use. It will keep there indefinitely as long as it is occasionally "fed." Feed it by stirring in a tablespoon of flour every week. It's easy to save some starter every time you use it to make a batch of bread.

Great tasting sourdough breads require nothing more than flour, water, and starter (see recipe by Nature's Bakery on pg. 126). Sourdough starter can be included in other doughs as well to add unique flavor. Please refer to **Laurel's Kitchen Bread Book** for a much more thorough and detailed accounting of working with sourdoughs.

Unyeasted Breads

Unyeasted breads are not hard to make and have their own unique appeal. They require basically the same methods as yeasted breads. However, since they have to develop their own yeasts, they need to rise for a long time. The dough is usually made the day before and left to sit overnight. Avoid using bowls made of aluminum or plastic, since the dough tends to absorb molecules of these materials.

After placing the loaves in the pans, cut deeply down the center of the loaf lengthwise, or make deep diagonal cuts across the top, to allow carbon dioxide to escape. Brushing the tops with oil or water helps avoid drying out during the last rising.

Unyeasted breads need to bake longer than yeasted ones—often up to 1½ hours at 350° F. The recipe will specify. The bread is done when the sides and bottom are darkish brown and hard, and the bread sounds hollow.

Essene Bread

Standing somewhat apart from the mainstream of Western baking tradition are the essene breads. Just the name seems to suggest something mysterious, even exotic, and certainly complicated to create. True, essene bread is different from the ordinary yeasted loaves with which we are familiar, but it is also simple to prepare, exceptionally nutritious, and best of all, a real taste treat.

What Is It?

With no pun intended, essene bread is the very essence of simplicity. The only required ingredients are sprouted grain and water, and you can easily make your own sprouts. The sprouts are ground to a doughy consistency, shaped into loaves, and baked at very low heat until crusty on the outside but still moist and chewy inside. Nothing else is needed: no yeast, sweeteners, flour, oil, salt, and of course, no chemical conditioners or preservatives! You can add other items to the dough—nuts, seeds, dried fruits, chopped apple, or spices—and they can give exciting new tastes and variety to your breads. But these ingredients are just nice, not necessary. Plain essene bread has a surprisingly sweet and nutty-rich flavor all its own.

Hard whole wheat berries are used most frequently, and work extremely well. When sprouted, they become very sweet (since, through sprouting, the starches in the grains are converted into sugars), and once ground, produce a workable dough which holds together well when shaped into loaves. But other grains can be used too, and each will have its own characteristics of taste and texture. Rye berries, for example, also become sweet when sprouted, yet they have a taste which is distinctly different from wheat. Other possibilities are soft whole wheat (more crumbly and milder-flavored than hard), triticale, barley, millet, and oats. Combining different grains produces interesting new flavors.

Historically, essene bread is one of the earliest varieties of bread. It derives its name from a recipe of the ancient Essenes as recorded in **The Essene Gospel of Peace**, a 1st Century Aramaic manuscript. The speaker is Jesus Christ.

" 'How should we cook our daily bread without fire, Master?' asked some with great astonishment.

'Let the angels of God prepare your bread. Moisten your wheat, that the angel of water may enter it. Then set it in the air, that the angel of air also may embrace it. And leave it from morning to evening beneath the sun, that the angel of sunshine may descend upon it. And the blessing of the three angels will soon make the germ of life to sprout in your wheat. Then crush your grain, and make thin wafers, as did your forefathers when they departed out of Egypt, the house of bondage. Put them back again beneath the sun from its appearing, and when it is risen to its highest in the heavens, turn them over on the other side that they be embraced there also by the angel of sunshine, and leave them there until the sun be set.' "(p.37)

How to Make It

You will need a few items of basic equipment to make your essene bread. Nothing special is required; most of the essentials will already be in your kitchen.

1. **Containers for sprouting.** Large-mouthed glass jars are ideal, but any container that holds water will work fine (a large plastic tub, soup pot, etc.)
2. **Breathable tops for the sprouting containers.** A piece of fine screening or cheesecloth is best, placed over the container's mouth and secured with a strong rubber band (or you can punch holes in a screw-on lid that fits your container). Anything which will allow air and water, but not sprouts, to pass through easily is fine.
3. **Grinder.** A hand-operated food or meat grinder is the least expensive and psychologically most satisfying, but a Champion Juicer or food processor works well.

4. **Miscellaneous items.** You will also need a large bowl to hold your dough, a cookie sheet, and, of course, an oven (except in the case of sun-baked, or dried, wafers and patties).

The Ingredients are unbelievably simple. Just buy a quantity of the grain you've decided to use. But remember, the grain must be suitable for sprouting; therefore, you need uncooked, unsprayed, **whole** berries. Neither cracked wheat or pearled barley, for example, will sprout. Hard red winter wheat works extremely well, and it is very inexpensive when bought in bulk from your local food coop or natural foods store.

To sprout the berries, follow these simple steps:

1. Measure the desired amount of berries. One cup of berries gives you about 2 cups of dough.

2. Soak berries overnight in the sprouting container, using twice the berries' volume in water.

3. In the morning, drain off the soaking water through the breathable top. Save this mineral-rich liquid for drinks, soups, or to water your plants.

4. Place the jar in a dark place, and rinse with cool water twice each day. Drain thoroughly. This helps make the sprouts less prone to spoilage. Occasionally shake the jar vigorously to keep the roots from matting together in a solid, unmanageable clump.

5. Sprouts are ready when the sprout hairs are about 2 times as long as the berry— usually 2½ to 3 days after soaking—and have a sweet, mild taste.

6. Skip the last rinse before grinding so that the berries won't be too moist.

To make your dough, take the sprouts when they have reached the right length, and put them through the grinder. Oiling the grinding parts before use helps prevent sticking. The result should be a juicy, sticky dough that is mottled light and dark brown in color; the consistency is somewhat similar to raw hamburger.

The dough is ready to use as soon as it emerges from the grinder. If you can't continue at that point, cover the dough tightly with food wrap and place in the refrigerator. Also, if you are going to add nuts or fruit to the dough, now's the time. Soaking dried fruit first (20-30 minutes in hot water) will give the fruit a pleasing, juicy texture.

To shape the loaves, wet your hands well and take a quantity of dough; one large handful will make a nice roll while a big two-handed scoop will give you a larger loaf. Work the dough with your hands briefly to produce a smooth surface and to insure that there are no air pockets inside. No kneading is required. Shape into round loaves, with slightly flattened tops. Rewet your hands (and working surface if necessary) before handling each new loaf. Place on a cookie sheet that is lightly oiled or dusted with cornmeal to prevent sticking. These are now ready to bake.

To bake essene bread, place in a 200° - 275° F oven for about 2-3 hours (less for rolls) till the outside is firm and the bottom, though not hard, is firm enough to spring back slightly after a gentle prod with the thumb. The inside will be quite soft—a firmer texture develops upon cooling. Essene can actually be baked at a wide variety of temperatures, from as low as 120° (for 8-10 hours) up to 300°. Bear in mind that if you bake the loaves too long, they will tend to dry out on the inside. Also, baking at too high a temperature will tend to overcook the outside of the loaves. And both of these probably cause excessive loss of nutrients. To help prevent drying out, some bakeries spray the loaves with water both before and during baking.

For storage, let the loaves cool on a wire rack after removing from the oven (try not to eat all of them while still warm). When completely cold, store in sealed plastic bags. If you're going to eat your essene bread within 3-4 days, keep it out of the refrigerator as it will stay moister this way. Otherwise refrigerate; it'll keep up to 4 weeks. Essene bread can be frozen.

Quick Breads and Muffins

These are quite simple and fast. They use baking powder or soda to achieve a light texture, and require no kneading or rising times. The same batter can be poured into a loaf pan or baked as muffins or cupcakes. You can produce a batch of hot muffins from scratch in not much more than half an hour, so they're ideal if you're short of time.

The most important thing to remember when making muffins and quick breads is to **mix gently and quickly** and, once mixed, to pour the batter into the pans and **bake right away.** The leavening agents will begin to act when combined with liquid or when stirred about—not so fast that you need to rush, but have your pans oiled and oven fully heated before the final mixing of ingredients. (You can preheat the oiled pans, too, if you like.)

- Combine all the dry ingredients in one bowl, sifting the baking powder or soda. Combine all the wet ingredients in another container, first creaming the oil or butter well with the sweetener to ensure lightness.
- Combine the wet with the dry ingredients, stirring lightly and just enough to moisten the dry ingredients (some lumps are ok). *Don't beat!*
- Fill oiled pans or muffin cups about ¾ full with batter (remember it'll rise in the oven).
- Place in fully preheated oven. The temperature is usually 350° - 400° for these baked goods. Muffins bake for 20-30 minutes, loaves for an hour or more. Test for doneness by inserting a knife, fork, or toothpick into the center—it should come out cleanly, and not be gooey. When done, the top will feel springy and the sides will brown a little and begin to pull away from the pan.
- Once out of the oven, let sit a few minutes before removing from the pan. Then cool on a rack. Refrigerate quick breads if you're keeping them longer than two or three days—they mold fairly fast. They will dry out somewhat, though, if refrigerated or frozen. Reheating in foil works well.

One final point about quick breads and muffins: since they don't require gluten, whole wheat flour isn't necessary. You therefore have a lot of leeway, and can substitute just about any flour (whole grain or legume) for the flour in the recipe. Have fun experimenting.

Cakes and Brownies

These are usually made in the same way as quick breads: combine wet—combine dry—mix them together lightly—pour batter into oiled or floured pans and bake right away. Test for doneness in the same way too. Cakes may call for mixing ingredients in a somewhat more elaborate manner—the recipe will give directions. Cake batters can usually be baked in muffin pans for light cupcakes.

Pies

Many people avoid pie-making because they think it's a special art. It's just not true. Pies are very satisfying and relatively simple to make. They also look and taste great! In particular, crusts are not difficult and can be put together quickly from a wide range of ingredients. We suggest below several different ways to make a pie a crust; these just indicate the potential. Experiment with your own ideas.

1. A crumb crust or granola crust; for example, cookie crumbs, toasted bread crumbs, or granola, bound together with oil, butter or juice, plus honey and spices if you like.
2. Raw bread dough, rolled out thin and baked without rising.
3. Slices of already-baked bread, laid overlapping and rolled out thin, to cover the pie plate.
4. A tasty blend of grains and nuts which can be served raw. For example, for an 8-9" pie, let 1½ cups rolled oats and ½ cup chopped almonds sit for half an hour

in about ½ cup cider or fruit juice. Press with wetted hands onto an oiled pie plate. This crust can be chilled (it'll stay crumbly), or baked (which holds it together well).

5. Just sprinkle the pie plate with wheat germ or crumbs, or forget the crust entirely and make pudding instead of pie!

6. Make a pie crust from flour and oil or butter, with a liquid to hold it together. Here are two—one buttery, the other dairyless—and both easy. In both cases, avoid overhandling and too much flour, for a lighter crust.

Buttery pastry crust—for an 8-9" single crust pie
   5-6 Tbl. cold butter
   1½ cups whole wheat pastry flour
   3 Tbl. cold water
   1 Tbl. vinegar

Work the butter into the flour, breaking it down into small lumps with a fork or your fingers. Rub it in until it's like fine breadcrumbs in texture. Mix in water and vinegar, adding a little flour, if needed, to make a soft, rollable dough.
Roll out on a lightly floured surface to fit pie plate. Rub buttered paper around plate to grease it.
Lift pastry carefully and press onto plate, trimming the edges and patterning with a floured fork, or fluting the edges with fingers or a spoon.
Prick the crust several times with a fork. Bake at about 375° for 10-15 minutes for full baking or 5-10 minutes for partial baking. It's OK to bake it longer at 350° or shorter at 400°.

Dairyless pie crust—for an 8-9" single crust
   ¼ cup mild oil (e.g. safflower or canola oil)
   1½ cups whole wheat pastry flour
   ½ cup water

Mix all ingredients together, adding a little extra liquid, if needed, to make a rolling consistency. Roll out and proceed as for buttery crust. Bake for slightly less time.

Cookies

The recipe instructions are usually adequate for these simple treats. Here are a few tips:

- Mix wet ingredients separately from dry ingredients, and combine them. Cream butter or oil well with the sweetener for a light, smooth texture.
- The batter needn't be spooned out right away unless it contains a lot of baking powder or soda.
- Spoon mounds of between 1 tablespoon and ¼ cup (depending on cookie size) onto oiled baking sheet. You can use a spoon, cup or ice cream scoop, dipping in water every now and then. Space cookies to allow for spreading if the recipe mentions this.
- To flatten cookies, use your fingers, a cookie press, the bottom of a tumbler, or a fork, dipping often in water to prevent sticking.
- Bake as directed in the recipe, usually at 350° for 10-20 minutes. Cookies will often still be soft when done, firming up as they cool. Look for light browning and firming around the edges. Gently lift one cookie with a spatula and see if the bottom looks nicely browned. In general, remove immediately from sheet and cool cookies on a rack.

One last point about baking powder or soda in cookies. This is usually given as an optional ingredient. We tested recipes both with and without it. Cookies made with thse leavening agents come out slightly lighter and with a more porous texture; omitting it produces a somewhat firmer cookie that needs a little longer baking time. Taste-wise, there isn't a great deal of difference, except for that hint of soda which some people don't like.

Substituting Ingredients

One of the most exciting aspects of whole grain baking is the opportunity it offers for exploring new combinations and tastes. A major feature of this in our bakeries is the active search for ingredients and methods that make our whole grain goods even healthier, but not less delicious. As we saw in "Foods for Whole Grain Baking," a growing number of people are becoming aware of undesirable effects associated with eating various foods: for example, dairy products, eggs, leaveners, fats, sweeteners, wheat, and salt. To accommodate these preferences, many bakers have experimented with ways to bake deliciously without using these ingredients. **Uprisings** contains a number of dairyless, eggless, and wheatless recipes, as well as the "Index by Special Dietary Characteristic" to help you find recipes which don't contain the food you wish to avoid.

Below we suggest some substitutions that should make it easier to alter any recipe in **Uprisings** to suit your dietary viewpoint, as well as convert an old favorite of your own to a more nutritious version. Or simply use these suggestions to increase the versatility of your baking, to replace an ingredient you're out of, or to save on costs. Don't expect the results to come out exactly the same as the original, and be prepared to experiment to see what works best in each case. The following substitutions are meant only as guidelines which some bakers have found helpful. Please let us know of any others you've had success with.

Suggested Substitutions

Brackets [ ] denote a more healthful variant of the undesired ingredient, but not a real alternative.

Asterisk (*) indicates when substituting a liquid for a solid or dry ingredient, to reduce other liquids and bake slightly longer at a lower temperature (by about 25°).

Wheat *(1 cup, unless noted)*
White flour
- 7/8-1 cup whole wheat flour (absorbency varies)

Whole wheat pastry flour
- Hard whole wheat flour (except in cakes)
- Other flours: rye, barley, rice, corn, oat, millet

Whole wheat bread
- 100% rye bread
- 100% triticale bread
- Essene bread (Most essene bread is made with sprouted wheat; however, many people who suffer reactions to wheat do not have the same problems when it has been sprouted.)

Dairy Products *(1 cup, unless noted)*
Whole Milk
- Soy Milk
- Seed or nut milk: grind sunflower or sesame seeds, almonds or cashews, then blend with water into milk; or soak, and blend with fresh water.
- [Skim milk]

Milk Powder
- Soy powder
- [Whey powder]

Yogurt, sour milk, buttermilk
- Soy milk curdled with 2 tsp. lemon juice
- Soy yogurt

Butter
- Soy or vegetable oil margarine
- ⅔ - 1 cup oil

Cream cheese
- Tofu
- Cashew cheese: grind or blend cashews to fine powder, then blend into thick cream with water or juice

Sour Cream
- Soy yogurt
- [Yogurt]

Solid Fats *(1 cup)*
- ⅔-1 cup vegetable oil*

Eggs

For one egg, substitute:

- 1 Tbl. tahini plus 3 Tbl. liquid
- 1 Tbl. garbanzo flour plus 1 Tbl. oil
- 1 Tbl. lecithin granules plus 3 Tbl. liquid
- 1 Tbl. arrowroot powder plus 3 Tbl. liquid
- 4 Tbl. of: 1 part flaxseed plus 3 parts water, blended smooth
- 3 Tbl. liquid plus 1 Tbl. of blend of: 2 parts arrowroot, 1 part tapioca flour, 1 part slippery elm
- [2 egg whites]

Salt

Quantities of salt substitutes should be determined according to taste. See our section on "Salt."

- Herbs, onion powder, caraway seeds
- Seasonings like vegetable powder or nutritional yeast
- Powdered kelp, other seaweeds
- Lemon juice (in goodies)
- [Tamari or miso] (contain salt from the fermenting process)
- [Sea salt or solar salt, instead of commercial table salt]

Leaveners

Yeasted breads

- Sourdough or unyeasted breads
- Essene bread
- Baking powder—or soda—leavened loaves

Baking powder or soda

- Add some cornmeal or coarse-ground rice flour; they tend to absorb water as they bake, expanding and creating some lightness.
- Replace some of the flour with rolled oats or granola; these contribute texture and may add some lightness.
- Try making a paste with a little yeast, water, and flour: let sit 30-60 minutes, then use.*

Commercial baking powder (equal quantities)

- [Commercial low-sodium baking powder]
- [Homemade baking powder: blend 2 parts arrowroot, 1 part baking soda, 1 part cream of tartar]

Sweeteners (1 cup, unless noted)
White sugar

- ½ cup honey or maple syrup*
- ⅔ cup malt syrup*
- ⅔ cup date sugar

Honey

- Maple syrup
- 1⅓ cups malt syrup

Honey, malt syrup, maple syrup

- Date butter: soak dates or date pieces in a little hot water till soft. Blend to a smooth paste. (Other dried fruits can be used, but date butter is sweetest and smoothest.)
- Fruit purees

Protein

This refers to the combining of different protein sources to make "complete" protein, a concept popularized by Lappe's first edition of **Diet for a Small Planet.** However, the 1982 edition emphasized that this is not necessary for good health. Add a little:

- Milk powder, other dairy products
- Whole or ground sesame or sunflower seeds
- Legumes, such as soy or garbanzo flour, tofu, or peanuts

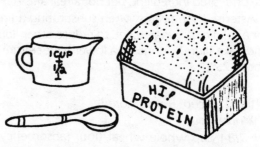

Problems and Solutions

Time

There are a number of breadmaking shortcuts which are simple, save time, assist planning, and help cope with interruptions:

1. *A bread sponge or dough can be refrigerated* (or put in any cool spot) to slow down yeast activity and hence rising. If you're interrupted while making bread, refrigerate covered dough until you return. Then allow to warm up and continue where you left off. This also enables you to prepare dough for later baking (for example, if you want fresh bread for dinner but have to go to work). Refrigerate the covered dough just before or just after shaping. When ready to prepare the dough for baking, place it in a warm place to rise (allow for warming-up time) and proceed as usual. Refrigerating preshaped cinnamon rolls or bagels overnight gives you the best kind of "fast food" breakfast!

2. *Dough can also be frozen.* Divide the dough into loaf-sized pieces, flatten (for even thawing), and wrap loosely. Trays of shaped rolls or bagels work very well when frozen for later use. Remove from the freezer, then allow to warm up and rise.

3. *Don't forget that dough can rise and be punched down several times,* if you're able to check back briefly at intervals (or have someone else do so). The cooler the spot it's left in, the less frequently it need be checked.

4. *One or more of the following shortcuts can help speed up the baking process. Yeasted doughs*: (1) omit the sponge step, but knead vigorously; (2) let dough rise only once before shaping; (3) provide a warm, moist place for rising; (4) bake at higher temperatures for shorter times (400° F for 30-35 minutes); (5) make rolls or bagels instead of loaves—they can require less kneading, and quicker proofing and baking.

Other baked goods: Unyeasted breads aren't usually a good idea for an emergency loaf. However, a few of the unyeasted breads in *Uprisings* are fairly fast (but not sweet); Irish soda bread and buckwheat bread are examples (see Index). The sweeter quick breads and muffins can be made at short notice as a substantial and appealing accompaniment to a hastily planned meal. You can rustle up a batch of hot muffins, for instance, in perhaps forty minutes. For a sweet treat, cookies are the fastest to produce. A time-saving practice used in our bakeries is gathering in advance the measured dry ingredients for a batch of goodies and storing them in a container in the fridge for use at a moment's notice. Fully mixed cookie batter (not containing baking powder or soda) can also be refrigerated for later scooping and baking.

Cost

A major cause of anxiety for almost everyone these days is the cost of food. Baking at home is an excellent way to save on your expenses. Here are some further tips:

1. *Locate the nearest food coop store or buying club*, to obtain cheap, bulk ingredients. Look in the phone book under "Health Food Stores" or "Grocery Stores," or ask at a health food shop or restaurant. Get involved with a buying club where groups of people buy supplies at wholesale prices. These aren't hard to start, by the way, and save a lot of money. Most health food stores and supermarkets are more expensive because they're making a profit.

2. *Choose cheaper ingredients whenever possible.* Compare the prices of oils, for

instance, and buy the lower-priced safflower rather than sesame oil. For sweetening, honey and malt cost less than maple syrup, and some honeys can be much cheaper than others. For both oils and honeys, however, be on the alert for the cheaper, highly processed versions which are best avoided. When choosing dried fruits, raisins will probably be less expensive than currants or dates, and preformed date pieces may be a good buy. For texture and crunch, sesame and sunflower seeds make a low cost addition to your baking; in particular, "sunnies" are a good replacement for the more expensive nuts. The prices of dried fruits and nuts may fluctuate over the year, perhaps being lowest after harvesting in the fall. Bulk amounts bought when prices are down can be stored for use over a period of time. Obviously, these are only rough guidelines—just shop with care and awareness. One final thought: "Substituting Ingredients" (see pg. 57) may give you some ideas for alternative ingredients that will save you money.

3. **Keep your baking simple.** Whole wheat flour isn't expensive and you can make a good, basic loaf without a lot of extra ingredients. Flour, water, yeast and salt make a fine bread, so home baking can be very economical. You can use herbs and vegetables from your own garden to flavor your bread. For variety, basic bread dough can be shaped into rolls, bagels, or cinnamon buns, or braided, glazed, and sprinkled with poppy seeds.

Quantity

If you want to feed a lot of people or have extra bread to store, here are some suggestions.

1. **Breads:** you can easily knead a four-loaf batch of dough (double any recipe in **Uprisings**). Stagger baking, if necessary, by letting half the dough rise an extra time, or put some in the fridge for later proofing and baking. You can also freeze unbaked dough (see above, under "Time").

2. **Other baked goods:** you can make up to four dozen muffins at once, if you have the oven space to bake them all at one time. If the batter sits too long between mixing and baking, it won't rise nicely in the oven. Virtually any cookie recipe can be multiplied as many times as you like. Don't use baking soda or powder if the dough will have to sit while the first batch bakes. Cookies or sweets such as unbaked halvah, fudge, or fruit and nut balls are the easiest things to produce in quantity. In addition, premixed doughs can be refrigerated for later spooning or shaping.

One Final Suggestion for finding solutions to your baking problems, whatever they may be. Get help! Involving other people can give you support and other opinions in a crisis, an extra pair of hands to halve the labor and save time, or merely a good time for everyone concerned. Buying supplies with others can reduce your food costs considerably. This is probably the most important thing we've learned in our bakeries—work together with other people and virtually any problem can be solved. Share your troubles and successes, don't be afraid to experiment, and most importantly, enjoy yourself.

Equivalents of Weights and Measures

Liquid Measure

3 teaspoons (tsp or t)	=	1 Tablespoon (Tbl or T)		
2 Tbl	=	1 ounce (oz)		
4 Tbl	=	¼ cup (cup or c)		
16 Tbl = 8 oz	=	1 cup	=	½ pint (pt)
2 cups	=	1 pt		
2 pt	=	1 quart (qt)		
128 oz = 16 cups	=	4 qt = 1 gallon (gal)		

Dry Measure

16 ounces (oz) = 1 pound (lb)

Volume/Weight Equivalents

Water:

1 pint = 1 pound = 2 cups

Honey:

1⅓ cups = 1 pound (1 cup = ¾ lb)

Whole Wheat Flour:

1 pound = 3½ cups (approximately)

American/Metric Conversions

Liquid:

1 tsp	=	5 milliliters (ml)
1 Tbl	=	15 ml
1 oz	=	30 ml
1 cup	=	235 ml (about ¼ liter)
1 qt	=	.95 liter (l)
1 gal	=	3.8 liters

Dry:

1 oz	=	28 grams (gm)
1 lb	=	454 gm
2.2 lb	=	1 kilogram (kg)

Temperature Conversions

° Fahrenheit		° Celsius
250	=	130
300	=	150
350	=	180
400	=	200
450	=	230

To convert °F to °C,
subtract 32, multiply by 5, and divide by 9.
$$[(°F - 32) \times 5 \div 9 = °C]$$

American/English Equivalents

1 U.S. tsp (5 ml)	=	1 English tsp (5 ml)
1 U.S. Tbl (14.2 ml)	=	⁴/₅ English Tbl
1¼ U.S. Tbl	=	1 English Tbl (17.7 ml)
1 U.S. cup (8 oz)	=	⁴/₅ English cup
1¼ U.S. cups	=	1 English cup (10 Imperial oz)
1 U.S. pint	=	⁵/₆ Imperial pint
2½ U.S. cups	=	1 Imperial pint (20 oz)
U.S. weights	=	English weights

For practical purposes, a two-loaf batch of bread in English measures would use:

just under 1 Tbl yeast
2-4 Tbl sweetener
1 pint or 2 cups water
4-5 cups flour

Bakery Locations

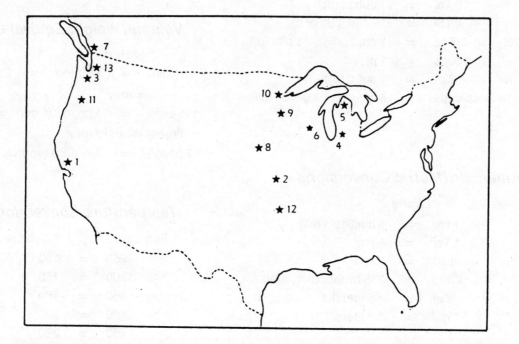

1. Alvarado St. Bakery
500 Martin Ave.
Rohnert Park, Ca 94928
(707) 585-3293

2. Amazing Grains
901 Mississippi
Lawrence, KS 66044
913-841-5510

3. Blue Heron Bakery
4935 Mud Bay Rd.
Olympia, WA 98502
(206) 866-2253

4. Grain Dance Bakery
243 East Michigan Ave.
Paw Paw, MI 49079
(616) 657-5934

5. Grain Train Natural Food Co-op
  421 Howard St.
  Petosky, MI 49770
  (616) 347-2381

6. Nature's Bakery
  1019 Williamson St.
  Madison, WI 53703
  (608) 257-363649

7. Uprising Breads
  1697 Venables
  Vancouver, B.C.
  Canada V5L 2M1
  (604) 254-5635

8. Open Harvest Bakery
  2637 Randolph
  Lincoln, NE 68510
  (402) 475-9069

9. People's Company Bakery
  1534 E. Lake St.
  Minneapolis, MN 55407
  (612) 721-7205

10. Positively 3rd Street
  1202 E. 3rd St.
  Duluth, MN 55805
  (218) 724-8619

11. Solstice Bakery
  645 River Rd.
  Eugene, OR 97404
  (503) 688-4868

12. Summercorn Bakery
  401 Watson St.
  Fayetteville, AR 72701
  (501) 521-9338

13. Touchstone
  501A N. 36th
  Seattle, WA 98103
  (206) 547-4000

ALVARADO ST. BAKERY

SANTA ROSA
CALIFORNIA

we are dedicated to providing
non-alienating work with decent
wages and benefits for the workers.
we supply our wholesale customers
with daily delivery service locally.
we recently moved and now do
some retail sales from the bakery,
though we'd like to expand this.
we are legally incorporated as a
co-operative under the california
co-operative corporation code.

PEASANT BREAD

2 x 1½ LB. LOAVES

A HANDY USE FOR OLD BREAD

2¼ CUPS WARM WATER
2 TSP MOLASSES + 1 TSP MALT
1 TBL YEAST
2 CUPS HARD WW FLOUR

1½ CUPS CRUSHED TOASTED BREAD
2½ CUPS HARD WW FLOUR
1 TBL VINEGAR
1 TSP KELP
2 TBL OIL
½ TSP SALT
(OPT.)

MIX TOGETHER FIRST FOUR INGREDIENTS, AND BEAT WELL. LET SIT UNTIL PUFFED UP. ADD REST OF INGREDIENTS, ADDING FLOUR AS NEEDED TO GET A SOFT TEXTURE. KNEAD DOUGH UNTIL IT'S ELASTIC. LET RISE TILL DOUBLED IN SIZE, PUNCH DOWN AND LET RISE AGAIN. PUNCH DOWN AND SHAPE INTO TWO LOAVES. PLACE IN OILED BREAD PANS AND LET RISE AGAIN. (THE SECOND RISING BEFORE SHAPING MAKES BREAD A LITTLE LIGHTER.) BAKE AT 350° FOR 45 MINUTES.

Carrot Celery
~ Bread ~

2 x 1½ lb loaves

A simple bread with a robust flavor.

2 cups warm water	½ lb grated carrot
¼ cup honey	½ Tbl celery seed
1 Tbl yeast	2 Tbl oil
5½-6 cups hard w.w. flour	1 tsp salt

Mix water, yeast and honey. When the yeast has dissolved, beat in about 2 cups of the flour. Let this sponge sit until doubled and puffy. Now add remaining ingredients, reserving flour and adding it to make a soft kneading texture. Knead dough well, until it's elastic. Let dough rise in a warm place until doubled in size. Punch down. Let rise again, shape into loaves and let rise in oiled pans.
Bake at 350° for 45 minutes.

POTATO DILL BREAD

2 - 1½ lb loaves

*Delicious with a fresh salad or
cool cucumber soup.*

2 cups warm water
¼ cup molasses
2 Tbl malt syrup
1 Tbl yeast
½ cup bran
1 tsp salt
3 Tbl vinegar
2 Tbl dill weed (dried)
1 medium potato, grated
5 cups hard w.w. flour

MIX TOGETHER WATER, MOLASSES AND
MALT. STIR IN YEAST AND LET IT DISSOLVE
BEAT IN 2 CUPS OF THE FLOUR. LET
THIS SPONGE SIT TILL PUFFED UP.
ADD ALL REMAINING INGREDIENTS,
ADDING FLOUR AS NEEDED TO MAKE
A SOFT TEXTURE. KNEAD DOUGH WELL
TILL IT'S STRETCHY. LET RISE IN A WARM
PLACE TILL DOUBLED IN SIZE. PUNCH
DOWN. LET RISE AGAIN AND SHAPE
INTO TWO LOAVES. LET THESE RISE IN
OILED PANS. BAKE AT 350° FOR 45 MINUTES.

Amazing Grains

Collective Whole Food Bakery
Lawrence, Kansas

The morning begins quietly at the Amazing Grains, as only two of the three member collective sleepily yet swiftly awaken the yeast and gather utensils and ingredients for the day's bake. And it is not long before the warm smell of bran muffins wafts its way through the moisture-filled air and into the noses of unsuspecting customers and employees at the Community Mercantile, a natural foods store located directly across the graveled neighborhood alley.

In August of 1988, Amazing Grains was born from Verbena, a 1 person owned and operated bakery of 14 years. Now a healthy collective of 3, the bakery continues on through transition and growth - (learn, learn, learn, then learn some more!), baking 6 days a week, selling wholesale to the Community Mercantile.

Our goals include baking wholesome foods using organic and/or locally grown ingredients whenever possible while striving to maintain a healthy work environment and contributing to the well being of the world around us.

Oatmeal Sun Bread

Makes – 2 loaves

Make sure you have :

3 Cups warm water
1 Tbl. yeast
1/4 Cup honey
3 Cups hard whole wheat flour
1/3 Cup rye flour
1/2 Cup rolled oats
1/3 Cup corn meal
1 Tbl. soy flour
1/2 Cup sunflower seeds
2 Tbl. safflower oil
1 Tbl. salt
3 more Cups hard whole wheat flour

1) Dissolve the yeast in the water. Add the honey. Mix in the 3 cups whole wheat flour and beat 100 times. Let rise 20 minutes.

2) Add remaining ingredients, reserving 1 cup of the whole wheat flour.

3) Knead the dough until it is elastic, adding the remaining flour only if necessary. This will take a while !.... Think of the muscles you are strengthening as well as the dough. Cover and let rise to double.

4) Punch down and shape into 2 loaves. Let rise to double again in oiled bread pans.

5) Bake at 350° for 40-45 minutes.

Golden Wheat Bread

Makes - 2 loaves

Dissolve 2 tsp. active yeast in 2 2/3 cups warm water. Let it sit until it bubbles.

Stir in 3 cups hard whole wheat flour and 1/2 cup barley malt syrup.
Beat that for about 5 minutes. Let rise about 45 minutes or until it doubles in bulk. Stir down.

Add 2 1/2 tsp. sea salt and 1 Tbl. cider vinegar and 2 Tbl. oil. Begin to work in 3 cups hard whole wheat flour. You may need a bit more than 3 cups or not quite that much. Turn onto a floured board and knead the dough for 8-10 minutes, until it becomes smooth, even and elastic. Set into an oiled bowl + lightly oil the top. Let rise to double.

Punch down and divide in 2 loaves and shape. Let rise to double in a warm place.

Bake at 350° for 45-60 minutes.

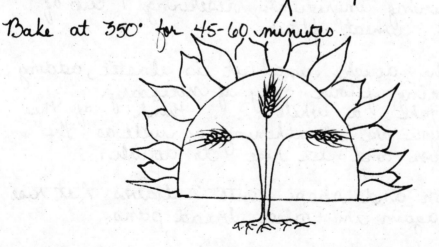

Bagels

Makes - one dozen

Have ready a 2-loaf size pieces of bread dough

Set 1 gallon of water to boil   Then begin :

4 oz lumps

Weigh dough out into 4 oz. lumps - the size of a small apple (1/4 pound)

Roll into logs about 6 inches long

Overlap the ends of the log and roll or pinch them closed. Make sure it's a tight connection

(Hand dropping bagel in water)

Drop bagels into boiling water and cook for 2 minutes turning them over once during that time.

Place on oiled cookie sheets and bake at 350° for 25-30 minutes - until the bottom is brown

Veggie Spy Rolls

Makes : 18 Rolls

Have ready on hand:

- ½ Pound of tofu
- ½ Pound of chopped onions
- 2 Cloves of garlic, minced
- ¼ Cup dried parsley
- 1 Tbl. dried basil
- 1 Cup spinach, steamed and chopped
- 4 oz. grated, pepper jack cheese
- 6 oz. dry curd, cottage cheese
- 8 oz. grated, medium cheddar cheese
- ¼ cup sunflower seeds
- 1 loaf of RAW bread dough

Roll the dough into a rectangle 24 x 18 inches.
Spread the tofu mixture over the rectangle so
it covers it with at least ½ inch thickness. Slowly
roll the dough, a little at a time, pinching the top
edge as you end. Cut into 18 pieces. Place on an
oiled pan, preferably with side. let rise for 25 minutes
Bake at 350° for 20 minutes

Spy Rolls II - Curry Cabbage

Makes: 18 rolls

Combine in a large bowl

- 1.½ Cup finely chopped cabbage
- 1 finely chopped onion   ◎ 1 Tbl. Cumin
- ¾ Tbl. tumeric   ◎ 4 cloves minced garlic
- 12 oz. cottage cheese ◎ 1 Tbl. ground Sage
- ½ pound of crumbled tofu
- ¾ pound of grated cheese - your choice
  (cheddar is lovely)

Mix Well. Proceed as for "Veggie Spy Rolls"

Spy Rolls III - Rainbow

Makes: 18 Rolls

Combine in a large bowl:
- 1 red onion, minced
- 1 small carrot, grated
- 1 small red bell pepper, diced
- 1 ½ cups green cabbage, chopped fine
- 4 cloves garlic, minced
- 1 small zucchini, diced
- 12 oz. cottage cheese (1½ cup)
- ¾ pound cheese of your choice, grated
- ½ pound tofu
- 2 Tbl. marjoram
- ½ tsp. salt
- ½ tsp. Cayenne

mix well. Proceed as for "Veggie Spy Rolls"

Bread Sticks

Have ready – One lump of dough that is the size for one loaf

Cut into 12 equal pieces – about 2 oz. each.

Roll out into skinny logs – about 10 inches long.

Roll into sesame seeds or sunflower seeds if so desired

Place on oiled cookie sheets

Spray with water until surface of dough is wet

Bake for 15 minutes at 350°

Spray again and bake 10 minutes more.

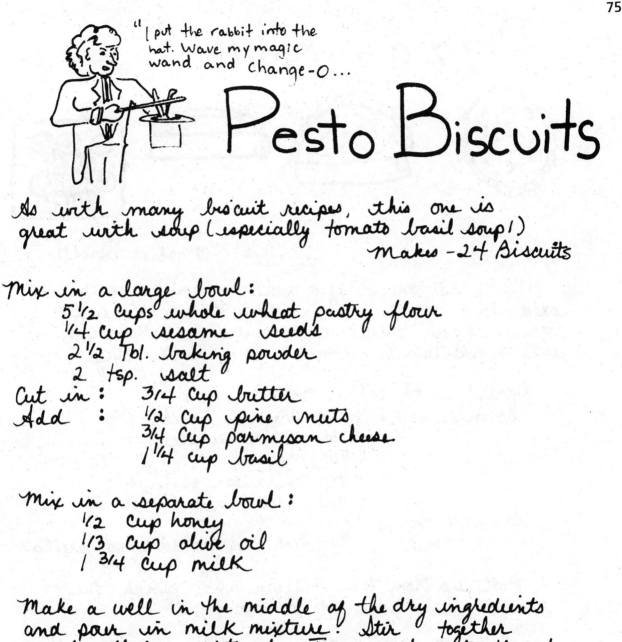

"I put the rabbit into the hat. Wave my magic wand and change-o...

Pesto Biscuits

As with many biscuit recipes, this one is great with soup (especially tomato basil soup!)

Makes - 24 Biscuits

Mix in a large bowl:
    5 1/2 cups whole wheat pastry flour
    1/4 cup sesame seeds
    2 1/2 Tbl. baking powder
    2 tsp. salt
Cut in :   3/4 cup butter
Add   :   1/2 cup pine nuts
            3/4 cup parmesan cheese
            1 1/4 cup basil

Mix in a separate bowl :
    1/2 cup honey
    1/3 cup olive oil
    1 3/4 cup milk

Make a well in the middle of the dry ingredients and pour in milk mixture. Stir together until all is moistened. Turn out onto floured board. Knead with hands just until it is evenly mixed. Roll out to a 1 inch thickness and cut with biscuit cutter.

Place on oiled cookie sheets and bake immediately for 15-18 minutes at 400°.

Pizza Rolls

Makes: 10 rolles

Make up one loaf's worth of any smooth, seed-less dough. The "Golden Wheat Bread" recipe is a good one to use. Roll dough into a rectangle, about 10 x 15 inches big.

Spread with: 4 oz. tomato paste
Sprinkle with: 1 Tbl. dried basil
2 Tbl. dried parsley
1 Tbl. oregano
1 tsp. granular garlic
2 Tbl. parmesan cheese.
Sprinkle over that: 1/2 - 3/4 cup grated mozzarella

Roll up from the bottom and pinch the seam when you get to the top.

Cut into 10 pieces and place on oiled cookie sheet. Flatten slightly. Let rise till it doubles.

Bake at 400° for 15 minutes.

Pumpkin Bread

Makes - 2 loaves

Mix together: ½ cup canola oil or melted butter
2/3 cup honey
½ cup sorghum or unsulfured molasses
2 eggs
1½ cup mashed pumpkin or squash

Blend in a medium bowl:
2 cups whole wheat pastry flour
1 tsp. baking powder
1 tsp. baking soda
1 tsp. freshly grated nutmeg
1½ tsp. ground cloves
2 tsp. cinnamon
¼ tsp. ground cardamom
¼ tsp. salt

Combine all the wet and dry ingredients together.

Pour into 2 loaf pans.

Bake at 350° for 30-40 minutes

Crumb Cake

The crumbs are yummy, the flavor's great. You might just want one more piece!

Makes—one 8 inch square pan
or 12 muffins

Mix and soak for 2 hours :
  2 cups pitted dates, chopped up
  12 oz. can of frozen, unsweetened juice concentrate, thawed

Cream together : ½ cup butter
  ½ cup canola oil

Add : 2 cups whole wheat pastry flour
  ½ cup brown rice flour
  2 cups coconut, flaked or shredded
  ½ cup sunflower seeds
  ½ tsp. salt
  1 tsp. baking soda

Mix in : juice/date mixture. Bake in oiled muffin tins or tins with cup cake papers or an oiled 8x8 inch pan. Place into your 350° oven for 18-25 minutes.

Mom, can't I just have one more crumb? Please..

Basic Biscuit

makes: 8-10 biscuits

<u>Plain Variety</u>

Mix together: 2 ½ Cups whole wheat pastry flour
2 Tbl. sesame seeds
1 Tbl. baking powder
1 tsp. salt

Cut in   :   6 Tbl. butter

mix up   :   3 Tbl. honey
2 Tbl. oil
1 cup milk

Then add that to your flour mixture

Knead 8-10 times. Roll out 3/4 inch thick. Cut out with biscuit cutter or a glass. Place on oiled cookie sheet with biscuits touching each other. Bake at 400° for 10-15 minutes.

Great with whipped cream and fresh fruit!

<u>Apple Variety</u> : Fold in one cup chopped Jonathan apples, 1 tsp cinnamon, ½ tsp. freshly grated ginger

<u>Cinnamon Raisin Variety</u> : Fold in 3/4 cup raisins and 1 tsp. cinnamon

Basil-Cheese Biscuits

—Makes: 15 Biscuits

Have ready:

2 1/4 cups whole wheat pastry flour
2 Tbl. sesame seeds
1 Tbl. baking powder
1 tsp. salt
6 Tbl. butter
3 Tbl. honey
2 Tbl. oil
1 cup milk
2 oz. grated cheddar cheese
3/4 cup dried basil

Stir dry ingredients together. Cut or rub in the butter. Mix in basil and cheese. Mix together oil, honey and milk. Add to flour mixture. Stir until dough cleans the bowl. Knead lightly – 8 → 10 times. Roll about 3/4 inch thick on a lightly floured board. Cut with biscuit cutter or glass. Place on an un-oiled cookie sheet with biscuits touching. Bake for 12–15 minutes at 400°

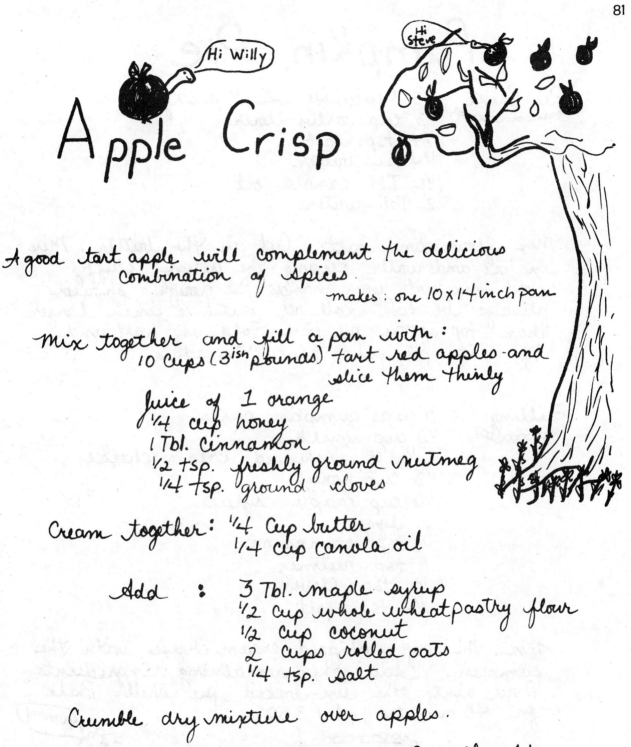

Apple Crisp

A good tart apple will complement the delicious combination of spices.

makes: one 10 x 14 inch pan

Mix together and fill a pan with:
10 Cups (3ish pounds) tart red apples - and slice them thinly

Juice of 1 orange
1/4 cup honey
1 Tbl. cinnamon
1/2 tsp. freshly ground nutmeg
1/4 tsp. ground cloves

Cream together: 1/4 Cup butter
1/4 cup canola oil

Add : 3 Tbl. maple syrup
1/2 cup whole wheat pastry flour
1/2 cup coconut
2 cups rolled oats
1/4 tsp. salt

Crumble dry mixture over apples.

Bake for 30-40 minutes at 325° until golden brown and apples are soft.

Pumpkin Pie

Pie Crust : 2/3 cup whole wheat pastry flour
1/3 cup barley flour
1/4 tsp. salt
1/4 cup butter
1 1/2 Tbl. canola oil
2 Tbl. water

Mix flour and salt. Cut in the butter. Mix in oil and water keeping the dough fluffy. Don't mix with your hands. Pie dough should always be cool. Roll out until 1/2 inch larger than top of the pie pan. Fold in half and lift into pie pan. Flute the edges.

Filling : 3 cups pumpkin puree
1/3 cup milk
2 1/2 oz. whipped cream cheese
1/3 cup honey
1/16 cup maple syrup
2 eggs
2 tsp. cinnamon
1 tsp. nutmeg
1/2 tsp. cloves
1/4 tsp. salt

Mix the soft, whipped cream cheese with the pumpkin. Add the remaining ingredients. Pour into the un-baked pie shell. Bake for 40 minutes at 350°.

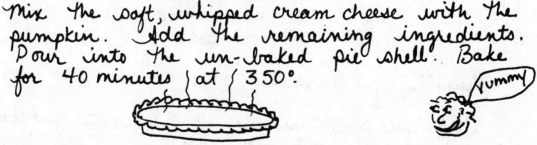

Yummy

Peachy Keen Pie

A lovely, light and fruity pie. Yummm!

Makes = one 8 inch pie

Have ready: one un-baked pie shell
4 Cups peaches, sliced
½ cup raisins
1 cup yogurt
3 eggs, whipped
½ cup maple syrup
1 Tbl. vanilla
1 tsp. nutmeg

Place sliced peaches in unbaked pie shell.
Mix remaining ingredients together and
pour on top of the peaches.
Bake at 350° for 35 minutes

Bread Pudding

Makes - 1, 8 inch square pan

1) Shred - 4 Cups of any whole grain bread

2) Mix together - 2 Eggs and beat them well
   - 5 Cups milk (soy works great)
   - 1/4 Cup honey
   - 1/4 Cup maple syrup

3) Combine milk mixture with bread

4) Add - 1/2 Tbl. nutmeg
   - 2 Tbl. cinnamon
   - 1 Tbl. vanilla
   - 3/4 Cup chopped apples
   - Juice of one lemon
   - 1/4 Cup raisins

5) Mix altogether and let sit for 15-30 minutes. Pour into oiled pan.

6) Bake at 350° for 45-55 minutes

Cashchews

a great Candy substitute
makes 12-16 balls

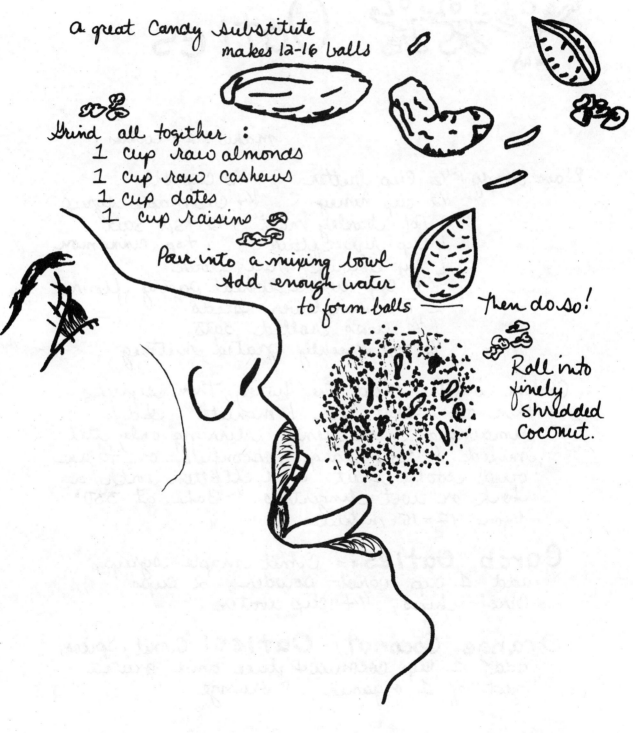

Grind all together :
    1 cup raw almonds
    1 cup raw cashews
    1 cup dates
    1 cup raisins

Pour into a mixing bowl
    Add enough water
        to form balls —— then do so!

Roll into finely shredded Coconut.

Oaties

makes: 24 cookies

Have ready: ½ Cup butter   ⅓ cup oil
            ½ cup honey   ¼ cup maple syrup
            2 Tbl. barley malt   ½ tsp. salt
            1 Cup rye flour   1 tsp. cinnamon
            1 cup brown rice flour
            3/4 cup whole wheat pastry flour
            2 Tbl. sunflower seeds
            1 ½ cups rolled oats
            ½ tsp. freshly grated nutmeg

Cream butter. Add the honey, then syrups, then oil. Beat for 1 minute. Add remaining ingredients, stirring only till mixed. Scoop large spoonfuls on to an oiled cookie sheet and flatten with a fork or wet fingertips. Bake at 350° for 12-15 minutes

Carob Oaties: Omit maple syrup, add 1 cup carob powder, 2 cups Carob chips, 1/4 cup water

Orange Coconut Oaties: Omit spices, add 1 cup coconut + juice and grated zest of 1 organic orange

JAMMIES
makes: 24 cookies

Whip : ½ Cup butter
Add & mix well : ½ cup canola oil
    ⅞ cup honey
    ½ tsp. almond extract
Add : 4 ¼ cups whole wheat pastry flour
    ½ tsp. nutmeg
    ½ tsp. salt

Mix the flour and spices in well. If the dough is sticky, add a touch more flour

Spoon out the dough onto a cookie sheet by teaspoonfuls. Make a dent in the top of each ball with a fingertip Spoon in ½ tsp. of jam into each impression. Bake for 12 –15 minutes at 350°, until lightly brown and jam bubbles a little.

VARIATIONS

<u>Lemon Cream</u> – Substitute ½ tsp. vanilla for almond extract and omit nutmeg.
    Filling — Omit jam. Use 8 oz. of softened cream cheese, 2/3 cup honey and grated rind of 1 lemon

<u>Maple Cream</u> – Use the same dough as for "lemon cream" cookies
    Filling – Soften 8 oz. cream cheese and ½ cup maple syrup whipped together

<u>Carob</u> – Use the same dough as for "lemon cream" cookies
    Filling – Soften 8 oz. cream cheese, add ¼ cup honey or maple syrup and ⅓ cup carob

<u>Peanut Cream</u> – Use the same dough as for "lemon cream" cookies
    Filling – Soften 8 oz. cream cheese and add ⅓ cup peanut butter and ½ cup honey

THE BLUE HERON BAKERY MAKES ITS HOME ON THE SOUTHERN MOST INLET OF THE PUGET SOUND IN THE PACIFIC NORTHWEST. THE INLET'S MOST UNIQUE INHABITANT, THE GREAT BLUE HERON HAS LENT THE BAKERY ITS NAME AS WELL AS SOME OF ITS SPIRIT. WE RISE EARLY LIKE THE HERON AND PLACE EQUAL EMPHASIS ON QUALITY AND RESPONSIBILITY. THESE IDEALS COULD NOT BE REALIZED WITHOUT PATIENCE AND DEDICATION. FINALLY, WE HAVE A COMMITMENT TO REGION, AN EXAMPLE BORROWED FROM OUR NON-MIGRATORY NAME SAKE.

Blue Heron Bakery

4935 Mud Bay Road
Olympia, WA 98502
866-2253

Whole grain naturally sweetened baked goods
Serving the community since 1977

AT THE BLUE HERON, WE ARE VERY PROUD OF LIVING IN THE CASCADIA BIO-REGION. WE FEEL THAT OUR EMPHASIS ON BAKING WITH LOCALLY GROWN ORGANIC PRODUCTS IS A TESTAMENT TO THIS PRIDE. WE PROVIDE THESE PRODUCTS AS AN EXAMPLE THAT WHOLE GRAIN BAKING, WITH UNREFINED SWEETENERS, CAN BE A DELICIOUS AND SATISFYING EXPERIENCE.

WE ALSO BELIEVE THAT INVESTMENTS IN A FLOUR MILL AND A BRICK OVEN AS WELL AS HAND KNEADING OUR BREAD AND HAND ROLLING OUR PASTRIES ARE THE PROPER DIRECTION TO BE TAKING IN THIS ERA OF EVER QUICKENING LIFE STYLES.

FINALLY, OUR COLLECTIVE MANAGEMENT SYSTEM, ONE OF EQUAL OWNERSHIP AND DECISION MAKING, PROVIDES IMPROVED BENEFITS FOR THE MEMBERS OF OUR BUSINESS, AS WELL AS FOR MEMBERS OF OUR COMMUNITY. SO- COME VISIT OUR HERONRY, JUST OFF HIGHWAY 101; WE THINK ENJOYING THE BREADS, PASTRIES, AND SWEETS ON OUR BRICK PATIO WILL PROVIDE A PERFECT RESPITE AS YOU TRAVEL TO THE OLYMPIC PENINSULA, SEATTLE, OR THROUGHOUT THE PACIFIC NORTHWEST; YOU JUST MIGHT HAVE A GREAT BLUE HERON FLY RIGHT OVER YOUR HEAD!

Potato Buttermilk Bread

Yeilds: 2 loaves

A PRETTY BREAD WITH A THICK CHEESY AROMA

DISSOLVE : 1 Tbl. YEAST
IN : 5 Tbl. WARM WATER

GRATE : ½ POUND RAW UNPEELED POTATOES
ADD TO : 1 ⅗ CUPS BUTTERMILK

COMBINE THESE MIXTURES

STIR IN : 1 tsp. SALT

KNEAD IN : 5½–6 CUPS HARD WHOLE WHEAT FLOUR

ADD FLOUR AS YOU WORK THE DOUGH ONLY IF YOU NEED IT.

KNEAD THE DOUGH SPRINGY, SOFT AND ELASTIC.

PLACE IN AN OILED BOWL. COVER AND LET RISE TILL IT DOUBLES.

PUNCH DOWN. SHAPE INTO 2 LOAVES. PLACE IN OILED BREAD PANS AND LET RISE TO DOUBLE AGAIN.

BAKE AT 350° FOR 45 MINUTES.

HEARTY WHOLE GRAIN

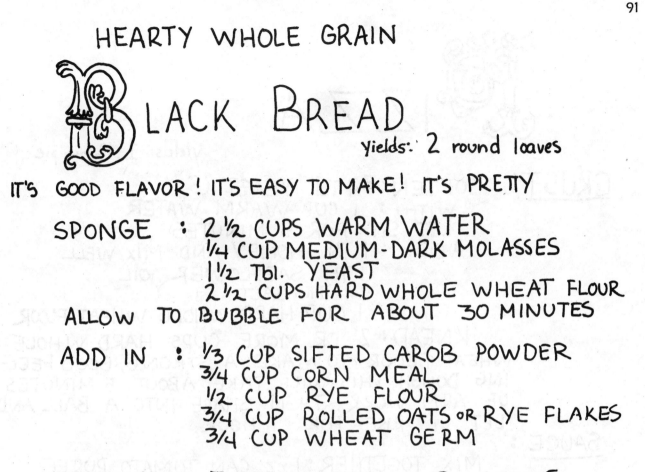LACK BREAD

yields: 2 round loaves

IT'S GOOD FLAVOR! IT'S EASY TO MAKE! IT'S PRETTY

SPONGE : 2 ½ CUPS WARM WATER
¼ CUP MEDIUM-DARK MOLASSES
1 ½ Tbl. YEAST
2 ½ CUPS HARD WHOLE WHEAT FLOUR
ALLOW TO BUBBLE FOR ABOUT 30 MINUTES

ADD IN : ⅓ CUP SIFTED CAROB POWDER
¾ CUP CORN MEAL
½ CUP RYE FLOUR
¾ CUP ROLLED OATS OR RYE FLAKES
¾ CUP WHEAT GERM

THEN ADD : 3 Tbl. OIL OF YOUR CHOICE
1 tsp. SALT

TURN ONTO FLOURED SURFACE AND KNEAD ADDING MORE WHOLE WHEAT FLOUR UNTIL THE MOIST STICKY DOUGH HAS BODY.

LET DOUGH RISE ABOUT 30 MINUTES IN A WARM PLACE COVERED WITH A DAMP CLOTH IN AN OILED BOWL. PUNCH. LET RISE 15 MINUTES. PUNCH DOWN AND SHAPE INTO LOAVES. PLACE ON OILED OR CORN MEAL- SPRINKLED TRAY. LET RISE TO ALMOST DOUBLE
BAKE AT 350° FOR 15 MINUTES THEN 325° FOR ANOTHER 35 MINUTES.

# IZZA

yields: **1**, 12 inch pie

CRUST:

SOFTEN: ¾ Tbl. YEAST (2¼ tsp)
WITH : 1 CUP WARM WATER
LET SIT FOR 5 MINUTES
ADD : 1 Tbl. HONEY AND MIX WELL
1 Tbl. SAFFLOWER OIL
¼ Tbl. SALT (3¼ tsp)
1 CUP HARD WHOLE WHEAT FLOUR
KNEAD: 2 OR MORE CUPS HARD WHOLE
WHEAT FLOUR TO MAKE A STRONG, GOOD FEELING DOUGH. THIS WILL TAKE ABOUT 5 MINUTES
OF ARM WORK. THEN SHAPE INTO A BALL AND
LET IT RISE FOR 1 HOUR.

SAUCE:

MIX TOGETHER: 1 oz. CAN TOMATO PUREE
1 SMALL ONION, FINELY DICED
1 tsp. OREGANO
1 tsp. BASIL
1 tsp. THYME
1 tsp. GARLIC POWDER
½ tsp. SALT

ROLL OUT THE DOUGH A LITTLE LARGER THAN
YOUR PAN. MAKE AN EDGE ALL AROUND TO
HOLD IN YOUR SAUCE. COVER WITH SAUCE.
SPRINKLE WITH PARMESAN CHEESE AND
½ CUP GRATED MOZZARELLA.

BAKE AT 400° FOR 10 MINUTES.

LUE CORN MUFFINS

Yield: 1 dozen

THESE SURPRISINGLY MOIST, TRULY BLUE MUFFINS ARE ONE OF OUR MOST POPULAR ITEMS AT OLYMPIA'S FARMER'S MARKET. THEY ARE MADE WITH A MIXTURE OF ORGANIC BLACK AZTEC AND HOPI BLUE VARIETIES OF CORN, BOTH OF WHICH HAVE UNIQUE FLAVOR AND SUPERIOR NUTRITIONAL QUALITIES

MIX TOGETHER IN ONE BOWL:

4 CUPS CORNMEAL- PREFERABLY COARSE AND BLUE IF POSSIBLE

1 tsp. SALT
1 tsp. BAKING POWDER
½ tsp. BAKING SODA

MIX IN ANOTHER BOWL:

2 CUPS SOY MILK
2 Tbl. CIDER VINEGAR

ADD TO THOSE LIQUIDS:

⅓ CUP MAPLE SYRUP
2 EGGS
⅓ CUP CORN OIL

MAKE A WELL IN THE DRY INGREDIENTS, POUR IN LIQUIDS AND MIX WELL. SPOON GENEROUS AMOUNT INTO WELL- OILED MUFFIN TINS. BAKE AT 350° FOR 18 MINUTES OR UNTIL TOP *SPRINGS BACK WHEN TOUCHED.

*MUFFINS ARE NOT AS FLUFFY AS CUP CAKES, SO THE SPRING WILL BE A LITTLE STIFFER.

ran Muffins

yields: 24 Muffins

Mix: 2 cups BARLEY MALT SYRUP
½ CUP CORN OIL
2½ CUPS WATER
½ CUP RAISINS
2 tsp. VANILLA
2 Tbl. FRESH GRATED GINGER

COMBINE: 4½ CUPS BRAN – WHEAT OR OAT
2 CUPS WHOLE WHEAT PASTRY FLOUR
½ CUP CORN MEAL
½ CUP OAT FLOUR
½ CUP POPPY SEEDS
2 Tbl. BAKING POWDER
2 Tbl. CINNAMON

STIR ALL INGREDIENTS TOGETHER. SPOON
INTO OILED MUFFIN TINS. BAKE AT 350°
FOR 25 MINUTES.

CARROT MUFFINS
WHEAT — FREE

yields: 12-16

COMBINE IN A BOWL:

    1 CUP SAFFLOWER OIL
    2/3 CUP RICE SYRUP
    1/2 CUP FINELY CHOPPED DATES
    3 EGGS - BEATEN
    1/2 CUP FINELY GRATED CARROTS
    2 Tbl. CURRANTS
    1 tsp. VANILLA

COMBINE IN ANOTHER BOWL:

    1 CUP CORN MEAL
    1 CUP + 2 Tbl. RYE FLOUR
    1/3 CUP RICE FLOUR
    1 tsp. BAKING POWDER
    1 tsp. BAKING SODA
    1 tsp. CINNAMON
    1/2 tsp. ALLSPICE
    1/4 tsp. NUTMEG
    1/3 CUP CHOPPED NUTS OF YOUR CHOICE

COMBINE "WETS" AND DRY INGREDIENTS.

SPOON INTO OILED MUFFIN TINS.

BAKE AT 350° FOR 35 MINUTES.

LET COOL SLIGHTLY BEFORE REMOVING
    FROM THE TINS.

innamon Rolls

yields: one dozen

THERE'S NOTHING LIKE A WARM CINNAMON ROLL!

DISSOLVE : 2 Tbl. YEAST
   IN   : 1⅓ CUPS WARM WATER
  ADD   : ¼ CUP HONEY
ALLOW THIS TO BUBBLE UP - ABOUT 10 MINUTES

MEANWHILE : 4½ CUPS WHOLE WHEAT PASTRY FLOUR
  COMBINE   ⅓ CUP DRY MILK
          1 tsp. SALT

COMBINE THE WET AND DRY INGREDIENTS

   ADD : 2 BEATEN EGGS

MIX OR KNEAD UNTIL IT LOOKS EVEN. THIS WILL TAKE A FEW MINUTES.

   ADD : ¼ CUP OIL — IN A STEADY TRICKLE. KEEP MIXING TO GET THE OIL EVENLY DISTRIBUTED. THE DOUGH WILL BE TACKY.

  ❋THIS DOUGH SHOULD NOT BE AS TOUGH AND STRONG AS BREAD DOUGH. — DON'T MIX IT TOO MUCH - ABOUT 5 MINUTES

   SHAPE INTO A BALL AND PLACE IN AN OILED BOWL. COVER. ALLOW DOUGH TO RISE 30-45 MINUTES

CINNAMON ROLLS (CONT.)

MEANWHILE : ¼ CUP BUTTER
WHIP   ½ CUP HONEY

WHEN DOUGH IS PUFFY, DON'T PUNCH IT DOWN.
ROLL IT OUT ON A TABLE, SHAPE IN A RECTANGLE.
A DUSTING OF FLOUR MAY HELP BUT DON'T USE
TOO MUCH. THE DOUGH SHOULD BE ONLY ⅓ INCH
THICK AND 20 INCHES LONG

POUR A PORTION (⅓) OF THE HONEY MIXTURE
OVER THE DOUGH, COVERING ALL OF IT.

SPRINKLE ON THAT WITH CINNAMON AND ½
CUP OF RAISINS.

ROLL THE DOUGH INTO A LOG TRYING TO KEEP
IT TIGHT AND EVEN.

CUT LOG INTO ¾-INCH WIDE SLICES OR 12 EVEN
SLICES. PLACE ON OILED COOKIE SHEET WITH
SPACE FOR ROLLS TO RISE.

LET RISE IN A WARM MOIST PLACE TILL THEY
DOUBLE OR FILL THE PAN.

BAKE AT 350° FOR 20 MINUTES, UNTIL GOLDEN.

THEN TURN UPSIDE DOWN ONTO A COOL COOKIE
SHEET. THEY SHOULD POP OUT

BRUSH THE TOPS WITH THE REST OF THE HONEY
BUTTER MIXTURE.

- BEST EATEN WHILE WARM.

 Carrot Cake

Yields: 1 9inch pan

THIS DELICIOUSLY RICH, MOIST CAKE IS ONE OF THE BLUE HERON'S BEST SELLERS FOR THOSE SPECIAL OCCASIONS

MIX : 1½ CUPS SOFTENED BUTTER
WHIP IN : 1 CUP HONEY
ADD : 4 BEATEN EGGS

COMBINE IN ANOTHER BOWL :
    1½ CUPS WHOLE WHEAT PASTRY FLOUR
    3/4 tsp. BAKING SODA
    3/4 tsp. CINNAMON
    3/4 tsp. SALT

GATHER IN ANOTHER BOWL:
    2¼ CUPS GRATED CARROTS
    ⅓ CUP RAISINS
    ⅓ CUP CHOPPED WALNUTS

ADD DRY INGREDIENTS TO THE WET ONES. THEN QUICKLY MIX IN THE CARROT MIXTURE.

LINE CAKE PAN WITH WAX PAPER. POUR BATTER INTO PAN.

BAKE AT 325° FOR 35—45 MINUTES AND CENTER IS FIRM, CHECKING THE CAKE PERIODICALLY. LET COOL. REMOVE FROM PAN. ICE CAKE IF DESIRED WITH OUR CREAMY CHEESE FROSTING

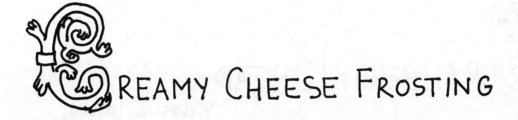REAMY CHEESE FROSTING

MIX TOGETHER UNTIL SMOOTH:

3/4 POUND CREAM CHEESE
1/4 POUND BUTTER, SOFTENED FIRST
2 Tbl. HONEY
2 Tbl. YOGURT
1 Tbl. + 1 tsp. VANILLA

FROST CAKE UNIFORMLY NOT MORE THAN THREE HOURS IN ADVANCE OF SERVING. ANY THIN SPOTS IN THE FROSTING OR LETTING THE FROSTED CAKE SIT TOO LONG, WILL ALLOW THE OILS FROM THE CAKE TO SOAK THROUGH.

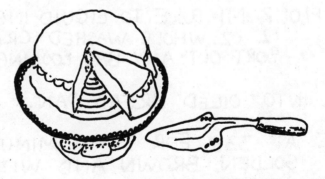

Cranberry Bread

Yields: 2 loaves

CREAM : 1¼ CUPS BUTTER
1¼ CUPS HONEY

ADD : 4 EGGS - MIXING IN ONE AT A TIME
2 CUPS ORANGE JUICE

COMBINE IN ANOTHER BOWL :
4 CUPS WHOLE WHEAT PASTRY FLOUR
½ CUP MILK POWDER
1 Tbl. BAKING POWDER
1 tsp. SALT
2 CUPS CHOPPED WALNUTS

ADD FLOUR MIXTURE TO LIQUID INGREDIENTS.
ADD : 12 OZ. WHOLE WASHED CRANBERRIES -
SORT OUT ANY BAD LOOKING BERRIES.

POUR INTO OILED BREAD PAN.

BAKE AT 325° FOR 55-65 MINUTES — UNTIL
GOLDEN BROWN AND WITH A FIRM
CENTER.

EVAN'S FAVORITE

PUMPKIN PIE

Yields: 1, 9 inch pie

THIS SIMPLE PUMPKIN PIE IS QUICK TO MAKE AND DELICIOUS TO EAT. A REAL HIT ANY TIME OF THE YEAR. PUMPKIN PIES ARE NOT JUST FOR THANKSGIVING!

FILLING - MIX IN ORDER
- 3 CUPS PUMPKIN PUREE
- 3/4 CUP HONEY
- 2 Tbl. MOLASSES
- 1/4 tsp. CLOVES - GROUND
- 1 Tbl. CINNAMON
- 1 1/2 tsp. GINGER
- 1 tsp. SALT
- 4 EGGS - BARELY BEATEN (OVER-BEATEN EGGS WILL MAKE TOP BUBBLED AND ROUGH)
- 1 CAN EVAPORATED MILK OR 2 CUPS OF SCALDED MILK

POUR INTO UN-BAKED 9 INCH PIE SHELL.

BAKE AT 450° FOR 10 MINUTES THEN AT 350° FOR 40 MINUTES

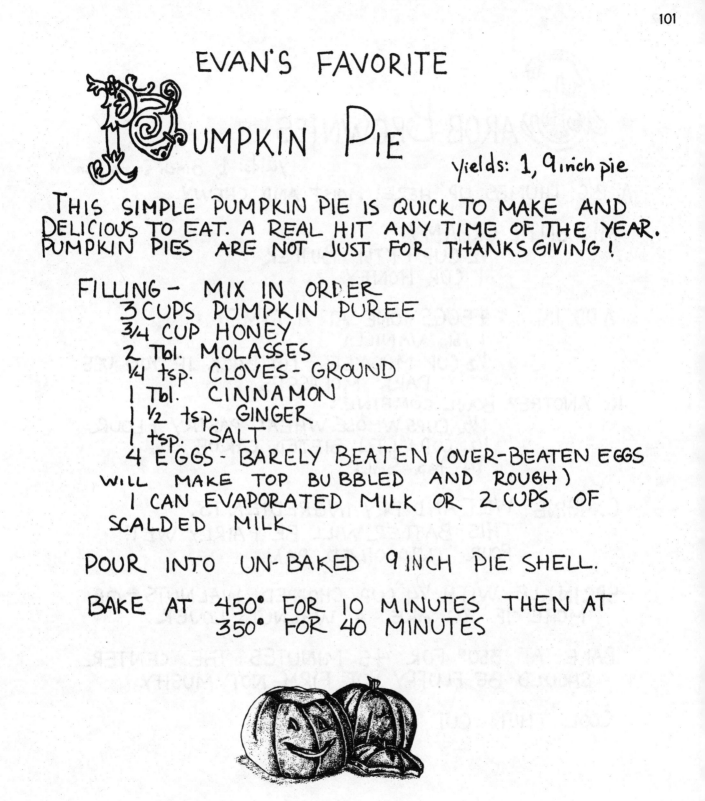

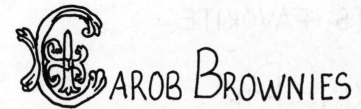AROB BROWNIES

yields: 1, 8 inch square pan

A BIG "THUMBS UP" HERE! MOIST AND CHEWY

MIX UNTIL CREAMY:
        ½ CUP + 1 Tbl. BUTTER
        1 CUP HONEY

ADD IN   : 4 EGGS - ONE AT A TIME
        1 Tbl. VANILLA
        ⅓ CUP MOLASSES - CUT BACK IF YOU USE
                DARK MOLASSES

IN ANOTHER BOWL COMBINE:
        1½ CUPS WHOLE WHEAT PASTRY FLOUR
        ½ CUP + 1 Tbl. SIFTED CAROB
        ¼ tsp. SALT

COMBINE WET AND DRY INGREDIENTS.
        THIS BATTER WILL BE FAIRLY WET.
        POUR INTO OILED PAN.

SPRINKLE WITH ¼ CUP CHOPPED WALNUTS - OR
        MORE IF YOU ARE A WALNUT LOVER.

BAKE AT 350° FOR 45 MINUTES. THE CENTER
        SHOULD BE FLUFFY BUT FIRM - NOT MUSHY.

COOL THEN CUT.

 PPLE BARS

Yields: one 8×12 pan
thus
24, 2 inch bars

THESE HOLD TOGETHER VERY WELL

<u>FILLING</u> : WASH, CORE AND CUT 4 LBS. ORGANIC APPLES.
IF YOUR APPLES ARE ORGANIC, LEAVE THE SKINS ON. THEY
WILL ADD SWEETNESS AND COLOR
<u>ADD</u> : ½ CUP MAPLE SYRUP
      ½ CUP APPLE BUTTER
      2 Tbl. VANILLA
      JUICE FROM ONE LEMON (AND RIND)
COOK SLOWLY TO APPLESAUCE CONSISTENCY

<u>CRUST</u> : MIX 3¾ CUPS WHOLE WHEAT PASTRY FLOUR
      ¼ CUP SESAME SEEDS
      5 CUPS ROLLED OATS
      ½ CUP RICE FLOUR
      ¼ tsp. SALT
<u>GATHER</u> : 1½ CUPS CANOLA OIL
      ½ CUP WATER
      ⅞ CUP HONEY

COMBINE WET AND DRY INGREDIENTS. THE RESULTING
DOUGH WILL BE STICKY AND CRUMBLY. LET REST FOR
20 MINUTES TO SOFTEN THE OATS.

DIVIDE DOUGH IN 2 PARTS. PAT ONE PART INTO THE
   BOTTOM OF YOUR OILED PAN, PRESSING FIRMLY. COVER
   WITH THE APPLE FILLING. CRUMBLE REMAINING
   CRUST OVER TOP AND PRESS SLIGHTLY.
BAKE AT 350° FOR 35-45 MINUTES, UNTIL TOPPING
   IS BROWNED SLIGHTLY. CUT WHILE WARM.

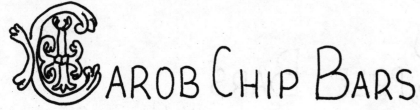arob Chip Bars

Yields: 1 16 x 12 inch pan —
or as close to it as possible

VERY RICH AND DELICIOUS

CREAM : 1¼ CUPS SOFT BUTTER
        ¾ CUP HONEY

ADD : ⅓ CUP BARLEY MALT SYRUP
      ⅓ CUP MOLASSES

BEAT IN: 3 EGGS

ADD : 1 Tbl. VANILLA

COMBINE : 2½ CUPS WHOLE WHEAT
TOGETHER   PASTRY FLOUR
          ¾ Tbl. BAKING SODA

COMBINE WET AND DRY INGREDIENTS.

STIR IN : 2 CUPS UNSWEETENED CAROB CHIPS
          1¼ CUPS SUNFLOWER SEEDS

SPREAD INTO OILED PAN.

BAKE AT 325° FOR 20-25 MINUTES — TILL
  LIGHTLY BROWN.

CUT WHEN SLIGHTLY COOL.

Coconut Dream Bars

yields: 1 16x12 inch pan

A LUXURIOUS TREAT FOR SPECIAL OCCASIONS

CRUST: CREAM: 1 CUP BUTTER
                        ½ CUP HONEY
            ADD : 2 tsp. VANILLA
        MIX IN : 2 CUPS WHOLE WHEAT
                                PASTRY FLOUR
                        ⅔ CUP RICE FLOUR

MIX THOROUGHLY BUT GENTLY.
SPREAD ON OILED PAN.
BAKE AT 325° FOR 10-15 MINUTES

TOPPING: BEAT : 2 EGGS
               ADD : ½ CUP YOGURT OR BUTTERMILK
                        1 CUP HONEY
                        3/8 CUP MOLASSES
                        2 tsp. VANILLA

        COMBINE: 3/8 CUP WHOLE WHEAT
                                PASTRY FLOUR
                        ½ tsp. BAKING SODA
                        ½ CUP FINELY SHREDDED
                                    COCONUT
                        ½ CUP WHEAT GERM
                        1 CUP CHOPPED WALNUTS
        MIX WET AND DRY INGREDIENTS.
        SPREAD OVER CRUST. SPRINKLE SOME
COCONUT ON TOP. BAKE AT 325° FOR 20-30 MINUTES.

WALNUT-RAISIN-DATE-CASHEW—
Ultimate Oatmeal Cookies

Yields: 24

THESE ARE BIG AND THICK AND CHEWY AND DELICIOUS

BEAT: 3 EGGS
ADD: 3/4 CUP WARMED HONEY
3/4 CUP LIGHT OIL

COMBINE: 4½ CUPS ROLLED OATS
1¼ CUPS WHEAT GERM
3/4 CUP MILK POWDER
3/4 CUP COCONUT FLAKES
2/3 CUP WALNUTS OR CASHEWS
2/3 CUP RAISINS OR DATES

POUR WET INGREDIENTS INTO THE DRY INGREDIENTS.

QUICKLY STIR MIXTURE WITH YOUR HANDS. WHEN EVENLY MIXED, LET IT REST 20-30 MINUTES. THIS WILL HELP THE COOKIES BIND AND NOT BE SO CRUMBLY.

DIVIDE OUT COOKIES ON TO OILED COOKIE SHEETS. PRESS TILL THEY ARE ABOUT 1/4 INCH THICK AND ROUND AND FLAT

BAKE AT 325° 15 MINUTES AND GOLDEN.

ALTERNATE OATMEAL COOKIES

Yield: 2 dozen large cookies

THIS IS A GOLDEN, CHEWY COOKIE WHICH IS DAIRY-FREE AND SWEETENED WITH RICE SYRUP. IT KEEPS VERY WELL. SERVES NICELY AS A SATISFYING, FILLING SNACK.

COMBINE IN A LARGE BOWL:
- 4 CUPS ROLLED OATS
- 2 CUPS WHOLE WHEAT PASTRY FLOUR
- 1/4 tsp. SALT
- 1 1/3 CUPS CHOPPED PECANS
- 2/3 CUP CHOPPED DATES

MIX TOGETHER IN ANOTHER BOWL:
- 1/3 CUP OIL (SAFFLOWER OR CANOLA)
- 1 3/4 CUPS RICE SYRUP
- 1 1/3 CUPS WATER

MIXTURE WILL BE SOUPY SO LET IT SIT FOR AN HOUR OR SO. THE OATS SOAK UP THE LIQUID—THIS IS WHAT BINDS THE COOKIE.

FORM 2 INCH BALLS AND PLACE ON COOKIE SHEET THAT IS OILED. PRESS DOWN UNTIL COOKIE IS 1/4 INCH THICK— THEY WILL NOT SPREAD IN THE OVEN.

BAKE AT 325° FOR 25 MINUTES, OR UNTIL THEIR TOPS SPRING BACK WHEN TOUCHED.

# RUGELACH

Yeilds: 32 cookies

MIX TOGETHER A DOUGH OF:

½ Tbl. UNSALTED BUTTER

8 OZ. CREAM CHEESE

2 CUPS WHOLE WHEAT PASTRY FLOUR

SPRINKLE WITH WATER IF NECESSARY.
MAKES A DRY DOUGH. REFRIGERATE.

* RAISIN FILLING:

1 CUP CHOPPED RAISINS

1 CUP FINELY CHOPPED ALMONDS

1 Tsp. CINNAMON

* JAM FILLING:

1 CUP JAM OF YOUR CHOICE

1 CUP FINELY CHOPPED ALMONDS

ADD WATER AS NEEDED TO MAKE YOUR FILLING
EASY TO SPREAD. DIVIDE DOUGH IN 2 PARTS.
ROLL INTO A CIRCLE AND CUT INTO 16 WEDGES.
SPREAD WITH FILLING. ROLL EACH WEDGE FROM
THE OUTSIDE TOWARD THE CENTER. PLACE ON
OILED COOKIE SHEET. BAKE 15 MINUTES AT 350°

PAW PAW, MICHIGAN

Grain Dance Bakery and Natural Foods, located in the fruit belt region of southwestern Michigan, employs a small group of hard working, enthusiastic, and dedicated bakers. We are part of a consumer owned food cooperative which has been operating since 1979. A natural foods grocery is housed under the same roof as the bakery, and is the primary outlet for our breads and goodies.

We strive to be an integral part of community life in Paw Paw and the surrounding rural area. Our loyal customers often come from as far as 25 miles away as we are the only whole grain bakery around.

We have watched with great satisfaction as more and more new faces join us for a fresh whole grain muffin or stuffed bagel (our specialty). As sales continue to grow we feel we are finally over the "will we make it" stage and have established a niche in Paw Paw.

Our bakery has developed a strong positive energy and a unique personality which makes it a very fulfilling place to work. The whole grain bakeries we have met through the Cooperative Whole Grain Educational Association have been a tremendous help and inspiration to us as we grow.

VEGGIE-CHEESE STUFFED BAGELS

Makes 16

Chop or dice into small pieces:
- 1 bunch broccoli
- 2 large carrots (¼ lb.)
- 3 stalks celery
- 1 medium onion

Season veggies with:
- 2 tsp. basil
- 1 tsp. marjoram
- salt (optional)

Grate:
- 16 oz. colby or cheddar cheese (keep this separate)

After making a stuffed bagel, you will see how fine you need to chop the veggies. Large pieces will poke through the dough and make holes.

Cut dough from the Eggless Whole Wheat Bagels recipe into 16 pieces. One at a time, flatten a lump of dough on a lightly floured board to form a rectangle of about 5"x 4." Be careful to flatten it evenly so it's not thinner in the center than at the edges. Place about ¼ cup (1 oz.) grated cheese along the edge closest to you. Next, place ½ cup of the veggie mix on top of the cheese. (fig.1)

Now lift the edge closest to you and wrap it around the veggies, rolling away from you (fig.2). Pull the far edge of the rectangle toward you, on top of the veggies (fig.3), stretching the dough gently. Pinch to seal, leaving one end open (fig.4). Pick up the roll and gently squeeze it to compact it and lengthen it slightly. Insert closed end into open end (fig.5) Pinch well to seal. (fig.6). It takes practice!

It's best not to let the bagels rise too much, so after you have made 3, it's time to start boiling. Place bagels in a large pot of boiling water and boil 30 seconds each side. Lift from water with slotted spoon, draining well. Place on oiled cookie sheet to await their fellow bagels, and when the tray is full, bake 20-30 minutes, till golden, at 400°

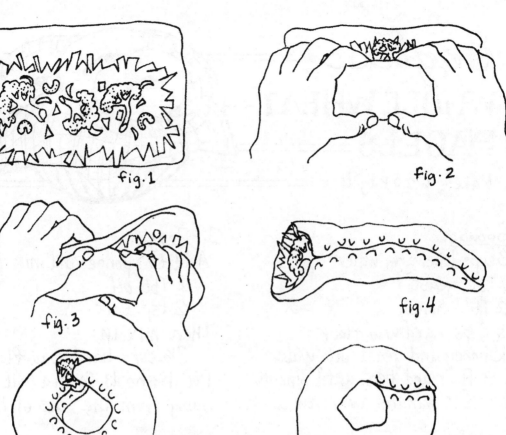

fig. 1

fig. 2

fig. 3

fig. 4

fig. 5

fig. 6

Helpful hints:

If you get holes in your bagels as you are forming them you can sometimes patch them by wrapping a small piece of dough around the weak area. If your veggies are too moist they will cause the dough to tear easily— try blotting the veggies with a towel before filling. Also, salt causes the veggies to "juice out" so sprinkle it on just before rolling. If some of the filling leaks out during baking, you can stuff it back in when the bagels come out of the oven.

At Grain Dance we have elevated bagel making to an art form. We make several stuffed varieties: pizza- bean burrito- sauerkraut- jalapeño- cream cheese and raisin- so be creative and try different fillings!
Happy Bageling!

Eggless
WHOLE WHEAT
BAGELS

Makes 16-20 Bagels

I <u>Sponge:</u>
3 cups lukewarm water
1 Tbl. yeast
2 Tbl. honey
3 cups hard w.w. flour
Wisk honey and yeast into water.
Mix in flour and beat until smooth.
Let rise 15 minutes away from draft.

II. <u>Dough:</u>
Add to sponge and mix in:
2 Tbl. oil
2 tsp. salt
Then mix in:
3½ cups hard w.w. flour
Dough should form a ball and come
away from the sides of the bowl.

III. Turn dough onto floured board and knead 15 minutes until smooth and elastic. Dough should be fairly stiff but still stretchy. Try to use no more than ¼ c. additional flour to keep dough from sticking to board.

IV. Let dough rest for 20 min. It doesn't have to rise as much as bread dough.

V. Cut dough into 20 pieces. Roll each piece into a snake, then connect the ends, pressing together well. Drop bagels into a pot of boiling water (no need to rise them first - the water does that). Boil for 1 minute, then turn with a slotted spoon and boil 1 minute on the other side. They should rise to the surface and get puffy. Remove from water with slotted spoon and place on oiled cookie sheet. If you want poppy seeds on top, sprinkle them on as soon as you remove the bagels from the water. Onions or raisins can be kneaded into the dough before it rests. Bake 20-25 minutes at 400° or until golden.

...oh muffin love.....oh muffin love....

OAT-APRICOT MUFFINS

makes 1 dozen.

First:
Soak 1 cup chopped dried apricots in ½ cup hot tap water for 30 min.
= Do not drain. =

Wets:
   ¼ cup flax mix* or 1 egg
   ¼ cup oil
   3/8 cup honey
   3/4 cup water
   ½ cup chopped walnuts
   the above apricots and their juice

Blend together with a wire wisk until smooth.

Drys:
   2 cups w.w. pastry flour
   ¼ cup oat bran
   ¼ cup rolled oats
   3/8 cup milk powder
   2 tsp baking powder
   ¼ tsp baking soda
   1 tsp cinnamon

Stir together drys. Add drys to wets, blending quickly with wisk until just combined. Scoop into papered or oiled muffin tins. Bake at 400° for 15-20 minutes or til done.

* How to make flax mix egg substitute:
Place ½ cup whole flax seeds in dry blender jar. Blend to an even meal. As you continue to blend, pour in 2 cups water. When the mixture begins to thicken and resembles a milk shake turn off the blender. Can be stored in the refrigerator for quite some time.
   Makes 2 cups. ¼ c = 1 egg. Try it in other muffins!

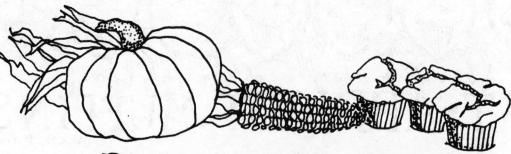

Pumpcorn Muffins
makes 12

½ cup safflower oil
½ cup honey
1½ cups pumpkin puree
1 cup water

Beat together
with a wire wisk
until smooth.

2¼ cups whole wheat
    pastry flour
1 cup cornmeal
1 Tbl. baking powder
1 tsp. cinnamon
½ tsp. ginger
¼ tsp. cloves
¼ tsp. nutmeg

Stir together drys.
Add to wets, blend
in quickly with wisk.
(do not overbeat)
Scoop into papered
muffin tins. Bake
at 375° about 30
minutes or til done.

the
grain train
Food Co-op
Petoskey, Michigan

The Grain Train Bakery grew out of the Mercado Restaurant, which was owned and operated by the Grain Train Natural Foods Cooperative in the early 1980's. Sales of bread from the restaurant were so brisk that a separate bakery operation evolved to supply the Coop store front. The bakery has blossomed ever since!

The Bakery now supplies the Grain Train Co-op with, among other things, breads, cookies, bars, granola, bagels, pecan and cinnamon rolls, muffins and special holiday treats.

The bakery, retail store-front and deli have been collectively managed for the past three years, and have always been committed to providing the community with excellent whole grain food.

Non-Dairy "Basic Bran" Muffins

yield 10-12 muffins

Blend thoroughly in a blender
    2 TBL. flax seeds
    3/4 cup water
Add to this
    2 1/2 cups water
    1/4 cup soy flour
Then mix in
    1/4 cup safflower oil
    1/3 cup honey

Combine together in another bowl
    4 cups whole wheat pastry flour
    1 1/2 cups bran (oat or wheat)
    1 1/2 TBL. baking powder
Fold liquid ingredients into the flour & bran Stir only until everything is moistened, then quickly spoon batter into oiled muffin tins. Bake at 350°F. for 45 minutes.

VARIETY II ~ HAZELNUT PRUNE
    to "basic bran" add~
    1/2 cup chopped hazel nuts
    3/4 cup finely diced prunes (pitted)
    1/3 cup water

VARIETY III ~ CORN BRAN
    to basic bran add ~
    1 cup cornmeal in place of 1 cup whole wheat pastry flour. Replace 1/4 c. safflower oil with 1/4 c corn oil. Add 2 cups organic raisins.

ALMOND MUFFINS

YIELD 8-10 muffins

This one is for the almond lovers, nice texture, good flavor!

CREAM TOGETHER:
    1 cup maple syrup
    ½ cup canola oil
    ¼ cup almond butter

Add:
    3-4 drops lemon oil (or ¼ tsp. lemon rind)
    2 tsp. vanilla

In another bowl combine:
    3½ cups whole wheat pastry flour
    3/4 cup chopped almonds
    2 tsp. baking powder

Add flour mixture to liquid ingredients, stirring in 1 ¼ cups soymilk. Spoon into oiled cup cake tins. Bake at 350°F for 20-30 minutes.

118

Pumpkin Bars

Dairyless, eggless. An easy way to have pumpkin pie that travels well in lunch boxes or to that pot luck dinner down the road!

yield one 8"×12" square

CRUST:

4 cups rolled oats
1½ cups soft whole wheat (pastry) flour
¼ cup honey
¾ cup soy margarine
½ tsp. vanilla extract

Blend together oats and flour. Cut in margarine, add honey and vanilla and mix well. The mixture should be moist but crumbly.

FILLING:

1⅔ cups mashed pumpkin
¾ cup soy milk
2 Tbl. arrowroot
2 Tbl. cashew or almond butter (or 1 Tbl. pumpkin seeds finely ground)

BLEND until smooth:

¼ cup honey	¾ Tbl. molasses
½ Tbl. vanilla	½ Tbl. cinnamon
¼ tsp. nutmeg	¼ tsp. ginger

⅛ tsp. ground cloves

Spread half of crust on a 8"×12" cookie sheet. It's not necessary to oil the sheet. Compressing with a rolling pin dusted with flour. Spread filling over the crust, smooth with spoon or spatula and crumble remaining crust evenly over filling. Bake 30 to 40 minutes at 350°F until lightly firmed and brown on top.

NON·DAIRY FROSTING

yield 1 cup frosting

CREAM together ~
   1/4 cup softened soy margarine
   1/4 cup maple syrup
BEAT IN ~
   2-3 Tbl. unsweetened soymilk
   1 tsp. almond extract
ADD IN & continue beating until light and fluffy
   2/3 -1 cup soymilk powder (not soy flour)
STIR IN if desired ~
   1/2 cup chopped almonds

NATURE'S BAKERY

NUTRITION IN GOOD TASTE
1019 William Street — Madison Wisconsin

As if Lakes Mendota and Monona were enormous yeasty sponges, their leavening power bubbling over into the isthmus, the cultural and political fermentation in Madison during the late 60's gave rise to Nature's Bakery. While teeming throngs of protestors gathered around the capitol, storefront windows shattered, tear gas rose above state street and bombs went off in the University's military math center, dedicated groups of people were forming co-ops and collectives, seeking to infuse these alternative structures with their convictions and passions, and in doing so help bring about a broad transformation of society.

This deep desire for social change has been a part of Nature's Bakery since it began over 20 years ago. Certainly the political climate in Madison has cooled to a degree — owing to a conservative high pressure system trickling down from an artic mass of white bread brain tissue.

But it's still possible to connect with the spirit of change born here in the late 60's— even without renting The War At Home from your local video boutique. There is still a strong network of alternative business, political organizations, lifestyles, values, and visions. and Nature's is still very much a part of it.

Our collective is currently seven members strong: three women and four men dedicated to cooperative work, consensus decision making, organic whole grains and pulling our bakery out of the finacial hole it has fallen into over the past few years.

The likelihood of our recovery seems, ironically enough, to be assured by the fact that one of the hottest capitalist marketing trends of the late 80's is natural foods. It's an odd dialectical situation: wanting to work more with distributors to gain a larger market for our products, and being told by one of our local co-op distribution networks that we're too small. (Small may be beautiful but the volume doesn't quite cut it); discussing changes in our marketing practices with a local store manager, who says of the 'old' bakery. "That wasn't a bakery. it was a spiritual experience."

But even while Nature's historical situation has changed, our "bottom line" has not. We know that our work can never be profitable simply by generating more money. We must continue to support and promote organic agricultures, and wholistic, sustainable methods for growing and distributing foods. We must continue our recycling work and our support of local charity and hunger networks. We must keep advancing our collective work: nurturing the non-exploitative and non-hierarchical approach to labor that so often <u>does</u> make our business a spiritual experience. We must continue creating healthful and delicious products: foods that delight the soul as well as the body.

And we must never stop working to create the wonderfully rewarding bonds between our customers and us, those incredibly satisfying moments when someone sensuously licks their fingers clean and sighs. "That's the best dang roll I've ever had!"

By remaining sensitive to all these facets of our business, we plan to enter our third decade more profitably than ever: cultivating and harvesting the fruits of our labor, and strengthening a bakery that, for generations to come, will continue to play a role in the transformation of our society, and the people within it.

Whole Wheat Bread
Makes 2 loaves

Sponge: 2 tsp. barley malt
2 ⅓ cups warm water
1 Tbl. yeast
4 cups hard whole wheat flour

Mix the malt, water, and yeast and let sit until yeast begins to bubble. Mix in the flour with 100 strokes. Let the sponge sit in a warm damp place or under a damp towel for 30 minutes.

4 tsp. oil (safflower works well)
2 - 2½ cups hard whole wheat flour
2 tsp. salt
3 Tbl. sunflower seeds (optional)

Add the remaining ingredients to the sponge. Mix then knead well until thoroughly smooth and elastic. Let dough rise until it doubles, in a warm moist place.

Divide in 2 and shape, and place in 2 oiled loaf pans. Let rise to double and bake at 375° for 40-50 minutes or until the bread comes easily out of the pans. The bottoms and corner of the baked loaf should be firm.

Swedish Rye Bread:~.

Makes 2 loaves
A lovely rye loaf with a distinctive anise flavor

Sponge:
- 1 Tbl. yeast
- 5 Tbl. molasses
- 2½ Tbl. oil
- 2 cups warm water
- 2 cups hard whole wheat flour

Mix well, the water, oil, molasses and yeast and allow the yeast to bubble. Then add the flour and let this sponge rise for 20-30 minutes in a warm place.

- 1⅔ cups hard whole wheat flour
- 2⅓ cups rye flour
- ½ orange - juiced then chop finely - the entire thing!
- 2 Tbl. anise
- 2 tsp. salt

Mix the rest of the ingredients together then add them to the sponge. Knead until well mixed - maybe 5 minutes-. Let rise to double in a warm damp place.

Knead on lightly oiled surface and place in well oiled pans. Allow to rise until it doubles in a warm damp place or with a damp towel over it. Bake at 325° for 75-80 minutes or until bottom corners are hard and golden.

Sinny Sunny Currant Bread

Makes Two Loaves

1½ Tbl. yeast
1¼ cups. warm water

Mix the yeast in the water and let it rest for 5 minutes.

2 beaten eggs
1 cup honey
2 Tbl. oil (maybe safflower)

Add eggs, honey and oil to the yeast mixture and mix it well.

3½ cups hard whole wheat flour

Add flour to that mixture, knead for 7-10 minutes until dough is smooth and elastic. Let rest in an oiled bowl for 10 minutes. Cover with damp towel

½ cup organic currants or raisins
⅓ cup sunflower seeds
1 tsp. salt
1 Tbl. cinnamon

Mix the dry ingredients together and knead in for 5 minutes.

Place in oiled bread pans. Let rise to double in a warm place. Bake at 350° for 35-45 minutes.

"yeast-free" Buckwheat Bread

Makes 2 loaves

A very versatile dough that can be used for pizza crusts, rolled thin for crackers, etc. It has the same delicious flavor as those old fashioned breakfasts.

½ cup buckwheat groats
1½ cups water

Roast groats gently, then add water, cover, bring to a boil, then turn down heat and simmer until the water is absorbed. Cool.

2 cups hard whole wheat flour
2 cups buckwheat flour
1¼ cups water
2 Tbl. sunflower seeds (optional)

Mix together all remaining ingredients with the groat mixture. If you decide to add sunflower seeds, a nice touch is to roast them gently. before adding. Knead dough 'till it is moist but no longer sticky.

Shape into round flat loaves that are about 1½ inches high. Decorate loaves with original designs and bake at 400° for 45 minutes or so.

Slow Magic
Sourdough

Makes 2 loaves

1 cup sour dough starter	Combine starter and water
2 cups water	in a glass, enamel or earthen-
5 cups hard whole wheat flour	ware bowl and let sit all night.

Add flour, the next day or 12-15 hours later, until a stiff dough is formed. knead for 20 minutes, adding flour only to keep the dough from sticking to you or the table. Lay the dough in a clean oiled bowl, cover with a damp cloth and rest it in a warm place until it doubles in size. - This could take all day or only a morning depending on how fast and active your culture is growing. Be patient.

When it has risen, punch it down. You may shape it now or let it rise, punch it down, then shape it. If you like it very sour, let it rise several times before you bake it.

Before the last rise, punch down the dough, shape it in two loaves. Use either loaf pans or oiled cookie sheets and shape in round or long loaves. Slit the tops with a sharp knife. Let rise. Bake at 375° - 400° for 45-60 minutes. With experience you will learn to gauge rising times, baking temperatures and baking times.

Sourdough Variations

Herb Sourdough

Just before adding the flour, stir the following into the liquid starter:

3/4 tsp. oregano   3/4 tsp. dill or celery seed
3/4 tsp. marjoram   1 tsp. granular garlic
3/4 tsp. basil or thyme

Proceed as for the basic recipe.

Rice Bread

Just before adding the flour, stir into the liquid starter, 4 cups cooked rice or any other whole grain and proceed as for the basic recipe. This will make 3 loaves rather than 2.

Rye Sourdough

Use all or part rye flour instead of the whole wheat flour.

Wheat Sprout Crackers

Makes 15 1x3 inch crackers

½ pound wheat sprouts (see "How to Bake Essene Bread"
1 Tbl. oil (corn or safflower)   in the front of this book)
A little pastry flour, whole wheat of course.

Grind the sprouts <u>fine</u> using an old meat grinder or
food chopper. Be careful, these sprouts will get very
sticky. Oil your parts before using them.

Add the oil and knead it all together until the dough
is uniform in consistency. Then knead in flour —
enough to make a dough that can be rolled out (the
amount of flour depends on how long the sprouts are —
the longer the sprouts, the more flour you'll need).
The dough should also be soft enough to roll out but
not sticky. The dough should not be able to fall apart.

Roll out on a floured surface to about an ⅛ inch
thickness. Cut into shapes. Place on slightly oiled cookie
sheets. Bake at 300° for about 20 minutes, until
slightly browned and stiff. They will still be soft
but become crisp as they cool off.

Blueberry - Coconut Corn Muffins

Makes 12 Muffins — that are distinctively tasty and not too sweet

3/4 cup whole wheat pastry flour
1/2 cup hard whole pastry flour
1 Tbl. baking powder
1/2 tsp. ground cardamom

Mix dry ingredients together in a bowl. Be sure there's no lumps in your baking powder. Whisk or sift these dries to make them fluffy.

Add 1/2 cup unsweetened coconut and 1 cup corn meal

2 eggs
1 cup soy or cow's milk
3/4 cup honey
4 Tbl. melted butter

In another bowl beat your eggs then add the milk, honey and butter and whisk.

Combine your wet and dry ingredients then add 1 1/2 cups fresh or frozen blueberries. If your berries are frozen, your batter will stiffen and cool when you add them. Don't worry. Scoop batter into oiled tins or papered tins. Bake at 350° for 25 minutes or until a toothpick comes out clean.

Apple Oat-Bran Muffins

Makes 2 dozen

1 cup dried apples
2 cups apple cider

Chop up the apples in small pieces, about ½ your pinky nail size. Then Soak them in the cider

⅞ cup oat bran
½ cup hard whole wheat flour
1½ cups whole wheat pastry flour
2 Tbl. baking powder
1½ tsp. nutmeg
2½ tsp. cinnamon
¼ tsp. allspice

Mix all the dry ingredients together.

In another bowl mix till frothy : 2 eggs - white

⅓ cup vegetable oil
1½ cups soy milk
1 cup honey
¾ tsp. lemon juice
pinch of salt

Mix all the wet ingredients and the salt together.

Mix the dry ingredients into the wet ingredients, gently and quickly. Then fold in the egg whites. Add the apples. Spoon into oiled muffin tins and bake at 325° for 20-25 minutes and until firm to the touch.

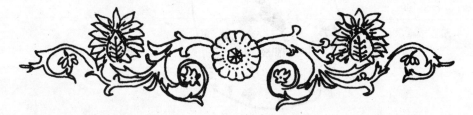

Ginger Snaps

Makes about 20 cookies

That traditional favorite with great ginger flavor.

3½ cups whole wheat pastry flour
1 Tbl. baking powder
¾ tsp. Salt
1 Tbl. cinnamon
½ Tbl. cloves
1½ Tbl. ginger *

Mix all the dry ingredients together in one bowl.
* If you use fresh, grated ginger rather than dry ginger, add a little less of it and add it to your wet ingredients.

1 cup soy margarine
1 cup honey
6 Tbl. molasses
2 small eggs

Cream margarine and honey. Mix up the eggs, then add the other wet ingredients to it.

Combine wet and dry ingredients thoroughly. Test bake one cookie to see how much it will spread. Drop on oiled cookie sheets. Bake for 12-15 minutes at 350°. Don't let them burn.   Don't let them burn.

Poppy Seed Cookies

Makes One Dozen

2 ¼ cups whole wheat pastry flour
¼ cup poppy seeds
2 tsp. baking powder

Combine flour, poppy seeds and baking powder in a bowl.

¾ cup margarine
¾ cup honey

In another bowl cream margarine and honey

1 beaten egg
1 Tbl. vanilla

Add your egg and vanilla to the honey and margarine. Then add your flour mixture

Scoop onto oiled trays. Press lightly with fingers. Bake for 12 minutes at 350°.

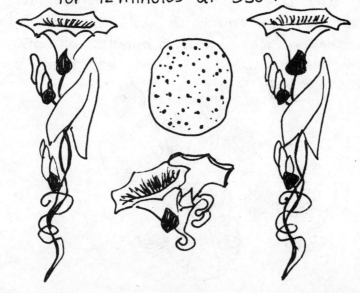

Carob Chip Cookies

A goodie with a few surprises - try this
one with your icecream!

½ cup tahini
¼ cup butter

Cream tahini & butter

1 cup honey
1 Tbl. vanilla
1 Tbl. tamari (yes, tamari)

Add honey, vanilla & tamari

2 cups whole wheat
      pastry flour
1 tsp. baking soda
1 cup rolled oats
½ cup chopped walnuts

In another bowl combine
flour, soda, oats, walnuts

Combine wet and dry ingredients, mixing quickly
and lightly. Add: 1 cup carob chips.

Spoon onto an oiled cookie sheet. Wet your fingers
and press or flatten with a fork.

Bake at 325° for 15 minutes and edges are golden.

Carob Nut Bars

Makes about 20 bars
One 6×10 inch pan

A very tasty snack or dessert, and much more nutritious than the familiar sugar and chocolate variety. The kids will love them — that is, kids of all ages!

¼ cup oil (safflower, canola, sunflower are suggestions)
¼ cup tahini
¾ cup maple syrup
¼ cup water

Combine wet ingredients in a bowl and beat well.

¾ cup chopped walnuts or pecans
½ cup carob powder
2 cups whole wheat pastry flour

Combine and thoroughly mix dry ingredients in a separate bowl.

Combine wet and dry ingredients and push into an oiled pan. Chill in the refrigerator for several hours or overnight. Then bake at 375° for 10-12 minutes.

Peanut Minus Cookies

Makes about 18 cookies

Eggless, dairyless, wheatless, but <u>Not</u> peanut less!

¼ cup millet
½ cup water

Place millet and water in a small sauce pan and bring to a boil. Lower heat and simmer until water is absorbed.

1 cup barley malt syrup
1½ cups peanut butter
¾ tsp. vanilla

Meanwhile stir together the malt, peanut butter and vanilla

¼ cup corn meal
¼ cup rye flour
¾ cup chopped dry roasted peanuts

In a separate bowl combine flour, meal, and peanuts.

Combine the sticky wet ingredients with the millet. Add the dry ingredients. The dough will be very sticky. Spoon dough onto oiled cookie sheets. Flatten with wet finger. Bake at 350° for 12-15 minutes. They should be nicely browned, and will firm up as they cool off. You don't have to wait to eat them!

on the Rise
WHOLE GRAIN BAKED GOODS
109 Walton St. Syracuse NY 13202   475-7190

A hot, humid, sultry dawn in the city, 80° and already the heat glazes the sidewalk while inside the bakery 6 women knead bread....

One of the most valuable gifts about working at On the Rise is the internal support we offer eachother. We are currently a women's collective baking whole grain bread in beautiful central New York. Our reasons for being an all women's partnership are as varied as the six of us. We all agree that a feminist work environment has enabled us to feel more powerful. It also helps us create a secure place in which to explore leadership roles. The responsibility of operating a non-hierarchical small business, which is not profit motivated, has been a challenge. We have shared intense feelings about this agenda and at present have clearly made conscious choices in order to provide empowering work for women.

We use organically grown grains and bake a variety of breads and pastries. We offer baked goods free of yeast, wheat, oil and/or salt; to satisfy customers with restricted diets and as an acknowledgement of the overuse of wheat in our society.

We support local organic farmers by preparing our lunches and baked goods with seasonal produce.

We prepare all of the foods without animal products. This decision evolved out of ethical, nutritional, and economic considerations.

On the Rise recently celebrated its 10th anniversary! As we move into our next 10 years we will, through our love of baking, continue to heal ourselves, our community, and our earth. We hope to be seen as a model and inspiration for peaceful global change.

At **on the Rise** we try to use only local, organically grown foods in season. We also want to cook as low on the food chain as possible. This is how we do it:

Flax seed Mixture

- we use this as an egg substitute. We also decrease the amount of oil in recipes as flax is an excellent source of whole fat. Blend 1 cup flax seed till decimated. Add 3 cups cold water and blend. This should have the consistancy of eggs. Use 1/4 cup of this mixture in replacement of 1 egg

Soy milk

- we use this as a substitute for milk. Soak 3/4 lb. soy beans overnight (in cold water). Drain and grind. Pour 8 cups boiling water over beans and let sit 10 minutes. You can strain out the pulp or use it as we do. Then you have a real whole food

Potato Water

- pour 9 cups boiling water on one lb. finely grated potatoes. Let sit for 10 minutes. You can then strain it, but we use it all.

Wheat free baking

- in changing recipes the conversion is 1 1/4 cup other flours to 1 cup wheat flour. For cookie recipes use barley/cornmeal in a 6/1 ratio. For muffins & cakes use a barley/oat in a 2/1 ratio or barley/oat/corn 2/1/1 ratio. Buckwheat flour can be used alone to replace wheat flour.

Experiment and enjoy!

Daily Bread

makes 2 loaves

Soften 1 Tbl. yeast
in   2 cups warm soymilk
        1 cup warm water
        3 Tbl. honey
Let that sit for 10 minutes.

Then add 4 cups hard whole wheat
    flour and let that sit for 20 minutes.

Then add ⅜ cup oil
        3 Tbl. molasses
        1 ½ tsp. salt

Mix altogether then begin adding
your whole wheat flour. As you need it, sprinkle
in the flour, as you knead it for 10-15 minutes.
Let dough rise to double.

Divide dough in 2 loaves.
Shape and place in oiled
pans. Let rise to double then
bake at 350° for 45 minutes.

Anadama Bread

makes 2 loaves

Story has it that when Anna and Dama got together to bake bread one day, there wasn't enough wheat flour or honey to make bread. "What shall we do?", moaned Anna. "Let us use this cornmeal. But the bread will not be sweet," said Dama. Somehow that gave Anna the idea of molasses. Thus together they created what we today call Anadama. It's true! It's delicious, too!

The night before pour 1 cup boiling water over 1⅛ cups corn meal. Stir in 3 Tbl. molasses and ¼ cup oil.

The next day add 1 Tbl. yeast to 1¾ cups warm water. Let it rest 5 minutes. Then add the yeast mix to the corn mix. Stir. Add ¾ Tbl. salt. Stir. Knead in hard whole wheat flour so it is workable (about 4 cups). Continue kneading for 5 minutes. Place in an oiled bowl. Cover with a damp towel and let rise 1½ hours. Punch down. Shape in 2 loaves. Place in oiled pans or cookie sheets. Let rise to double. Bake at 350° for 45 minutes.

A WARM CUP OF BREAD

Chico's 3-Seed Bread

Makes 2 loaves

Over 1½ cups rolled oats, pour ¾ cup boiling water let sit until warm but not hot.

Add 2¼ cups potato water
  ¼ cup honey
  1 Tbl. yeast

Let that bubble, then add 3 cups hard whole wheat flour. Let that rest 20 minutes.

Add ⅓ cup safflower oil
  ¼ cup honey
  1 tsp. salt
  ⅓ cup sunflower seeds
  ⅓ cup poppy seeds
  ⅓ cup sesame seeds

Begin kneading dough, adding flour only to keep dough from being too sticky. Knead for 10-15 minutes. Let rise in a warm place 'til it doubles. Punch down and shape in 2 loaves. Place in oiled pans and let rise to double again. Bake at 350° for 45-50 minutes.

Pumpkin Cider Bread

Makes 2 loaves

In 2 cups warm water, mix 1½ Tbl. yeast
    let that sit for 5 minutes
Add 4 Tbl. honey and 2 cups hard whole wheat flour
    let that sit for 20 minutes

Add in   ¼ cup safflower oil
        ½ cup grated apple
        ½ cup pumpkin or winter squash that
has been cooked and mashed

In another bowl combine ¼ cup corn meal ½ tsp. salt
                              ¼ tsp. cinnamon ⅛ tsp nutmeg
                                  ⅛ tsp. ground cloves
Mix the spices, then add to the
dough. Knead, adding more whole
wheat flour as you need it. let
rest 1 hour. Shape in 2 loaves.
Place in oiled bread pans.
        let rise to double.

Bake at 350°
for 45-55
minutes.

7-Grain Bread

Makes 2 loaves

Some cooked, some milled, some rolled, some roasted

① Cook ahead of time in
1 cup water
1/4 cup brown rice
1/4 cup millet
Let it cool down to room temperature

② Lightly brown, in the oven or in a dry fry pan,
1 cup barley flour

③ Combine in
1 1/2 Tbl. yeast
1 1/2 cups potato water
(see beginning of this chapter)
Let that bubble for 5 minutes

④ Add to that
1/2 cups rolled oats
1/4 cup honey
Add to that 1 1/2 cups hard whole wheat flour
Let that bubble for 15 minutes

⑤ Add to that, the cooked grains and barley
flour. Mix, then add 1 cup corn meal
1/2 cup rye flour
3/4 Tbl. salt
1/2 Tbl. brewer's yeast
1/4 cup safflower oil

⑥ Begin kneading, adding more whole wheat flour
to keep from sticking. Knead for 10 minutes
Let rise to double. Punch down and shape. Let rise.

⑦ Bake in oiled pans at 400° for 35-45 minutes.

100% Rye Bread

makes 2 loaves

A "take-your-time" type bread

Mix 2 Tbl. yeast
in 2½ cups potato water
Let rest for 15 minutes

Add: 2 tsp. salt
⅓ cup safflower oil
1½ Tbl. chopped parsley
⅓ cup whole flax seed
¼ lb. crumbled tofu or
¼ cup okara (soy bean
fiber left over from the
production of tofu)

Add in 2 cups rye flour.
Mix for 5 minutes. Let rise 30 minutes.
Then add rye flour to dough, kneading it in
so it is not so sticky (remember, it will feel
different than a wheat flour dough) knead for
5-10 minutes. Let rise in a warm place, covered
with a damp towel, for 1 hour. Shape into
2 balls. Place on oiled cookie sheets.
Cut a design on top of each. Let rise
one more hour. Bake at 350° for 45-60
minutes. A denser bread that doesn't rise
as much needs longer baking time.

Parsnip · Cake ·

makes one 10 inch square pan or 24 muffins

Cook until tender, then mash:
    1 1/4 cups parsnips

Mix with that :
    1/2 cup corn oil
    1/2 cup honey
    3/4 cup soy milk
    1/2 Tbl. vanilla

Combine in another bowl:
    2 1/4 cups soft whole wheat pastry flour
    1 Tbl. baking powder
    1/2 tsp. baking soda (with no lumps)
    1/4 tsp. nutmeg

Mix wet and dry ingredients together. Pour into an oiled pan or cupcake tins. Bake until firm, about 25-35 minutes at 350°.

Carrot Cake

Makes one 10 inch pan

Combine in one bowl:

1 cup corn oil 1 1/3 cups honey
1 Tbl. vanilla 3 cups grated carrots
3/4 cup flax seed mixture (see beginning of
                          this chapter)

Combine in another bowl:

4 cups whole wheat pastry flour
1 tsp. salt 1 Tbl. cinnamon
3/4 tsp. nutmeg 1 tsp. baking soda
1/4 tsp. baking powder

Stir both mixtures together. Pour into an oiled pan. Bake at 350° for 45 minutes or until center is firm.

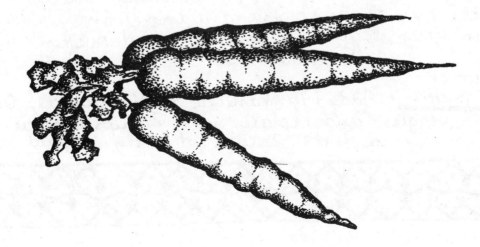

Basic Wheat Free Muffin

Makes 10-12 Muffins

This is a wonderful recipe to mark the seasons. Use zuccini, carrots, blueberries, apples, pecans or anything you like in season. Play with your spices, too!

Prepare ahead: 2 cups finely chopped vegetables (May we suggest a combination of bell peppers, broccoli & onion.)

Mix in one bowl: 3/4 cup oil
3/4 cup honey
3/4 cup flax seed mixture
(see beginning of this chapter)
1 cup soy milk

In another bowl: 2 cups barley flour
Combine   1 3/4 cups oat flour
1 1/4 cups corn meal.
1 tsp. baking soda
1 Tbl. baking powder

Quickly mix the wet and dry ingredients together. Fold in your veggies. Spoon into oiled muffin tins.
Bake at 350° for 35 minutes

Nut or
<u>Fruit Muffin</u> - Add 1 Tbl. vanilla to the liquids. Omit veggies and replace with 2 cups chopped fruit or replace with 2 cups of finely chopped nuts.

Blueberry Muffins

Makes 16 muffins

Rich & Moist & Dairy-less

Mix together 4 cups whole wheat pastry flour
1 Tbl. baking powder
1 tsp. ground cardamom
1 1/3 cup blueberries

Blend and then add 1/2 cup safflower oil
1/2 cup honey
1 1/2 cups soy milk
1/2 cup ground flax
seed mixture

Mix it all together!

Scoop into oiled cupcake tins.
Bake at 350° for 30-40 minutes
or until tops are lightly browned.

* You can substitute peaches and pears for
the blueberries.

Corn — Cakes

Makes 24 cup cakes or 2, 8 inch square cakes

This makes a crunchy cake and moist cornbread. Slices are especially good when toasted later!

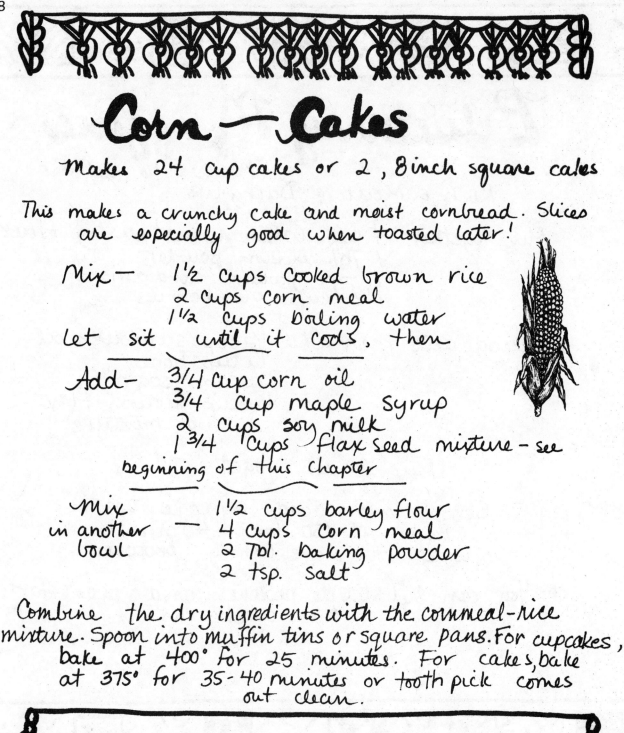

Mix —
1½ cups cooked brown rice
2 cups corn meal
1½ cups boiling water
Let sit until it cools, then

Add—
3/4 cup corn oil
3/4 cup maple syrup
2 cups soy milk
1 3/4 cups flax seed mixture — see beginning of this chapter

Mix in another bowl —
1½ cups barley flour
4 cups corn meal
2 Tbl. baking powder
2 tsp. salt

Combine the dry ingredients with the cornmeal-rice mixture. Spoon into muffin tins or square pans. For cupcakes, bake at 400° for 25 minutes. For cakes, bake at 375° for 35-40 minutes or tooth pick comes out clean.

Honey - Rye Cakes

Wheat - Free

makes 18 cupcakes

A spicy cake with nutty rye flavor and a dried fruit surprise... lots to chew on!

Mix together: 1¼ cups honey
½ cup molasses
2 cups water

In another bowl combine:
5½ cups rye flour
½ Tbl. baking soda
1½ Tbl. baking powder
3 Tbl. cinnamon
½ Tbl. ground cloves
½ Tbl. allspice
¼ tsp. cardamom

Combine wet & dry ingredients.

Fold in 1¼ cups chopped dried apples
¾ cup roasted sunflower seeds

Spoon into oiled cupcake tins. Move quickly and carefully.

Bake at 350° for 45 minutes and centers are soft yet firm (not gushy)
Enjoy them warm or cool.

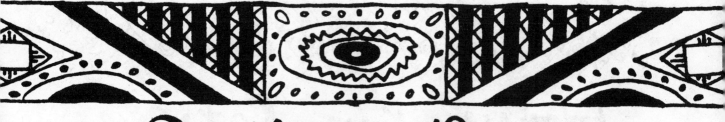

Soy Milk Biscuits

makes 18 Biscuits

Whisk together: ½ cup corn oil
1¼ cup soy milk

In another bowl: 3 cups whole wheat pastry flour
Combine 2 Tbl. baking powder
¾ tsp. salt

Mix gently until all ingredients are
combined. Roll dough to a ¾ inch
thickness, sprinkling gingerly with flour
to keep pin from sticking. Cut with a
biscuit cutter, drinking glass or
cookie cutter. Place on oiled cookie
sheets and bake at 400° for 15-20
minutes, until the edges are golden.

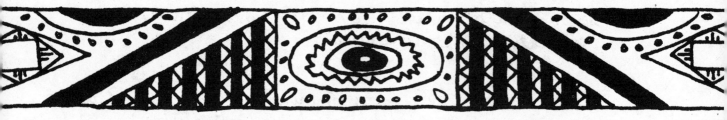

Oatmeal Raisin Cookies

Makes 24 Big ones

Lightly toast in a dry fry pan
4 Cups rolled oats
1 cup sunflower seeds — Cool them.

Mix with   2 cups whole wheat pastry flour
4 tsp baking powder
4 tsp. cinnamon
2 cups raisins

In another bowl cream   1 cup safflower oil
1½ cups honey
½ cup water
1 cup ground flax
seed mixture
1 tsp. vanilla

Combine both mixtures.
Make big balls of dough.
Drop on oiled cookie sheets.
Flatten with wet fingers.
Bake at 350° for 20-25 minutes.

Peanut Butter Cookies

Makes about 15 cookies

Mix —
in one bowl
- 3/4 cup corn oil
- 1 3/4 cups peanut butter
- 1/2 Tbl. vanilla
- 1 tsp. molasses
- 3/4 cup maple syrup

Mix —
in another bowl
- 2 1/2 cups barley flour
- 1 1/2 cups corn meal
- 1/2 tsp. baking powder
- 1/2 tsp. salt

Add the peanut butter mix to the dry ingredients and combine.

Spoon out teaspoonsful of dough onto an oiled cookie sheet. Press with a cookie press or fork. Bake for 25-30 minutes at 325° and edges are golden brown.

Oat Cookies

Wheat- Free   Makes 24

Combine in one bowl
1 cup oil (any light oil will work)
1½ cups maple syrup or a mixture of honey and maple syrup
½ cup flax seed mixture (see beginning of this chapter)
1 Tbl. vanilla

Combine in another bowl
4½ cups rolled oats
2 cups barley flour
1 cup oat flour
2 tsp. baking powder
1 tsp. salt

Mix the wet and dry ingredients together.
Place ¼ cup's worth of dough at a time onto oiled cookie sheets and bake at 350° for 25 minutes.
Be sure you take a little time and shape the batter round and flat. They will look the same after you bake them as they do before.

OPEN HARVEST BAKERY

Open Harvest Bakery in Lincoln, Nebraska, is a part of Open Harvest, Inc., a not-for-profit natural foods co-operative which opened it's doors in 1975.

Open Harvest was formed to provide a non-profit alternative food market place where minimally processed quality food is distributed through the co-operative energy of the membership. It is our belief that this process contributes to the positive growth of our non-exploitative human relationships and to the development of awareness of our interdependence with our Earth.

We strive to meet the needs of urban residents who have limited choice in the selection of foods and local farmers who benefit from a non-profit market for their farm products.

The ultimate goal of Open Harvest is good health through good nutrition for all our shoppers. We seek to establish business patterns that relate to the local economy through support of local producers and sustainable agricultural practices. As a cooperatively owned business, Open Harvest provides products through honest, fair, and ethical business practices. We operate according to the internationally accepted Rochdale Principles of Cooperation: open membership, 1 member 1 vote, limited return on investments, profits returned to members, commitment to education, and cooperation among cooperatives. Our goal is to share information about good food, nutrition, and health with people who come into our store and to the community.

Open Harvest Bakery began in 1977 in the basement of a local church and has grown since then to provide baked goods to the local community on a regular basis. Our baking is done using whole grain flours and minimally processed foods such as honey, nuts, seeds, farm eggs and fresh & dried fruits, vegetables...all of the highest quality available. As much as possible, we use organically grown foods in our baked goods. Many of our ingredients come from local growers and others from Blooming Prairie Warehouse in Iowa City, Iowa. Blooming Prairie is cooperatively owned by retail natural food cooperatives and food buying clubs throughout the Midwest.

The baking is done by a staff of 3. A wide variety of baked goods are produced including breads, bagels, sweet rolls, cookies, muffins, cakes and granolas. One of our new bakers is creating some very delicious egg-less, dairy-less, honey-less pastries. We have been experimenting with puffed amaranth and amaranth flour as high protein additions to some of our products. A new area of production is hot lunch items which are available every day. These include several kinds of pizza, tofu pot pies, vegetable cheese rolls, calzone and curried cauliflower pockets. These are available both fresh and frozen for customers to prepare at home. Providing ready to eat, nutritious, delicious, whole food entrees helps spread the message of good eating.

Open Harvest is in the process of relocating and expanding. We look forward to the opportunity to provide high quality foods to more people, making a greater impact in the community at large.

 CHALLAH

A rich and beautiful bread for special occasions

Yields 2 large loaves

Sponge:
2½ cups warm water
2 Tbl. yeast
4 Tbl. honey
4 eggs, lightly beaten
4 cups hard whole wheat flour

When sponge is fluffy, add and knead in:
¼ cup oil or melted butter
2 tsp. salt
4-5 cups hard whole wheat flour

Continue kneading for 7-10 minutes.

Let rise in an oiled bowl, covered with a damp towel, for about 1 hour, till doubled in size. Punch down.

Divide in 2 and let rise a little longer until dough is a little airy. Shape. Traditionally, this bread is braided in many different ways. Be sure your ends are tucked in when you finish your design.

Place on an oiled baking sheet and let rise until double or 1 hour, whichever comes first. Brush top of bread with 1 egg yolk, beaten. Sprinkle with poppy or sesame seeds. Bake for 30-40 minutes at 375.

PITA

Makes 10 pitas

Pita is also called pocket bread. It is baked at a high temperature, which causes it to puff up, leaving a hollow center. You can cut it in half or split it at the top and stuff it with your favorite sandwich filling.

Mix together, stirring 100 times:
  1½ cups warm water
  1 Tbl. yeast
  1 tsp. salt (optional)
  1½ cups hard whole wheat flour

Then let it sit to rest for 15 minutes.

Knead to yield a stiff dough, adding 2-2½ cups more hard whole wheat flour. Continue kneading 7-10 minutes. Let the dough rise for 45 minutes.

Cut dough into 10 pieces. Shape into smooth balls. Roll out into circles 5 inches in diameter. Place on cookie sheets sprinkled with cornmeal or sesame seeds. Let rise for 30 minutes keeping moist and warm. Bake in a pre-heated oven at 450°-475° for 6 minutes. Serve while still slightly warm.

VEGETABLE VCR's CHEESE ROLLS

Excellent for lunch or for a light supper.   Makes 12

Have ready 1½ lbs (1 loaf's worth) of your favorite dough

Chop finely: 1 medium green pepper
                             1 medium onion
                             1 cup mushrooms

Grate, then mix in: ¾ cup cheddar cheese
                             ¾ cup mozzarella cheese

Roll out bread dough into a rectangle 7 x 14 inches big. Cover dough with veggie mix, leaving clear 1½ inches at top. Brush top 1½ inch with water. Roll carefully from the bottom up and pinch when you get to the top, forming a log. Cut into 12 pieces and place in an oiled pan with sides, about 9 x 13 inches big. Let rise about 30 minuts.

Bake at 350° for 25 minuts.

LEMON WEDDING CAKE

Makes 2, 8 inch pans
of cake

A light springy cake with a wonderful lemon flavor

You will need 1 cup honey   2½ tsp. vanilla
               ½ cup light oil   1½ tsp baking soda
               1 cup milk   juice & rind of 3 lemons
               2 eggs, separated   2⅓ cups whole wheat
                                             pastry flour

Preheat oven at 350°. Oil and lightly flour your cake pans.
Whip your egg whites to make stiff peaks. Set aside.

Whisk together the honey and oil. Add the milk, egg
yolks, vanilla and lemon.

In a separate bowl, combine flour and baking soda.
Add this to the liquids. Fold in your egg whites.

Pour into prepared pans. Bake for 25-35 minutes.

Lavina's
DATE COFFEE CAKE

Makes 1 9×13 inch cake

½ cup mashed banana
½ cup butter, softened
3 eggs
1 tsp. vanilla

Beat together bananas and butter. Add eggs and vanilla. Beat again.

3 cups whole wheat pastry flour
1 tsp. baking soda
2 tsp. baking powder

Mix your dry ingredients all together. Add them to your banana mix.

1½ cups chopped dates in
1¼ cups water

Add your dates (soaked in the water) with the water, to the above mixture.

Spread into your buttered pan.

Sprinkle with a topping of:
    ½ cup chopped dates
    ½ cup chopped walnuts
    ½ cup flaked coconut

Bake at 350° for 25-35 minutes.

BANANA MUFFINS

A light moist muffin. With a dab of frosting, you have an instant cupcake.

Mash 2½ ripe bananas. Add 1 beaten egg, 2 Tbl. honey, 1½ Tbl. water, ⅓ cup oil, 1 tsp. vanilla.

In another bowl combine 1⅓ cups whole wheat pastry flour, 2 tsp. baking powder, ¼ tsp. nutmeg

Make a well in the center of your dry ingredients. Pour in the liquids.
Stir just enough to combine everything.

Spoon into oiled muffin tins. They should be about ⅔ full.

Bake at 350° for 35 minutes.

CORN MUFFINS

Absolutely Heavenly.   Makes 12

1 cup whole wheat pastry flour
3/4 cup corn meal
2 1/2 tsp. baking powder
1/2 tsp. mace
1 egg, beaten
2 Tbl. corn oil
4 Tbl. honey
1 cup milk

Mix together the oil, egg, honey and milk.

In another bowl mix flour, corn meal, baking powder and mace.

Combine wet and dry ingredients.

Spoon into muffin tins that are oiled. Bake at 325° for 20-25 minutes.

Let them cool a bit before you pop them out of the tins.

Enjoy these muffins as a complement to scrambled eggs in the morning!

Muffin (Re) Production

7-GRAIN CURRANT MUFFINS

Makes 18 Muffins

3½ cups 7-grain flour *
2 Tbl. baking powder
½ tsp. nutmeg
2 eggs, beaten
¼ cup oil
½ cup honey
2 cups milk
¼ cup + 2 Tbl. currants

Preheat your oven at 350°.
Mix together flour, nutmeg, & baking powder
In another bowl, combine eggs, honey, oil, & milk

Stir the liquids into the flour mixture, then fold in the currants.
Pour into oiled muffin tins.
Bake for 25 minutes.

LEC

* 7-Grain flour — Use ½ cup of each:
Barley, Millet, Rice, Rye, Soy, Buckwheat and
Soft whole wheat pastry flour.

ORANGE-DATE SCONES

Makes 12

Surprise the people in your life — get up a little early and whip up a batch for breakfast.

Cut butter, 3/4 cup, into a mixture of
　　　　4 cups whole wheat pastry flour
　　　　2 Tbl. baking powder
　　　　1 tsp baking soda
Add　　2 eggs, beaten
　　　　2 Tbl. honey
　　　　1 orange, juiced, and grated rind
　　　　1 cup dates, chopped
Moisten　mixture with 2/3 cup of milk or yogurt
　　　　　　　　　　　　　　or buttermilk.

Combine lightly with your hands. Pat onto a floured surface, 3/4 inch thick. Cut in biscuit-size rounds and place on an oiled cookie sheet.
Bake at 350° for 12-15 minutes.

 JAM ROLLS

Bake and eat these non-dairy treats, right out of the oven! Makes 10

Cut : ½ cup margarine
in   2 cups whole wheat pastry flour.
until margarine pieces are the size of peas. Make a well in the center and add ½ cup of soy milk, stirring with a fork to incorporate the flour. Knead gently, just enough to bring it all together.

Roll dough on a flour board, ½ inch thick. Fold in thirds and roll out again to a rectangle about ¼ inch thick. Spread jam over rectangle evenly, leaving ½ inch on top and bottom without jelly. Roll into a log, not too tightly.

Cut into 10 pieces. Place on a greased cookie sheet.

Bake at 400° for 10 minutes.

SUNNYSEED COOKIES

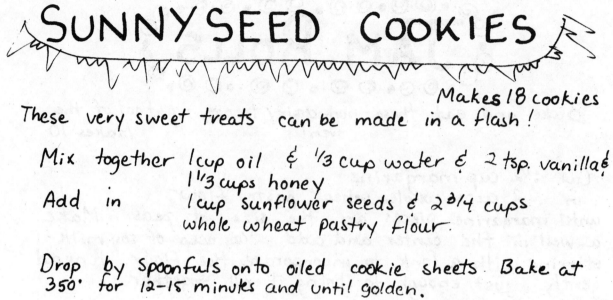

Makes 18 cookies

These very sweet treats can be made in a flash!

Mix together 1 cup oil & 1/3 cup water & 2 tsp. vanilla &
1 1/3 cups honey

Add in 1 cup sunflower seeds & 2 3/4 cups
whole wheat pastry flour.

Drop by spoonfuls onto oiled cookie sheets. Bake at
350° for 12-15 minutes and until golden.

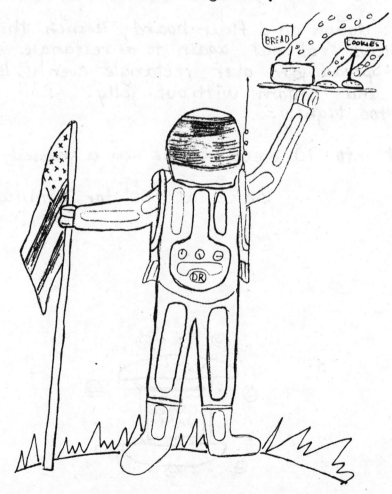

Peanut Butter Crunchies

Makes 24 cookies

1 cup peanut butter
1/2 cup honey
1 tsp. vanilla
3/8 cup oil
1 cup whole wheat pastry flour
1/2 cup wheat germ
1/2 cup coconut
1/2 cup sunflower seeds

Mix peanut butter, honey, vanilla and oil together.

In a separate bowl mix flour, coconut, wheat germ and sunflower seeds.

Combine wet and dry ingredients. Place by spoonfuls on oiled cookie sheets. Press slightly. Bake at 350° for 10-15 minutes. Let them cool before removing them from the pans.

Beverly's Puffed AMARANTH COOKIES

Yields 16 cookies

Cream together..
3/4 cup honey
1/2 cup butter
1/2 cup soy margarine
1 tsp. vanilla
2 eggs, beaten

Sift together..
3 1/2 cups whole wheat
pastry flour
1 tsp. baking soda

Combine honey and flour mixtures together. Add into that:
1 1/2 cups puffed amaranth (or other puffed cereal)
1 1/4 cups rolled oats
1/2 cups chopped walnuts

Place by rounded spoonfuls on buttered cookie sheets. Flatten with the bottom of a dampened glass. Bake at 350° for 12-14 minutes.

Raisins, orange rind, carob chips, and chopped dates may be added for variations.

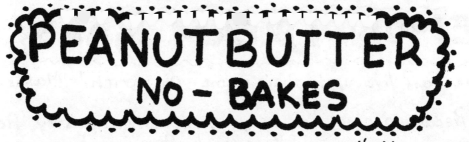

PEANUT BUTTER NO - BAKES

Yields 30 cookies

Combine: 1 cup peanut butter
½ cup honey
1 tsp. vanilla

Mix in: 2 cups rolled oats
½ cup milk powder
½ cup raisins

Use your hands and work everything together well. Shape into balls. Eat now or store in the refrigerator and have them when you want them.

LEMON DREAM BARS

These bars live up to their name.. Oh, so rich! Makes 16

Step 1 - Prepare a <u>crust</u> of 1 cup whole wheat pastry flour
            ½ cup butter
            1½ tsp. honey

Cut butter into the flour until all pieces are pea size or smaller. Add honey and work that in. Pat mixture into an 8×8 inch pan, greased on the bottom. Bake at 350° for 10 minutes.

Step 2 - Prepare the <u>topping</u> while crust is baking.
Beat 2 eggs. Add 3 Tbl. lemon juice, 3 Tbl. whole wheat pastry flour, ¾ cup honey. Mix well. Just before pouring this topping into the hot crust, add 1½ tsp. baking powder. Pour into crust and bake, again at 350° for 15 minutes.

Step 3 - Prepare <u>frosting</u>, while the bar is cooling.
            ½ pound of cream cheese
            2½ Tbl. butter, softened
            2½ Tbl. honey
            1 tsp. vanilla
            1 tsp. lemon juice

Soften the cream cheese. Add the softened butter. Whip in the other ingredients. Ice the bars with this frosting when they are completely cooled.
    Keep these bars stored in the refrigerator.

Breads, Cereals and Goodies Baked Daily
1534 E. Lake St.
Minneapolis. MN. 55407
(612) 721-7205

People's Company Bakery has continued to grow during the last several years, in spite of sharpening competition from at least four privately owned whole grain wholesale bakeries that opened in Minneapolis/St. Paul since 1980.

PCB supplys all the co-op groceries in the Twin Cities, and many in rural Minnesota and in neighboring states as well. We have also been increasing our distribution through non-co-op retailers, including a major Twin Cities chain which features a natural foods department in most of its stores.

We are outgrowing our current production space, and are planning for major equipment improvements that should save labor and help keep us competetive.

People's Company Bakery is proud to be the first and only worker-owned bakery in the Twin Cities. We pioneered whole grain, organic flour baking here in 1971. Our success and acceptance has been made possible by the support and vitality of the co-op, whole foods, and alternative agriculture communities of Minnesota and the Upper Midwest.

Veggie Bread

Yield: Two 1½ lb. loaves

No eggs or dairy

A meal in a slice! This bread is delicious — it smells like pizza. Excellent with soup or salad, or with grilled cheese on it.

1²/₃ cups warm water

1 Tbl. yeast

1½ Tbl. honey

Chopped Veggies:
- 2 medium tomatoes
- 2 medium carrots
- 1-2 sticks celery
- 1 medium onion
- ½ green pepper

1½ Tbl. oil

5-6 cups hard whole wheat flour
1 tsp. salt (optional)

Dried Herbs:
- 2 tsp. oregano
- 2 tsp. garlic powder
- 2 tsp. basil
- 1 tsp. marjoram

Mix water, yeast, and honey. Let sit a few minutes til frothy. Add all remaining ingredients, reserving some flour. Mix in well — begin to knead the dough when soft but not too sticky. Add flour as needed — the veggies will release some liquid as you knead, but watch you don't add too much flour and make the dough stiff. When springy and pliable, leave dough covered in an oiled bowl to rise. When doubled in size, punch down and shape into two loaves. Let rise again in oiled bread pans. Bake at 350° for 45 minutes.

Sesame Honey Bread

Makes 2 loaves

2 ½ cups water

1 Tbl. yeast

5-6 cups whole wheat flour

1 cup honey

2 Tbl. oil

1 tsp. salt

½ cup sesame seeds

Dissolve yeast in water. Add flour and then add the remaining ingredients. Knead the dough until it is smooth and elastic. Let rise in a covered bowl until it is doubled in size. Punch down the dough and shape into desired loaves. Let rise again in the pan. Bake at 350° for 45 minutes.

Russian Rye Bread

Makes 2 loaves

2½ cups water

¼ cup dehydrated onion

¼ cup molasses

1 Tbl. yeast

5-6 cups whole wheat flour

½ cup rye flour

1 tsp. sea salt

1 Tbl. caraway seeds

1 Tbl. whole fennel seeds

2 Tbl. oil

Soak onions for 10-15 minutes in 1½ cups water. Put 1 cup of water in a bowl with yeast. First add half of the flour and then the remaining ingredients, including the soaked onions. Add the remaining flour and work in thoroughly. Knead the dough until smooth and elastic. Let rise in a covered bowl until doubled in size. Shape dough into loaves and let rise again in oiled pans. Bake at 350° for 45 minutes.

Carrot Muffins

Makes about a dozen

Stir together:

1 cup honey

3/4 cup oil

1 tsp. vanilla

3 eggs

1/2 cup water

Blend in a separate bowl:

3 cups whole wheat
pastry flour

1 Tbl. baking powder

1/4 tsp. baking soda

2 tsp. cinnamon

1/2 tsp. nutmeg

1/2 tsp. sea salt

Combine the flour and spices with the liquid ingredients. Fold in:
1/2 cup grated carrot.
Spoon batter into oiled muffin tins about 3/4 full. Bake at 350°
for about 25 minutes.

*added:
ginger
cinnamon
cloves*

Poppy Seed Cookies

Yield: 3 Dozen Cookies
These cookies are delicious and beautiful!

2/3 cup butter

1/3 cup tahini

1/2 cup honey

1/2 cup maple syrup

2 eggs (or 3 tbl tahini)

2 1/2 cups whole wheat
pastry flour

1 cup rice flour

1 tsp baking powder
(optional)

1/2 cup poppy seeds

Cream butter, tahini, honey, and maple syrup together. Add eggs
(or tahini substitute). Add pastry flour, rice flour, baking powder.
Mix together, then add the poppy seeds. (Dough is sticky). Spoon
onto oiled sheets. Bake at 350°, about 10 minutes or until brown.

Date Nut Cookies

Makes about 2 dozen

½ cup honey

½ lb. butter

3 eggs

⅓ cup milk

½ cup walnuts

4 cups pastry flour

¾ lb. chopped dates

1 tsp. cinnamon

1 tsp. baking soda

Mix together honey and butter. Add eggs, milk, walnuts, and dates. Blend together flour, cinnamon, soda. Add to the other ingredients and stir together. Spoon out walnut-sized pieces on a cookie sheet and flatten with fingers. Bake at 350° for 12-15 minutes.

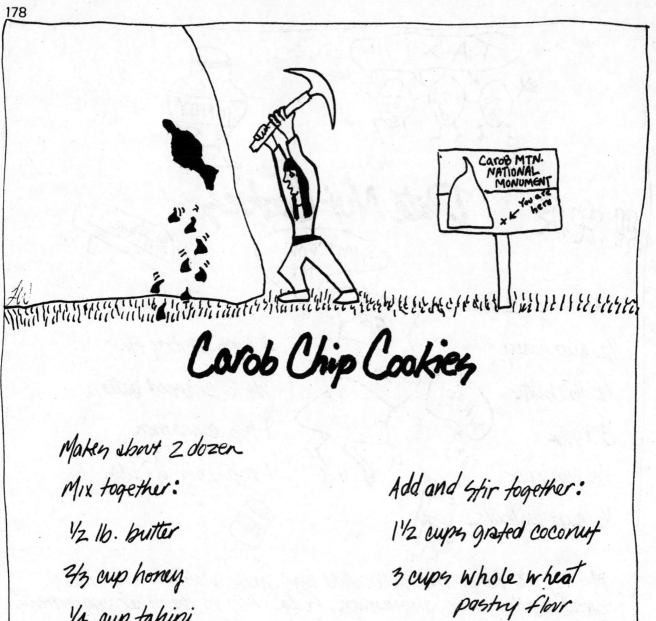

Carob Chip Cookies

Makes about 2 dozen

Mix together:

½ lb. butter

⅔ cup honey

¼ cup tahini

¼ cup maple syrup

1 egg

Add and stir together:

1½ cups grated coconut

3 cups whole wheat pastry flour

1½ cups carob chips

Spoon out walnut-sized pieces on a cookie sheet and flatten with fingers. Bake at 350° for 12-15 minutes.

Krunch Bars

16 bars approx. 1½" × 2½"

Mix together:

3/4 cup peanut butter

1 cup honey

1 tsp. salt

Add:

3 cups sesame seeds

2 cups sunflower seeds

1 cup grated coconut

½ cup cashews

→ I baked for 20 minutes!

Press flat on to oiled 9" × 13" baking pan with fingers or wax paper (to keep from sticking). Bake 12 minutes at 350°, until edges start to brown. Remove from oven and cool before cutting.

Maple Nut Granola

Makes about 10 cups

Mix together:

8 cups oats

½ cup almonds

¼ cup sesame seeds

¼ cup sunflower seeds

Add and toss together:

½ cup maple syrup

¼ cup oil

½ cup honey

Bake on a cookie sheet in a 350° oven. Stir while baking if the layer is thick. Take out when the oats are slightly toasted, (about 30 minutes). Cool and store in tightly closed container.

POSITIVELY 3RD STREET BAKERY

1202 E. 3rd Street   Duluth, Minnesota

Positively 3rd Street Co-operative Bakery of Duluth, Minnesota has been providing whole-grain baked goods to Northern Minnesota and its surrounding area for over 5 years. Our 12 types of whole-grain breads, 7 flavors of bagels, many cookies and assorted sweets have become very popular with health conscious consumers in the northland. Because there are few "natural foods" bakeries in the area, we also distribute to health food stores in North Dakota, Northern Wisconsin and the upper peninsula of Michigan, besides stocking local grocery stores. We are particularly well known for our incredible chocolate chip cookies. Many customers come in the bakery specifically for them but also try our other products.

What is unique about Positively 3rd Street Bakery is that most of our staff is affiliated with PROUT - the Progressive Utilization Theory — an international socio-spiritual organization that promotes economic decentralization, local self-reliance and social reform. PROUT also encourages self-transformation through physical, mental and spiritual growth. Meditation is the most important aspect of this process. We at the bakery try to do our small part in making the world a more humane and progressive place to live.

Positively 3rd Street Bakery's

Blueberry Muffin

makes 1 dozen

Combine: 1/4 cup wheat bran
1/4 cup wheat germ
2 1/3 cups organic whole wheat pastry flour
3/4 Tbl. baking soda
3/4 tsp. salt
1/3 cup powdered milk or buttermilk

In another bowl
Combine: 1/3 cup safflower or canola oil
2/3 cup honey
1 1/3 cups filtered water

Stir liquid ingredients into dry ingredients
only enough to moisten and then
Fold in: 1 1/4 cups blueberries

Spoon into muffin tins. Bake 25-35 minutes
at 350°. Enjoy!

EUGENE, OREGON

SOLSTICE BAKERY IS A WORKER OWNED AND OPERATED BUSINESS IN EUGENE, OREGON. WE PRODUCE WHOLE GRAIN BREADS, GRANOLAS, AND TREATS USING 100% ORGANICALLY GROWN FLOURS AND BERRIES AND THE BEST INGREDIENTS AVAILABLE.

WE BEGAN ON SUMMER SOLSTICE 1978 PRODUCING GRANOLA FOR THE OREGON COUNTRY FAIR. TODAY SOLSTICE MAKES 9 VARIETIES OF YEASTED BREAD, 5 KINDS OF ESSENE BREAD, 9 FLAVORFUL GRANOLAS, MUESLIS, AND NUMEROUS COOKIES AND TREATS. WE DISTRIBUTE THROUGHOUT OREGON AND SOUTHERN WASHINGTON.

CINNAMON DATE BREAD

2 loaves

1 Tbl. yeast
2 C warm water
4 Tbl. barley malt
3 Tbl. honey

4 Tbl. oil
1 tsp. salt
1 Tbl. cinnamon
4-6 C hard whole
        wheat flour
1 C date pieces

dissolve yeast in warm water and mix with barley malt, honey and 1 C flour to make sponge. let sit for 20 minutes. add cinnamon.

add salt, oil and ½ of remaining flour and mix briskly until all ingredients are thoroughly mixed. slowly add the rest of the flour until you can knead the dough with your hands. knead for about 10 minutes, add date pieces and knead for 10 more minutes. let dough rise for 10-15 minutes, then punch down and form into 2 loaves. place loaves in oiled bread pans and let rise until dough reaches top of pan or slightly over. bake in an oven preheated to 350° for 45 minutes.

variation: cinnamon raisin bread
        replace the dates with 1 C raisins

ALMOND YOGURT COFFEECAKE

yield: 1 9"x9" pan   (12 servings)

½ c butter (or soy margarine)
2¼ c whole wheat pastry flour
¾ c date sugar mixed with
    ¼ c water
1 c honey
1 c plain yogurt
2 tsp. peanut butter

1 tsp. vanilla
1 tsp. baking soda
1 tsp. cinnamon
¼ tsp. ground cloves
¼ tsp. nutmeg
¼ c chopped almonds

mix together butter, date sugar and 2 cups pastry flour. set aside ½ cup of this mixture. add the baking soda, spices and the rest of the flour to mixture and stir in well. add the yogurt, honey, peanut butter and vanilla. mix thoroughly and pour into an oiled and floured 9"x9" cake pan. add the chopped almonds to the ½ cup of flour and butter mixture that was set aside. sprinkle over top. bake at 350° for 45-50 minutes. delicious!

hint: if you can't find date sugar you can use the following substitution:
blend 1 cup chopped dates with ¾ cup water. if you do, reduce the amount of yogurt called for in the recipe to ½ cup.

COCONUT SHORT BREAD

a fairly simple recipe that results in a luscious, light treat, almost like french pastry.

2 dozen squares

1	lb.	soy margarine
1½	C	honey
1	tsp.	almond extract
1	tsp.	vanilla
4	C	whole wheat pastry flour
4	C	coconut, shredded
4	C	oats

cream margarine and honey. mix in the extracts. combine flour, coconut and oats. add to creamed mixture. press evenly into a cookie sheet. poke fork holes every 2" or so. (maybe a nice pattern.) bake at 350° for 35 minutes. cut into squares while still warm.

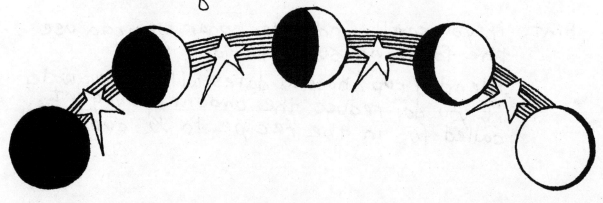

OAT BRAN MUFFINS

makes 8-10 muffins

1 C oat bran
1 C wheat bran
3/4 C hot water
1 C apple sauce
3/4 C honey

2 eggs beaten
2 C whole wheat
    pastry flour
3 tsp. baking soda
1/2 tsp. salt

bring 3/4 cup water to a boil. add to oat and wheat bran and mix. let cool. then add apple sauce, honey and eggs. mix thoroughly, then add flour, baking soda and salt. stir until uniformly mixed. spoon into muffin tins and bake for 30-35 minutes at 350°.

DATE BARS

a deliciously chewy bar !

makes 12 bars

2 ¼ C date pieces (dry)
½ C canola oil
⅓ C honey
2 Tbl. barley malt
2 ¼ C oat flour
3 C rolled oats

optional ingredients:
    chopped walnuts to add to crust
    cinnamon, apples and raisins to add to the filling

soak date pieces in enough warm water to just cover for 30 minutes. mix oil, honey and malt together well. add oats and mix. then add oat flour and mix thoroughly. dough should be crumbly yet stick together when pressed in your hand. if too sticky, add a little more flour.

oil and flour an 8" x 12" pan. press most of the crust into the bottom of the pan, saving some to sprinkle over the top. spread wet dates evenly over crust and sprinkle rest of the flour mixture over the top and pat down lightly. bake at 350° for 35-45 minutes. cut into squares and eat !

CHEESECAKE BARS

easier to make than cheesecake filling —
almost fool-proof baking.

makes 12-15 bars

½   C   soy margarine (or butter)
¼   C   honey
½   C   walnuts, chopped
2¼ C   organic whole wheat pastry flour

*   *   *   *   *   *   *

¼   C   honey
8   oz. cream cheese
2   tbl. milk
1   egg
2   tsp. lemon juice
½   tsp. lemon peel, grated
½   tsp. nutmeg
¼   tsp. vanilla

mix first four ingredients on recipe to make
a crumbly dough: set aside ¾ cup of mixture.
press the rest in bottom of a 9"x9" pan. mix
together honey, cream cheese, milk, egg, lemon
peel and spices. then spread over crust.
sprinkle remaining crust over top and bake
at 350° for 25 minutes.

PECAN SANDIES

a favorite of co-operative bakeries across the country!

makes 20 cookies

1 ¼	C	butter (or soy margarine)
½	C	maple syrup
¼	C	honey
1	tsp.	vanilla
2 ¼	C	whole wheat pastry flour (organic is best!)
1 ¼	C	pecan meal or blended pecans

mix butter, maple syrup, honey and vanilla well. add flour and pecan meal. mix thoroughly. place a small spoonful of batter on a cookie sheet and flatten to ¼ inch thick. press a pecan on top of each cookie for a lovely touch. bake for 25 minutes at 350°.

SUMMERCORN
FAYETTEVILLE ARKANSAS

Summercorn Bakery and Soyfoods is a worker-owned, collectively managed state non-profit corporation started in 1974. We have a small retail trade and also distribute wholesale to stores, coops and buying clubs in a seven state region. Stone-grinding our flour fresh before each bake, with organically grown grain from neighboring Kansas, makes for some wonderful aromas coming out of our bakery. We buy direct from local growers whenever possible. Our focus is producing for and educating the public about whole grains and the urgency of making use of plant sources of protein.

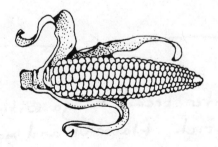

OLD WORLD RYE BREAD

Makes 3 1lb. loaves

"This recipe came to us from a Scandinavian woman who grew up in a bakery family. The only changes we made are the substitution of carob for roasted, ground coffee beans and an addition of slippery elm and kelp powder."

SPONGE INGREDIENTS:

3 cups water, 1/4 cup unsulphured molasses, 2 TBL. yeast, 3 1/2 cups hard whole wheat flour

Develop sponge, allow to rise 20 minutes, and add remaining ingredients:

4 tsp. corn or safflower oil, 2 tsp kelp powder,
1 tsp. salt, 2 tsp slippery elm powder,
1/4 cup dark roast carob powder, 1 1/2 TBL caraway seeds, 3 cups rye flour, 2 cups (approximately) hard whole wheat flour

Knead well. Allow to rise once, divide into 3 rounds and allow to rise again for 20 minutes before placing in preheated 350° oven for 1 hour.

"A dense, winter bread to go with a bowl of soup." Very rich, flavorful and moist with a thick, chewy crust.

Cinnamon Currant Bread

2   1½ lb loaves

We bake this bread in a two piece cylindrical strap pan. The round slices with a swirling of cinnamon + honey in the currant whole wheat bread dough make great toast. It works fine in regular pans too. Make a basic whole wheat dough, such as the one from Nature's Bakery, Madison.

To 3 lb bread dough add: 1 cup currants (or you can substitute raisins) that have been soaked in 3 TBL boiling water to soften, and 3 TBL. whole wheat flour to balance this added moisture from adding the currants. Allow to rise once, punch down, rise again, (this 2nd rising may be omitted but what's the hurry), + cut into 2 loaves, flatten into a rectangle + spread approximately 2½ TBL. honey (or more) evenly over the flattened dough leaving one edge without honey. Shake cinnamon generously over this same area leaving one edge clean. This is our future "seam"

← honey + cinnamon
← plain dough

Turn ½" edge on either side in to enclose honey + cinnamon. Roll up leaving unhoneyed edge to seal the outside edge. Pinch all seams well to stop honey oozing out while baking. Bake for 50 minutes at 350°F.

start rolling this end
unhoneyed edge
fold in

Ozark Barley Bread

Makes 2 1½ lb loaves

* UNLEAVENED *

This is a favorite in Fayetteville. The recipe is an adaptation from the Tassajara Bread Book, (The "Bible" of basic bread baking".)

2 cups roasted barley flour
1 TBL oil
1 tsp salt
3½ cups hard whole wheat flour
1 tsp kelp powder
½ cup corn meal
3 TBL sesame seed
⅓ cup corn oil
3 cups boiling water

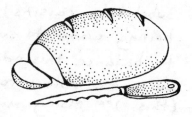

Roast barley flour in 1 TBL corn oil, stir continually. Mix flours, meal, salt & kelp. Add oil and mix with hands, rub through well. Add boiling water, knead well. Allow to rest briefly, covered with a damp towel before cutting & shaping into rounds. Cutting shallow slits (¼" deep) in tops will prevent cracking while in oven. Cover & proof 4-8 hours. Re-moisten if necessary during proofing. Bake at 350° for 2 hours.

Carob Nut Brownies

Makes 9 Brownies
8" x 8" pan or equivalent

½ cup safflower oil ⎫
1 cup honey   ⎬ mix well
¼ cup egg replacer * ⎬
½ cup water   ⎭

1½ tsp vanilla
2 cups whole wheat pastry flour
2 tsp baking powder
½ cup carob powder
½ cup chopped nuts (save some to sprinkle on top)

Blend liquid ingredients well. Add dry ingredients and mix.
Pour into a pan that has been oiled and floured.
Press evenly into pan. Bake 25 minutes at 350°.
Allow to cool before cutting.

* Egg Replacer
  1 TBL dry + 1-2 TBL water = 1 egg
  Mix together well:
  2 parts arrowroot powder
  1 part tapioca flour
  1 part slippery elm powder

Peanut Butter Cookies

Makes 24

This cookie will reflect the use of a sweet organic peanut butter if you are so lucky as to find one. Try a variety from Deaf Smith.

Blend in a bowl or mixer until smooth:

    1 cup butter or soy margerine
    1 1/4 cup peanut butter
    7/8 cup honey

Mix separately from the wet ingredients:

    3 cups whole wheat pastry flour
    2 tsp. baking powder
    1/2 tsp. salt
    1/8 - 1/4 cup water (as needed)

Add dry ingredients to wet ingredients and mix briefly. Spoon onto an oiled cookie sheet and flatten with a fork, making a cross-hatch design if desired.

Bake at 350° for 10-12 minutes.

Tofu-Carob Frosting

Makes 2½ cups

2 cups (1 lb.) tofu, crumbled
½ cup honey
½ cup roasted carob powder
4 TBL oil or melted margarine
1 tsp vanilla
1 TBL coffee substitute (Cafix, Pero, etc.)

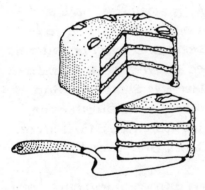

Combine all ingredients in a bowl, preferably with a wire whisk. Blend in small batches. In a blender or food processor until smooth and creamy, adding enough water to make it easy to blend.

TOUCHSTONE B·A·K·E·R·Y

501 A. N 36th SEATTLE, WA. 98103 (206) 547-4000

Touchstone Bakery, established in 1983, is a whole grain baking collective. In Seattle, a community abounding with bakeries and espresso joints, Touchstone has the distinction of being the only bakery that is organic, whole grain and collectively run.

If you were to come into Touchstone, you would see stacks of organic whole wheat flour, packaging tables, racks of golden breads such as Walnut Wheat, Orange Breakfast, Buckwheat Sunflower, Challah, Caraway Rye, Herb and Onion, Sourdough, Anadama, Seven Grain, trays of buns and rolls waiting to be sliced, packaged and delivered to coops, specialty stores and small restaurants around Seattle. Come further into our bakery and see two mixers - a Hobart and Century, five pizza ovens, and a beautiful new Rainer five shelf rotating oven (our only new piece of equipment, the rest bought at auctions or second hand shops - all paid for in cash, keeping us loan free). Finally see our beautiful wooden loafing table around which loaves and friendships are formed.

Meet the Touchstone bakers, seven men and seven women. A few have been here for years (2 are original members), but most are new. Although Touchstone Bakery has only four collective members and ten employees, the time feels ripe for changing this ratio. The positive energy in the bakery is tangible. Through personal and collective struggle over the years, we've gotten to a place where we work much more reasonable hours for more reasonable pay. We've learned the need for more structure and a common vision, and we will attract new collective members with this in mind.

From its inception, Touchstone has been committed to using organic ingredients whenever possible. We use organic whole wheat flour (milled locally), some organic grains and fruits. By using organic ingredients we are supporting farmers who practice sensible and regenerative agriculture. Touchstone Bakery is proud to offer the people in our community a product that is not only good for them, but good for the planet as well.

Dolly's Pumpkin Pie

A Seattle favorite. We make hundreds every year between Halloween and Christmas. Create your own holiday tradition.

Slice whole pumpkin, cutting out seeds. Cook about 35-40 minutes covered with water. Peel when cool.

For <u>one</u> pie, toss in blender:

½ cup honey
¼ cup maple syrup
½ tsp. salt
2 tsp. cinnamon
½ tsp. ginger
½ tsp. nutmeg

½ tsp. ground cloves
2½ cups cooled pumpkin
½ cup milk
1½ cups cream or half and half
2 eggs

Whip it until well blended. Pour into unbaked pie shell. Bake at 400° for 15 minutes. Turn down oven to 350° and bake 20-30 minutes.

Pie <u>Crust</u>:
  ½ cup unsalted butter - very cold
1½ cups whole wheat pastry flour
  ⅓ cup <u>very</u> cold water
  ½ tsp. salt

Cut butter into flour with salt until coarse. Add only enough water to hold mixture together, forming a ball. Roll out and fit into 10 inch pie plate.

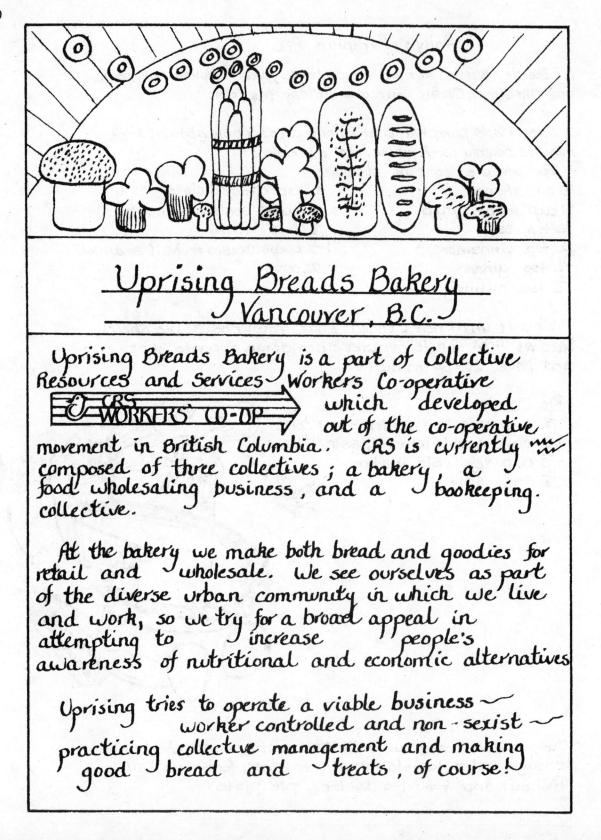

Uprising Breads Bakery
Vancouver, B.C.

Uprising Breads Bakery is a part of Collective Resources and Services Workers Co-operative which developed out of the co-operative movement in British Columbia. CRS is currently composed of three collectives; a bakery, a food wholesaling business, and a bookeeping collective.

At the bakery we make both bread and goodies for retail and wholesale. We see ourselves as part of the diverse urban community in which we live and work, so we try for a broad appeal in attempting to increase people's awareness of nutritional and economic alternatives.

Uprising tries to operate a viable business — worker controlled and non-sexist — practicing collective management and making good bread and treats, of course!

Peanut Butter Cookies with carob chips or raisins

Yield: 3 doz. good size cookies
Oven: 350°

1. Cream together wet ingredients.

2. Combine dry ingredients.

3. mix the dry into the wet just until dryness disappears.

2 cups w.w. pastry flour
1⅛ cups oats
1⅓ cups sunflower seeds
1 tsp. baking soda
1 tsp. cinnamon

1⅓ cups carob chips or raisins

6 ounces butter
(1½ sticks)
1⅓ cups honey
2 cups peanut butter

ummh

4. Drop by spoonsful onto oiled cookie sheet and bake about 15 minutes 'til golden. Let cool on sheet before removing, as they are quite soft.

Sourdough Pumpernickel

(2 risings)

Yield: 2 large loaves

Oven: 375° 45-55 minutes

*Dark, delicious, and great smelling, if you're afraid of sourdough this recipe is meant for you.

The STARTER is a pleasure to make! It's ALIVE!

Mix ½ cup of rye flour and ½ cup of cold water. Let this sit, open to the air, or loosely covered, 24 hours.

Now you FEED THE STARTER the next day by adding a little more flour and a little more water, about half and half. Continue to feed every day 5-7 days depending on temperature of environment. A sour, bubbly concoction is achieved as the starter grows, picking up yeast organisms in the air, and will later give the bread a rise.

When you make sourdough bread, ALWAYS SAVE SOME STARTER for the next time. After using, feed and mix to a loose, but not watery, consistency. After feeding allow starter to remain out for several hours, then refrigerate.

NEXT →

The Recipe & Loafing it

2½ cups water
1 cup Sourdough starter
1 heaping Tbl. molasses
1 Tbl. safflower oil

5 cups hard w.w. flour
4 cups rye flour
½ cup rye meal
¼ cup cracked wheat
2 tsp. salt

Mix together all the wet ingredients. Add to them the salt, then all other dry ingredients.

The dough will be more sticky than a regular dough, but knead it very well for 10-15 minutes. You can keep a bowl of water at hand, or use oil, to keep the dough from sticking to your hands and the kneading surface.

Place dough in an oiled bowl, oil the top or turn dough bottom up, cover, and let rise 3-4 hours.

Cut and shape dough into 2 loaves. Cut deeply but gently with a sharp, wet knife, after placing in loaf pans. Let rise again 3-4 hours. Try making rolls in a round pan or baking loaves on open flat trays S.F. style.

with ♡
from the folks of
CRS at
Uprising

BAKE
'til darkest brown

BAGELS

Yield: 1½ dozen
Oven: 350° or 425°; also boiling H₂0.

BASIC RECIPE

Tasty and fun to make, let the children help. If you like, these can be frozen raw for later. Directions are below.

Ingredients:
- 7 cups hard w.w. flour
- 2 eggs
- 1 Tbl. oil
- 2 tsp. salt
- 2 tsp. yeast
- 1 Tbl. honey
- 2 cups water

Add yeast to water, stir slightly, and add honey. Next, stir in the oil, eggs, and salt, adding the flour last. Knead well for about 10 minutes until the dough is smooth and elastic. Let dough <u>rest</u> for 30 minutes.

The shaping: Cut dough into 18 pieces. Shape dough into thick cylinder, long enough to wrap around your hand.

Shape pieces into doughnut forms. Have a pan of water boiling. (Honey may be added to the water for a sweeter taste and a nice glazed look.) Drop bagels into water for 30-60 seconds. Lay bagel on oiled tray and sprinkle with poppy or sesame seeds.

Bake: 425° or 350° / 20 min / 30 m.

If frozen, allow about 1½ hrs. for thawing, then prepare as above.

BAGEL (bā'gəl) n:

A ring-shaped roll with a tough, chewy texture made from a plain yeast dough that is dropped briefly into boiling water and then baked;

From the Yiddish 'beygel' and Middle High German 'bouc', meaning ˌring or braceletˌ and the Indo-European root 'bheug' meaning ˌto swellˌ related to bent, pliable, or curved ˌobjects.

UPRISINGS BAKINGS COLLECTIVE

Berkeley, Ca.

Uprisings Baking Collective is dedicated to producing the best tasting, most nutritious breads and baked goods available today. There are no dough conditioners, stabilizers, preservatives, or other chemical surprises in any of our products. We bake exclusively with organic stoneground whole wheat flour and other fine ingredients including fresh fruits and vegetables, expeller pressed safflower oil, honey and molasses.

Established in 1975 to produce bread for a local not-for-profit community food store, we have since grown so that as we enter the nineties, our twenty-two workers are producing over 6,000 loaves of bread, over 1,000 muffin packs and hundreds of bags of cookies and granola each week. We deliver our baked goods to supermarkets, health food stores and produce markets throughout the Bay Area and currently sell at two EastBay Farmers Markets as well.

We are a worker owned and managed business. There is no boss to tell people what to do. All decisions are made by the workers and conflicts are solved cooperatively. There are regular meetings of the work shifts, and of several commitees, as well as meetings of a representative steering committee and of the whole collective. All members are required to take an active role in managing the bakery as we strive towards the development of each worker to their fullest potential.

Uprisings is very much a community bakery, with its workers involved over the years in a cross section of progressive causes and groups. The bakery has distributed hundreds of thousands of label sized inserts in its bread publicizing countless solidarity meetings, counterculture institutions, anti-nuclear, anti-racist and anti-imperialist events and campaigns. We are well aware that an Uprisings Bakery constructed on our principles will only survive in the long run if we encourage uprisings in every phase of society.

Honey Bran Bread

makes 2 1½ lb. loaves

1 ⅛ cup warm water
1 Tbl. barley malt
3 Tbl. honey

2 cups whole wheat flour
1 Tbl. yeast
1 cup wheat bran
1 cup water

Combine malt and water. Stir in yeast until dissolved. Beat in flour well; let rise until doubled in size. Soak the wheat bran in 1 cup water for a few minutes.

3 ¼ cups whole wheat flour
2 Tbl. soy flour
3 Tbl. safflower oil
¼ tsp. salt.

Mix the sponge, the bran, and all the other ingredients together. Knead well until the dough has a uniform feel. Let rise until doubled. Punch down and shape into 2 loaves. Let rise until doubled again.

Bake 35 minutes at 375°

Nine Grain Bread

x x x x x x x x x x x   makes 2 loaves

We use a locally produced 9-grain cereal mix of wheat, oats, barley, rye, corn, brown rice, millet, soy beans, triticale and flax seed.

1 ¼ cup water

¼ cup barley malt syrup

1 ½ Tbl. molasses

1 Tbl. yeast

2 cups whole wheat flour

Mix together malt molasses and water. Stir in yeast until dissolved, then add flour. Mix and let rise until doubled.

1 cup water

3 cups whole wheat flour

1 ½ cups 9-grain cereal mix

3 Tbl. safflower oil

¼ tsp. salt

Add to above sponge. Knead until smooth, then let rise until doubled. Punch down and shape into 2 loaves. Let rise in 2 oiled bread pans. Bake at 375° for about 35 minutes.

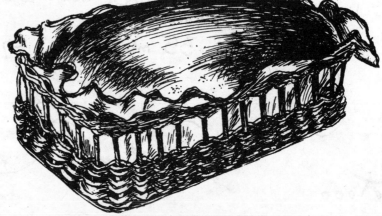

RAISIN BREAD

2 1/2 lb loaves

A light spicy, medium-sweet loaf with juicy raisins. The kids will love it — and so will you. Try it for french toast, using extra-thick slices, and topping with real maple syrup — yum!

■ 1 1/4 cups warm water   1 Tbl. yeast
6 Tbl. malt syrup   2 cups hard whole wheat flour

Cream malt with water, stir in yeast until dissolved. Beat flour in well, then let rise until doubled.

■ 1/2 cup oats   1/2 cup water

Mix oats with water and let sit 15 minutes.

■ 1 cup raisins   1/3 cup oil
1/3 cup sunflower seeds   1/4 tsp. salt
1 Tbl. cinnamon   3 cups hard whole wheat flour
1/2 tsp. nutmeg

Add oat mixture and all other ingredients to sponge. Mix and knead until dough has a uniform smooth feel. Let rise till doubled, punch down, shape into 2 loaves. Let rise in oiled bread pans. Bake at 350° for 50 minutes.

Carrot Herb Bread

···deliciously flavorful···

2 1½ lb
loaves

SPONGE
- 1 2/3 cups warm water
- 1/3 cup malt syrup
- 1 Tbl. yeast
- 2½ cups hard whole wheat flour

- 1 cup grated carrots
- 2/3 cup finely chopped scallions
- 1 tsp. garlic powder
- ½ tsp. sage
- 2 tsp. dill weed
- 2 tsp. ground basil
- 2 tsp thyme
- 1½ tsp. cumin
- 1 Tbl. poppy seeds
- ¼ cup oil
- 1 tsp salt
- 3½ cups hard whole wheat flour

Mix malt and water well, stir in yeast until it dissolves. Beat flour in, then let rise until sponge is doubled in size.

Add all remaining ingredients. Mix well, then knead dough until it's pliable and elastic. Let rise, covered, in warm place, till doubled. Punch down. Let rise a 2nd time, if desired, or shape into 2 loaves and place in oiled pans. Let rise again in pans. Bake at 350° for 50 minutes.

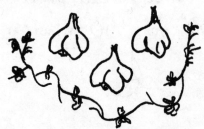

Lemon Sesame Bread

A delicious lemon-flavored yeasted bread.

2 1½ lb loaves

1²/₃ cups warm water
3 Tbl malt syrup
1 Tbl yeast
1²/₃ cups hard w.w. flour

cream malt with water, stir in yeast till dissolved. beat flour in well, then let rise till doubled.

1 cup chopped dates or date pieces
¹/₃ cup lemon peel & juice
½ cup sesame seeds
¼ cup oil
½-1 tsp. salt
4 cups hard w.w. flour

add all remaining ingredients. mix and knead the dough well, till its smooth and elastic. Let rise, covered, in oiled bowl till doubled in bulk. Punch down. shape into 2 loaves. let them rise in oiled bread pans. bake at 350° for 45-50 minutes.

Sesame millet bread

yield: 2 1½ lb. loaves

½ cup millet   ½ cup water

   bring water to a boil. add millet and return to a boil. cover, turn off heat and let steam. cool.

1 cup warm water   1 Tbl. yeast
⅓ cup honey   2 cups whole wheat flour

   mix honey and water and stir in yeast until dissolved. add flour and let rise until doubled.

1¼ cups water   ⅓ cup toasted sesame seeds
3⅔ cups whole wheat   3 Tbl. safflower oil
        flour   ¼ tsp. salt

   combine with above ingredients. knead, cover, and let rise for 1 hour. form into 2 loaves. place in oiled pans to rise until doubled. bake at 375° for 35 minutes.

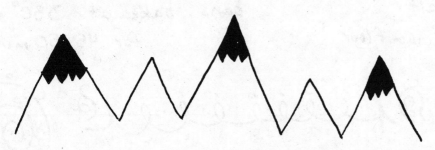

Oat Sunflower Bread

makes 2 1½ lb loaves

part A
- 1¼ cup warm water
- 1 Tbl. yeast
- ¼ cup malt syrup
- 2 cups whole wheat flour

mix malt syrup with water and stir in yeast until dissolved. Add flour, mix and let rise until doubled.

part B
- 3⅔ cups whole wheat flour
- ⅔ cup oats
- ½ cup sunflower seeds
- ¼ cup soya flour
- 3 Tbl. safflower oil
- ¼ tsp. salt
- 1 cup warm water

Add remaining ingredients, mix and knead well until the dough has a smooth, uniform feel. Let rise until doubled, punch down and shape into 2 loaves. Let rise in oiled pans until double again. Bake at 375° for 30-35 minutes.

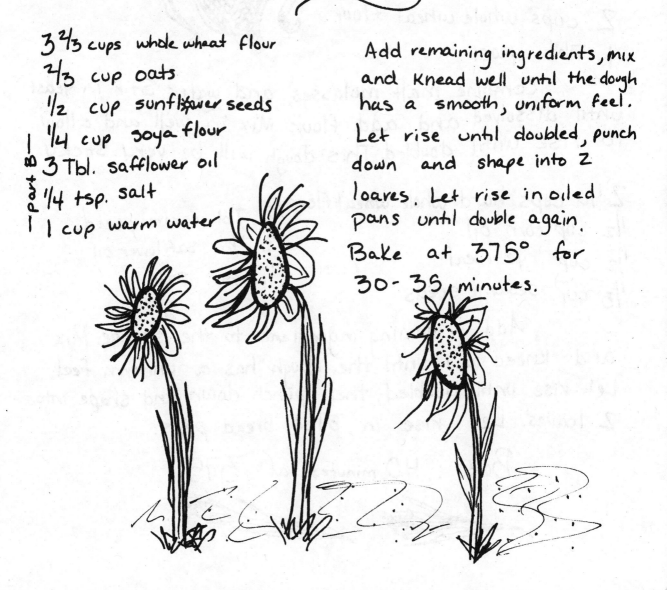

Corn Rye Bread

makes 2 loaves

1 cup warm water
1/3 cup barley malt
2 Tbl. molasses
2 cups whole wheat flour
1 Tbl. yeast

Combine malt, molasses, and water. Stir in yeast until dissolved and add flour. Mix in well and allow to rise until doubled. This dough will be very sticky.

2 1/4 cups hard whole wheat flour
1/2 cup corn oil
1/2 cup rye meal
1/3 cup sesame seeds

2 Tbl. caraway seeds
3 Tbl. safflower oil
1/4 tsp. salt

Add remaining ingredients to the sponge. Mix and knead well until the dough has a uniform feel. Let rise until doubled, then punch down and shape into 2 loaves. Let rise in oiled bread pans.

Bake: 40 minutes at 375°

Irish Soda Bread

great for dunking in your tea!

Yield: 2 loaves

Mix in 1 bowl:
- 1/4 cup safflower oil
- 1 lemon rind, grated
- 1/2 cup water
- 1/2 cup buttermilk
- 1 Tbl. honey

In another bowl combine:
- 2 1/2 cups whole wheat pastry flour
- 1/4 cup currants
- 1/2 Tbl. caraway seeds
- 1/8 tsp. salt
- 1 tsp. baking soda

Combine liquid ingredients and dry ingredients separately, then mix together. Shape into 2 round loaves. This dough will be somewhat floppy, like very stiff cake dough, not a yeasted bread dough. If you flour your hands to shape the loaves, that will help. Place on oiled cookie sheet and bake at 325° for 60-65 minutes, until the center is firm to the touch.

Orange Surprise Bread

yield: 2 loaves

this makes wonderful toast!

1 cup warm water	1 Tbl. yeast
1/4 cup malt syrup	2 cups whole wheat flour

Combine malt syrup with water. Stir in yeast until dissolved. Beat flour in well, then let rise until doubled.

Soak 1/2 cup rolled oats in 1/2 cup water for 15 minutes.

juice and grated rind of 2 oranges
1 1/2 Tbl. poppy seeds
3/4 cup date pieces
2 1/3 cups whole wheat flour
3 Tbl. safflower oil
1/4 tsp. salt

Add soaked oats and remaining ingredients to the yeast sponge. Mix and knead well until the dough has a uniform feel. Let rise until doubled, punch down and shape into 2 loaves. Let rise in oiled bread pans. Bake for 45 minutes at 375°.

...WOW...

RICE POPPY SEED CAKE

no eggs
no wheat

2 x 8" pans
or 1 bundt pan

A particularly delicious moist cake. Just smelling it - especially warm from the oven - transports you back to some wonderful childhood memory. At least, thats how it affected the recipe testers.
See what it will do for you!

3/4 cup butter, melted or very soft

1 cup honey

4 Tbl. oil mixed with ⎱ = 4 eggs
4 Tbl. garbanzo flour ⎰

1 1/2 - 2 cups buttermilk

2 1/2 cups rice flour

2 tsp. baking powder

spices ⎰ 1 Tbl. cinnamon
      ⎱ 1 tsp. nutmeg
      ⎱ 1 tsp. cardamon

add last ⎰ 1 cup coconut
        ⎱ 1/4 cup poppy seeds
        ⎱ rind of lemon, grated
        ⎱ 2 tsp. vanilla

Cream butter and honey together. Add garbanzo/oil mixture and beat well. Combine flour, baking powder and spices. Add in stages to creamed mixture, alternating with buttermilk, stirring each time. Now add last 4 ingredients; stir in gently. Pour into oiled pans. Bake at 350° for 35 minutes (50-60 for bundt.).

BANANA
Muffins or Bread

12 muffins ✳ 2 small loaves

✳ "Umm, good!" The banana's sweetness really comes through.

Combine in one bowl:

1 lb. mashed banana
3 Tbl. buttermilk
1/2 cup honey
1/3 cup safflower oil
1/2 Tbl. vanilla
1/2 Tbl. lemon extract

In another bowl combine:

2 cups whole wheat pastry flour
2 tsp. baking soda
1/2 tsp. baking powder
1/8 tsp. salt

★ Add the flour mixture to the liquid ingredients.

★ Add 1/2 cup chopped walnuts.

★ Spoon into oiled muffin tins or small bread pans.

★ Bake at 350° for 30-45 minutes.

Apple Bran Muffins

nice and
moist

approx.
1 doz.

3/4 cup raisins
3/4 cup water
2 eggs
1/4 cup safflower oil
1/2 cup honey
1 1/2 Tbl. molasses
5 oz. buttermilk
1 large apple, chopped in small pieces

3/4 cup wheat bran
2 cups whole wheat pastry flour
1 heaping cup chopped walnuts
1 tsp. baking soda
1/2 Tbl. baking powder
2 tsp. cinnamon
1/4 tsp. ground cloves
1/4 tsp. nutmeg

Soak raisins in water. Beat eggs and then add oil, honey, molasses, buttermilk, apple pieces and raisins. In another bowl combine dry ingredients. Add contents of both bowls together, stir thoroughly and spoon into a well-oiled muffin tin (or paper muffin cups in a tin).

Bake at 350° for 30 minutes.
(20 minutes for mini muffins)

Raisin Bran Biscuits

YIELDS 1 DOZEN

1 cup raisins

Soak raisins in enough water to cover them, set aside.

Mix together:

3 Tbl. honey

2 Tbl. molasses

3/4 cup buttermilk

1 egg, beaten

3 Tbl. safflower oil

1 1/4 cup bran

In another bowl gather:

1 cup whole wheat pastry flour

1 Tbl. baking powder

1/8 tsp. salt

Drain raisins (this juice can be used for many other things like the water for your next bread!). Add raisins to liquid ingredients. Mix in dry ingredients. Spoon into papered muffin tins.

Bake at 350° for 25-30 minutes.

Ginger Snaps

Let them cool to get that real snap!

yield: 12-15

Cream Together:
1/4 lb. butter
1/2 cup molasses
1/2 cup honey

Mix and Add to the above:
2 cups whole wheat pastry flour
1 1/2 Tbl. ginger
1 tsp. cinnamon
1/4 tsp. ground cloves
1 2/3 tsp. baking powder
1/8 tsp. salt

Spoon onto an oiled cookie sheet.
Bake at 350° for 10-13 minutes.

Cranberry Muffins

makes 1 dozen muffins

1 beaten egg
7/8 cup honey
2 1/2 Tbl. safflower oil
juice & rind of 1 orange

2 1/4 cups whole wheat pastry flour
1 tsp. baking soda
1/2 Tbl. baking powder
1/4 tsp. salt
1 1/3 cups cranberries
3/4 cup raisins
1/3 cup walnuts

In a small bowl mix together wet ingredients. In a large bowl mix dry ingredients. Combine together only enough to moisten flour mixture. Pour into well-oiled muffin tins. Bake at 350° for 25-30 minutes.

Lots of fruits and nuts. If you like cranberries, you'll enjoy this one.

AUNTIE NUKE'S NUGGETS

Solar Power!

NO EGGS   proceeds to a non-nuclear future   NO DAIRY

Fans of this sweet rich cookie pay a higher price, which Uprisings donates to People Against Nuclear Power, a San Francisco anti-nuclear group.

5 dozen medium cookies

Dry:
1 Tbl nutritional yeast
1 cup chopped cashews
1 cup date pieces
1 cup shredded coconut
3⅝ cups w.w. pastry flour
1½ tsp baking powder

Wet:
2 cups maple syrup
1 Tbl vanilla
1 cup oil

Combine dry ingredients. Combine wet ingredients. Mix them together until batter has the consistency of thick peanut butter. Drop spoonfuls onto oiled cookie sheet. Bake at 325° for about 17 minutes. Cookies should be crispy.

Sesame Crunch Bars

makes about 30 2 inch squares.

use an 8" x 14" pan, or similar.

5/8 cup peanut butter
1 1/4 cups honey
2 tsp vanilla
1 1/4 cups oats
1 1/4 cups cashews
1 cup wheat germ
6 1/4 cups sesame seeds
5/8 cup sunflower seeds

Cream together peanut butter, honey and vanilla. Add the rest of the ingredients and mix well with your hands — it works best and saves on dishes. With wet hands or rolling pin, flatten mixture to uniform thickness on oiled pan. Dough will be stiff — be patient. Bake at 350° for about 25 minutes. Let cool.

~ no wheat ~

ALMOND RICE COOKIES

24 medium cookies

This recipe yields a soft and delicately-flavored cookie. Now popular at several other bakeries across the country!

1 cup butter
½ cup honey
2 eggs
1½ tsp almond extract
2 cups rice flour
2 cups finely chopped almonds

Let butter soften to room temperature.
Cream with honey, eggs and extract.
Mix in separate bowl flour and almonds.
Add to wet mixture, mix in. Scoop
small mounds onto baking sheet.
(Dough is fairly loose).
Bake at 325° for 12-15 minutes.
Cool before removing
from sheet.

Almond Date Granola

2 lbs.

1/2 cup molasses
2 Tbl. safflower oil
1 tsp. almond extract

~~~~~~~~

6 2/3 cups rolled oats (thick if possible)
3/4 cup wheat bran
2/3 cup sunflower seeds
2/3 cup almonds

~~~~~~~~

1/2 cup date pieces

Mix wet and dry ingredients separately and then combine. Spread on 2 cookie sheets and bake at 350° for 35 minutes. Turn every 10-12 minutes to keep mixture browning evenly. When cool, add date pieces.

Raisin Nut Granola

makes 2 lbs.

1/2 cup   molasses
1/3 cup   safflower oil
1 tsp.   vanilla
1/8 tsp.   salt

〰〰〰〰〰〰〰

5 3/4 cups rolled oats (thick cut, if available)
1/3 cup   peanuts
1/2 cup   sesame seeds
1/3 cup   cashews
3/4 cup   wheat bran
1/2 Tbl.   cinnamon

〰〰〰〰〰〰〰

1/4 lb. raisins (3/4 cup)

Mix wet and dry ingredients separately and then combine. Place mixture on two cookie sheets. Bake at 350° for 35 minutes. Turn every 10 - 12 minutes to keep the mixture browning evenly. Allow to cool and add raisins.

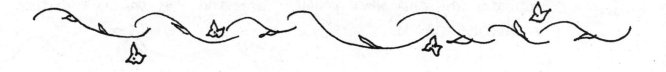

WILDFLOUR COMMUNITY BAKERY

Ann Arbor, Michigan

MILT KEMNITZ

Wildflour Community Bakery sits next to the 4th Ave. People's Food Coop, one block from Ann Arbor's colorful Farmer's Market. Wildflour is a whole grain, non-profit, co-operative bakery, managed by a collective of, currently six members. Decision-making is based on the consensus model.

There is little specialization of labor at Wildflour. Work shifts are shared equally (we all do some of the baking and some of the cleaning), other operational responsibilities are rotated.

However, Wildflour is more than a bakery managed by a production collective, it is a community bakery. People of all ages come to volunteer their labor in return for a discount, (which can be applied to all local food coops) and a "free" loaf of bread. These volunteers are an essential part of the bakery. The only machines we use are the mixer, oven and bread slicer. The bakery depends on people power to scoop its cookies, shape its dough and bag its bread.

Wildflour is also a co-operative. Although there is no official membership, input is sought from the community around the kneading table, in the store, and at Community Involvement Meetings, held every few months. At these meetings, repricing co-ordinator pay and other policies affecting the bakery's future are discussed. ☮

Going hand in hand with community involvement is Wildflour's concern with education. Since 1978 the bakery has sponsored its "Rolling-In-Dough" program, through which co-ordinators become guest teachers in Ann Arbor Elementary schools. Showing the students stalks of wheat, we talk about the relationship between the land, agriculture and a healthy society. Then, in small groups the children make bread on their desk tops. This brings up some of the dynamics of working collectively. Later, each child has her or his own bread sculpture, baked in the school ovens, to take home and enjoy.

The bakery also participates in the State and County Deferred Sentencing Program. This allows first offenders to erase their record by working a required number of hours at a non-profit organization of their choice. This often brings people to the bakery who have never been exposed to a democratic workplace or to whole grains. Time and again, the process of working in an atmosphere where people are enjoying themselves, and have control over their lives provides an enriching experience. Many people continue to volunteer at the bakery long after completing their hours.

We are also very fortunate to have a mill in Ann Arbor, The Daily Grind. The mill grinds organic grains, producing whole grain flours. Wildflour is committed to the use of organic produce and grains whenever possible. We understand the importance of organic farming as a key to the health and longevity of our Earth.

Since 1975 Wildflour has thrived on the loyal support of the Ann Arbor community. Our existence depends upon it. That is why at Wildflour, "Community" is our middle name. Join us in celebrating Wildflour's many years of community service. We know we only got here because we all worked together. In the years ahead, with all our efforts, we will continue to grow and work for the ideals that we all share.

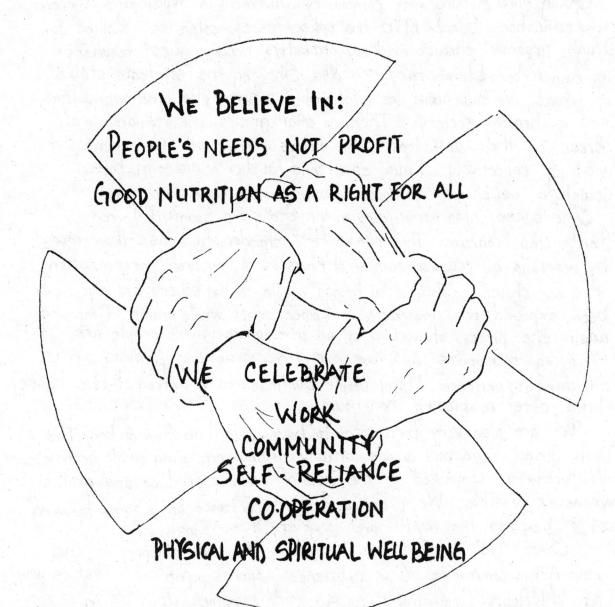

WE BELIEVE IN:

PEOPLE'S NEEDS NOT PROFIT

GOOD NUTRITION AS A RIGHT FOR ALL

WE CELEBRATE

WORK

COMMUNITY

SELF-RELIANCE

CO-OPERATION

PHYSICAL AND SPIRITUAL WELL BEING

We renew our commitment to a world community where education and work are productive and joyful; wealth and natural resources are shared by all, and all living things enjoy peace, harmony and freedom.

Sesame Sunflower Bread

Yields 2 Loaves

Proof
1 3/4 cups warm water
1 Tbl. yeast

Add and Let Rest
1 1/2 Tbl. barley malt
1/2 cup whole wheat hard flour

Mix In
3/4 Tbl. salt
2 Tbl. safflower oil
1 1/2 Tbl. soy flour

Knead In for 5 minutes
5-7 cups hard whole wheat flour

Keep Moist. Add:
2 Tbl. sesame seeds
2 Tbl. sunflower seeds

Knead well, let dough rise to double. Shape into loaves, and place in oiled pans, let double. Bake at 375° for 35-45 minutes.

Sour Dough Rye

YIELDS 2 LOAVES

MAKE 1 CUP RYE STARTER (see pg 127)

ADD and PROOF:
1 cup warm water
½ Tbl. yeast

MIX TOGETHER:
2 Tbl. honey
1 cup 'rye' meal
1 tsp. salt

KNEAD IN 2-4 cups hard whole wheat flour until firm but moist. Let rise to double.

SHAPE INTO LOAVES. Put dough in oiled pans, and let rise double again.

BAKE at 350°F for 35 minutes or at 375°F for 25 minutes.

Just Rye Bread   yields 2 loaves

A heavy bread that can be sliced
thinly once it cools...

Make 1 ½ cups rye starter the day before (see pg. 127)

The next day add:
  ¼ cup honey
  2 ½ cups water
  ¾ Tbl. salt

Knead in 2 - 3 ½ lbs rye flour (about 7 to 12 ¼ cups)

This will be a sticky dough. Think of it as clay.
Knead for 10 minutes if you can. Shape and let
rise to double. Bake at 350°F for 45 minutes

Seven Grain Bread
Yields 2 Loaves

This is an exciting loaf to bake, even for skilled bakers!
It needs a little preparation that can be done a day ahead.

Combine: ¼ c. cooked rice   (about 3 Tbl. raw)
    ⅓ c. cooked millet   (about 2 Tbl. raw)
    ⅓ c. cooked barley (about 2 Tbl. raw)
    these grains can be cooked together in one pot

Sponge: 1 ½ Tbl yeast
    2 c. warm water   } Mix and let rest
    3 c. hard ww flour   } 10 to 15 minutes
    1½ Tbl. molasses
    1 Tbl honey

Then Add: 1½ Tbl. safflower
    1 tsp. salt
    2 Tbl. vinegar
    ½ c. rye flour
    ¼ c. cornmeal

Work in · 3 c. hard w.w. flour
Knead until elastic, about 100 times. Finally add the cooked grains, cooled to at least room temperature. Knead till mixed in.

Place in an oiled bowl. Cover with a damp cloth. Let rise to double. Divide in 2 and shape into loaves. Place in oiled bread pans. Let rise to double. Bake at 350°F for 45 minutes, or until done.

Pecan Raisin Essene Rolls

A dairyless delight

1. <u>Soak</u> for 8 hours or more:
   2 lbs. Hard whole wheat berries
2. <u>Rinse</u> sprouts 2 or more times per day until the tails are 1½ times longer than the berries
3. <u>Skip</u> the last rinse before grinding the sprouts (or sprouts will make the dough too sticky & wet)
4. <u>Grind</u> the sprouts in a meat grinder, using the finest dye, or use a **Champion** juicer to homogenize sprouts.
5. <u>Knead</u> into the dough:
   2 cups raisins
   2 cups pecans
   Continue kneading, it will be <u>sticky</u>. Use a little water on your hands and counter to keep from sticking.
6. <u>Shape</u> into rolls and press a pecan in the center of each roll. Place on a greased cookie sheet.
7. <u>Bake</u> at 275°F for about 1 hour. The bottom should be browned and moist and spring back to the touch. These harden as they cool.

SESAME · OATMEAL ROLLS

It's hard to beat this one right out of the oven!

yields 24 rolls

Proof:
  1 Tbl. yeast
  2½ cups water

Add to make a sponge:
  2 cups oats
  1 cup honey
  1 cup hard whole wheat flour

Add in:
  1 Tbl. salt
  3 Tbl. oil

Keep dough a little sticky. Then add <u>1</u> cup sesame seeds. Knead well, and let dough double. Punch down, divide dough and shape into 24 rolls. Place on an oiled tray. Let rolls double in size, bake at 375° for 20 minutes.

Onion Rolls

dairyless / eggless

yields 1 dozen
large rolls

Sponge: ★★
- 1½ c. warm water
- 1 Tbl. yeast
- ¼ c. honey
- 2 c. hard whole wheat flour

Add and Knead briefly ★★★★
- 2 Tbl. safflower
- 1½ tsp. salt
- 1½ c. rye flour
- 2⅓ – 3 c. hard whole wheat flour (add as needed)
- 1 lb. fine chopped raw onions

As you add the onions, your dough will moisten up.
So, aim for a drier dough, it will make roll forming easier.

When ingredients are fully combined, place in an oiled bowl. let rise to slightly less than double, punch down.

Divide into 12 pieces and knead like bread dough, turning in sides, keeping one smooth surface down.

Dip the smoothest side into a little water, then into a bowl of poppy seeds.

Arrange on an oiled pan, poppy seed side up. Give them plenty of room to rise.

When they are not quite doubled, bake at 350°F for 30-40 minutes until browned on bottom.

Enjoy !

PIZZA

Yields 2, 12 inch
pizza pies

There are five basic steps to our pizza:

(1) Cheese grating, (2) Vegetable cutting, (3) tofu cooking (4) sauce
(5) Dough. You can cook the sauce a day ahead of time.
In fact tomato sauce, flavors are said to blossom with a day or two
of early preparation!

<u>The DOUGH</u> will take 45-60 min. so give yourself time

Sponge: 1½ c warm water

(MIX & SIT)
1 Tbl. honey
2 Tbl. yeast
2 c. hard whole wheat flour

ADD:
1 Tbl. oil (safflower)
¼ Tbl. salt
1 Tbl. oregano
½ tsp. cayenne
½ Tbl. basil

KNEAD IN: 1½ c. hard whole wheat flour, until elastic
This dough should not be quite as stiff as regular bread
dough. Set aside in an oiled bowl. Cover with a damp cloth.
Let double.

<u>Cheese Grating</u> - Grate a total of <u>1</u> lb. of cheese. We mix
mozzarella and provolone. Set aside.

Pizza con't.

Sauce

Whisk together:
- ½ cup water
- 1 Tbl. oregano
- 1 Tbl. basil
- 1 tsp. granulated garlic, or 3 cloves garlic, diced
- 1 tsp. granulated onion, or 1 small onion, diced
- 2 Tbl. honey
- 1 tsp. salt
- ¼ tsp. black pepper

Then add:
- 8 oz. tomato paste
- 18 oz. canned tomatoes

Whisk all together and cook on low heat until it bubbles.

Tofu

(Ah tofu!) Begin to sauté 1 onion & 3 cloves garlic. When they look a bit clear, add ½ lb. cubed tofu (add 1 lb. if you are a tofu fan). Add 2 Tbl. tamari, stir until tamari is absorbed. Take off heat and set aside.

Vegetables

Use what's in season! Generally we use:
- 1 green pepper diced
- 1 yam, diced and steamed
- ½ bunch broccoli, diced
- 1 small zucchini diced
- 1 small onion, diced

Set aside.

continued on next page...

Pizza con't.

<u>Begin</u> by dividing dough and all other ingredients in half.
 Roll out to a 12 inch round. Place on a pizza pan sprinkled
with cornmeal. Flute edge to keep filling in. Prick all over with
a fork and bake for 10 minutes at 350°.
 Cover with 1 c. sauce, spread evenly.
 Divide tofu and sprinkle evenly over pizza.
 Cover with diced vegetables, add cheese, and repeat for
 second pizza. Bake at 400° for 20 minutes or until golden on top.
As always, ENJOY THE FRUITS of YOUR LABOR!

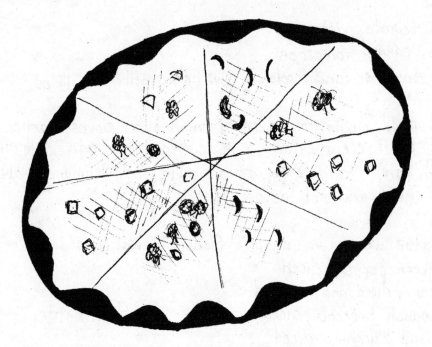

Honeyless Cake

The goodness of dates and fruit juice is all that's needed to sweeten this delicious cake.

Blend:
    <u>1</u> cup dates with 3/4 cup water (this will be <u>thick</u>)
Cream
    1/3 cup butter or margarine
Add the two above together and mix in:
    2 eggs
    1/2 cup fruit juice (such as apple or cherry)

Combine in another bowl:
    1 1/2 cups whole wheat pastry flour
    1/2 tsp. baking soda
    1/2 Tbl. baking powder
    1 Tbl. cinnamon
    1/2 tsp. nutmeg

Combine the liquid ingredients with the flour and spices, mixing gently. The batter should be a little stiff. Add 1/2 cup chopped walnuts. Pour batter into oiled 9" square pan. Bake at 350°F until firm, about 45 min.

APPLE MUFFINS
Makes 15 muffins

Mix together:
    3/4 cup safflower oil
    1¼ cups honey
    1¼ cups water

In another bowl combine:
    2 Tbl. arrowroot
    4 cups whole wheat pastry flour
    1½ Tbl. baking powder
    1 tsp. baking soda
    ½ tsp. salt
    1½ Tbl. cinnamon
    1 tsp. allspice

Combine liquid ingredients with flour and spices. If batter seems stiff, add ¼ cup water.

Add:
    2 cups finely diced organic apples
    1 cup chopped walnuts

Spoon into oiled muffins tins. Bake at 350°F for 35-40 minutes.

CHERRY MUFFINS
·MAKES 12 MUFFINS·

MIX WELL:
   1/2 cup safflower oil
   3/4 cup honey
   1 Tbl. lemon (juice and rind combined)
   2 cups chopped cherries
          (fresh or frozen)

ADD 2½ cups water

COMBINE IN ANOTHER BOWL:
   1 TBL. Arrowroot
   2 2/3 cups whole wheat pastry flour
   1 TBL. Baking powder
   1 TSP. Baking soda
   1/4 TSP Salt
   1 TBL Cinnamon

★ Combine liquid ingredients with dry. This will be a slightly stiff batter. Pour into oiled muffin tins.
★ Bake at 350°F for 35·45 minutes.

Peanut Butter Cake
A light and moist treat
Makes one 9" square cake

Cream Together:
- 1/2 cup peanut butter
- 1/3 cup butter
- 3/4 cup honey

Beat into Above Ingredients:
- 2 eggs
- 1 1/2 tsp. vanilla

Sift Together and Add Alternately with 1 cup Cold Water to above ingredients
- 2 cups soft whole wheat flour
- 1 tsp. baking powder
- 1 tsp salt
- 1/2 tsp cinnamon
- 1/4 cup milk powder

Pour into Oiled 9" Pan. Bake at 350°F for 45 minutes or until center springs back when touched. Take out of pan when cooled if you plan to frost it.

CAROB FROSTING   yield 2¼ cups

CREAM TOGETHER:
        1 cup peanut butter
        ½ cup butter
        ½ cup honey

ADD SLOWLY TO THE ABOVE INGREDIENTS:
        ½ cup carob powder, sifted
        1 Tbl. vanilla

BUTTERCREAM ICING   yield 3 cups

CREAM WITH A HAND MIXER:
        1 cup butter
        ¾ cup honey

ADD:

        3 Tbl. dry milk powder (non-instant works best)

SCRAPE BOTTOM OF BOWL AND MIX A LITTLE LONGER.

ADD SLOWLY (the pouring thickness of a pencil):
        1 cup whipping cream, cold (test to be sure it's
            sweet, not sour)

✱ IF you pour too quickly, the mixture gets lumpy. Don't worry just continue to mix it. When all ingredients are smooth, add 1 Tbl. vanilla. ✱

❋ FRUIT BARS ❋
wheat-free & dairyless

The Crust:

Mix together in the following order —
7/8 cup soy margarine
1/2 cup honey
— Mix above well — then add the next ingredients —
3 cups oats
2 3/8 cups oat flour

This will be quite sticky. Press firmly, 1/2 of this mixture, into a greased 8 × 8 pan. Reserve the remainder for the top.

Apple, Apricot-Peach, Date Fillings

Apple - 2 1/2 lbs diced apples
2 Tbl. cinnamon

A-P - 3 cups dried apricots } soaked
2 3/4 cups dried peaches } overnight
1 Tbl. cinnamon

Date - 3 1/2 cups pitted dates } soaked for
1 1/4 cups raisins } 1/2 hour
1 Tbl. cinnamon

Mix above for 5 minutes with an electric mixture on low.
Spread the filling over the bottom crust. Press remaining crust on top of filling
Bake at 350°F until golden (20 to 30 minutes)

Fresh Fruit Filling
For Fruit Bars

Use the simple crust recipe and fill with one of these fresh fruit fillings or any fruit in season.

Cook down fruit at low heat, so it won't burn. This may take an hour or so.

As fruit cooks down it makes its own juice. If your fruit is not juicy, as is the case with peaches sometimes, you may have to add 3/4 cup water or other juice to get the process going. When cooked fruit has produced about 3/4 cup of juice, drain off and <u>cool</u>. Add it to the arrowroot, stirring until all lumps are dissolved.

When fruit begins to boil, add the arrowroot mixture, keeping fruit boiling and stirring constantly. This will become cloudy and thicken immediately. When your mixture becomes clear, turn off the heat.

<u>Cherry</u> · Start with 2 1/4 lbs. pitted cherries. Add 1/2 Tbl. lemon juice and <u>1</u> Tbl. honey. Use 1/4 cup arrowroot.

<u>Peach</u> - Start with 2 1/2 lbs. diced peaches. Add 1/4 c. honey, and 1/4 cup arrowroot. Add 1/2 Tbl. cinnamon at end of cooking process.

<u>Blueberry</u> - Start with 2 1/4 lb. fresh blueberries. Use 1/4 c arrowroot.

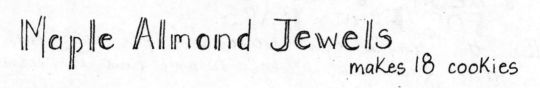

Maple Almond Jewels

makes 18 cookies

CREAM: ¾ cup **margarine**
½ cup maple syrup

ADD : <u>1</u> Tbl. vanilla
1 Tbl. almond extract

GATHER: 1 ¾ cups soft whole wheat flour
1 ¾ cups finely chopped almonds
½ tsp. baking powder

HAVE AVAILABLE : One whole almond for
each cookie

<u>Mix wet and dry</u> ingredients together. <u>Spoon onto</u> an oiled tray. These cookies will hold their shape. Place a whole almond on top of each cookie. <u>Bake at 350°F</u> for 25 minutes until the bottoms are golden brown.

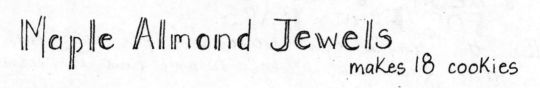

Peanut Butter Raisin Cookies
~ a chewy cookie that keeps well ~

makes 12 cookies

Cream:
- 1/3 cup margarine
- 1/3 cup peanut butter, organic if possible
- 1/3 cup honey
- 1/2 Tbl. vanilla

In another bowl combine:
- 1/2 cup whole wheat pastry flour
- 1/3 cup milk powder
- 1/4 tsp. baking powder
- 1/4 tsp. baking soda

Mix creamed ingredients with flour and milk powder. This will be somewhat sticky.

Add
- 3/4 cup rolled oats
- 3/4 cup raisins

Spoon onto an oiled cookie sheet and flatten with a fork. Bake at 325°F for 20-25 minutes, till edges brown. This cookie will brown quickly.

Variation: Carob Chippers
Replace 3/4 cup raisins with 3/4 cup carob chips. Yum!

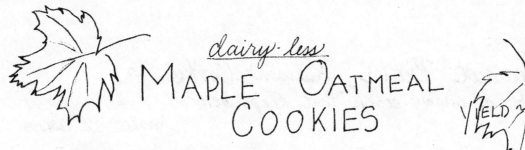

dairy-less

MAPLE OATMEAL COOKIES

YIELD: 24

CREAM TOGETHER WELL:
1 cup soybean margarine
1/3 cup maple syrup
1/3 cup honey
1 tsp. vanilla

ADD TO #1:
1 cup WW Pastry flour
1 cup walnuts
2 3/4 cups rolled oats

DROP BY ROUNDED TBL. ONTO A GREASED COOKIE SHEET. FLATTEN TO 1/2 INCH WITH A WET COOKIE PRESS (OR YOUR HAND!). BAKE AT 350°F FOR ABOUT 15 MINUTES, OR UNTIL GOLDEN BROWN.

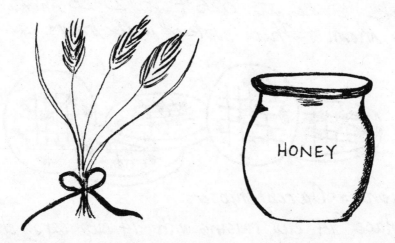

HONEY

Date Crunch

YIELD: 3½ lbs.

An amazing granola ; date sweetened, no oil, no wheat, no salt, no nuts, no dairy. Purely delicious.

3¼ Cups Date Pieces, or Pitted Dates   (1 lb)
1   cup Very Hot Water
9¼ cups Rolled Oats   (2 lbs)
1½ cups Sunflower Seeds   (½ lb)
¾ cups Sesame Seeds   (¼ lb)

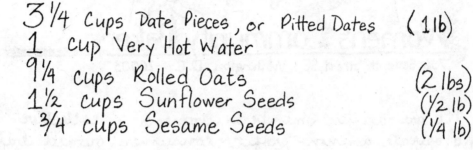

1. Combine dates with water, and let stand 'till dates are softened. Beat, blend or puree until a smooth butter is obtained.
2. Add oats, then seeds and stir gently until all coated.
3. Spread evenly on unoiled baking sheets - about ½ in. thick, just so you can't see the metal of the pans.
4. Bake at 350° for 20-25 minutes. When cooked, the surface is golden brown and a rich aroma is given off. It will be soft, but crisps as it cools.
5. Crunch can burn easily, so check during baking and rotate pans in case of darkening around edges.
6. Cool on sheets, then store in an airtight container or a plastic bag.

a not-for-profit collective

Women's Community Bakery

736 Seventh Street, SE   Washington, D.C.   20003

We are a ten member women's collective who operate a non-profit consumer owned bakery. Our aim is to provide good whole foods to people at the lowest possible prices. We place an emphasis on selling to consumer groups, food co-ops, and non-profit stores. We encourage people to organize with their co-workers in their apartment buildings and with their neighbors, to buy food collectibely at non-profit prices.

We choose to be a women's collective in order to provide opportunities for women to accept responsibility, develop self esteem, acquire business skills, learn to work co-operatively with other women, and to trust one another.

Being a women's group does not mean that we are separatists or sexists. We find roles for women in our society oppressive. We are trying to break out of those roles and to help others do the same.

Onion Rye Bread

Yielding
2 loaves

A favorite bread with
a wonderful blend of flavors

Dissolve: 1 Tbl. yeast in 1⅓ cups warm
water. Add 1½ Tbl. molasses and
1½ tsp. barley malt syrup. Mix in 1½
cups hard whole wheat flour. Let sit
until bubbly.

Mix in: 1½ Tbl. vinegar, 1½ Tbl. safflower
oil, ¼ cup buttermilk, 1 small onion that
is diced fine.

Then add: 1 tsp. salt, 2 tsp. caraway seeds,
2 cups whole rye flour.

Knead in: 2½ – 3 cups hard whole wheat
flour as needed to obtain a good springy
texture. This may take up to 10 minutes.

Let dough rise in a bowl until it
doubles. Punch down and shape into
2 round loaves. Place on oiled
sheets and let rise until it doubles
again.

Bake at 375° for 35-45 minutes

Warm Morning
Cinnamon Granola Bread
Yielding 2 loaves

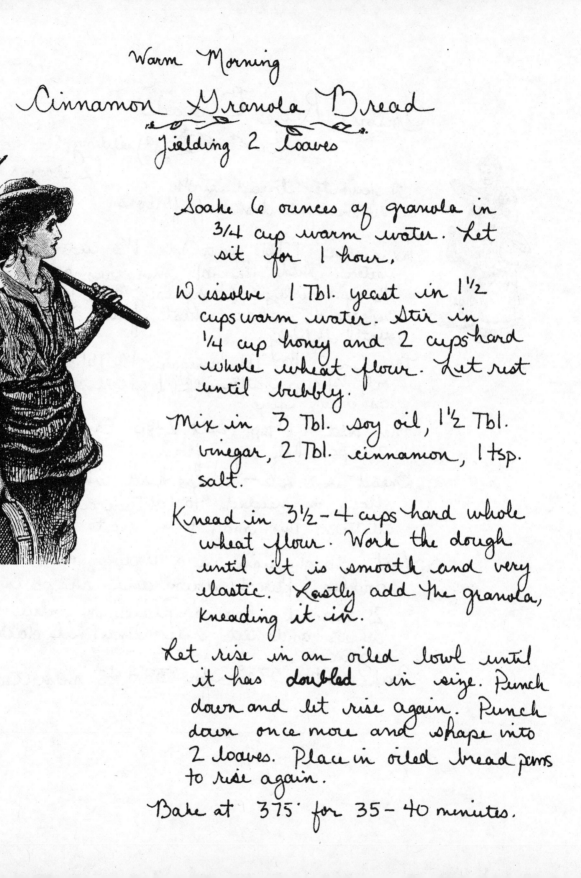

Soake 6 ounces of granola in 3/4 cup warm water. Let sit for 1 hour.

Dissolve 1 Tbl. yeast in 1½ cups warm water. Stir in ¼ cup honey and 2 cups hard whole wheat flour. Let rest until bubbly.

Mix in 3 Tbl. soy oil, 1½ Tbl. vinegar, 2 Tbl. cinnamon, 1 tsp. salt.

Knead in 3½-4 cups hard whole wheat flour. Work the dough until it is smooth and very elastic. Lastly add the granola, kneading it in.

Let rise in an oiled bowl until it has doubled in size. Punch down and let rise again. Punch down once more and shape into 2 loaves. Place in oiled bread pans to rise again.

Bake at 375° for 35-40 minutes.

Sandwich Rolls

Yielding 8 rich 5 oz. rolls

Plain

Mix together:
- 2 tsp. yeast
- ½ cup warm water
- 2 Tbl. honey
- 1 cup hard whole wheat flour

Let rest until it gets bubbly.

Add in:
- ½ cup milk
- 1 small egg
- 4 Tbl. soy oil
- 1 tsp. salt

Knead in until the dough is elastic:
- 2 – 2¼ cup hard whole wheat flour

Let rise in an oiled bowl until it is double in size. Divide in **8 pieces**. Shape into rolls. Brush the tops with egg wash or water and, if you'd like, dip them in poppy or sesame seeds. Let them rise in an oiled pan until puffy.

Onion

Combine:
- 1 chopped onion
- 1 clove garlic, crushed
- ½ tsp. rosemary
- 1 Tbl. poppy seeds
- Just enough oil to moisten

Mix ½ of this mixture in the above dough towards the end of the kneading. After shaping rolls smush the rest on top. Let rise.
Bake at 375° for 20 minutes.

Breakfast Bran Muffins

Yielding about 2 dozen
Very light, very good, not too sweet

Mix together thoroughly:

    ½ cup light oil
    2 eggs
    3 Tbl. molasses
    6 Tbl. honey
    3 cup water

Combine in a separate bowl:

    4 cups bran
    2½ cups whole wheat pastry flour
    3/4 cup milk powder
    1½ Tbl. baking powder
    1 cup currants or raisins

Combine wet and dry stirring just until the dry ingredients become wet.

Spoon into oiled muffin tins and bake at once.

Bake for 25 minutes at 400°

Cool a little before easing them out of the pan.

Oat Bran Muffins

Yielding about one dozen

Mix in a mixer until creamy:
- 1½ cups dates
- 2 cups water

Then add:
- ½ cup water
- ½ cup soy oil

Combine in another bowl:
- 1½ cups oat bran
- 2 cups brown rice flour
- 2 Tbl. flax meal (ground flax seed)
- 2 tsp. cardamom
- 1 tsp. salt
- 2 Tbl. baking powder

Combine both mixtures.

Spoon into well oiled muffin tins and bake at 350° for 25 minutes.

Holiday Fruit Cake

Yielding 1 cake

Even people who don't eat fruit cake, like ours.
We don't use any funny green things and of course
no white sugar. Try it! You'll be pleasantly surprised.

Mix together, one at a time, in this order:

    1/4 cup butter
    1/4 cup honey
    2 eggs
    2 tsp. black strap molasses
    1/4 cup buttermilk mixed with 2 Tbl. brandy

Combine dry ingredients in another bowl:

    1 2/3 cups whole wheat pastry flour
    3/4 tsp. baking powder
    1/2 cup dried, shredded, unsweetened coconut
    1 tsp. cinnamon
    1 tsp. nutmeg
    1 tsp. ground cloves
    1/4 tsp. allspice
    1 tsp. salt
    1 1/4 cups currants
    3/4 cup pecans
    1 cup dried, diced apricots
    1 cup dried, unsulphured apples
    3/4 cup dried unsulphured or sweetened and
        diced, pineapple

Mix everything together. Bake in buttered loaf pan at 250°
for 1 1/2 hours. Put a pan of water in oven to keep it moist.
Cool 10 minutes before removing from pan. Soak a cheese cloth in 1/4
cup brandy and wrap cake in it. Wrap in plastic to keep moist.

Cranberry Cake

Yielding 2 small loaves or 1 bundt cake
This batter also yields very tasty muffins

Mix together: ½ cup soy oil
2/3 cup honey

Add in : ¾ cup orange juice
4 eggs well beaten

Combine in another bowl: 3 cups whole wheat pastry flour
2 Tbl. milk powder
¾ tsp. salt
½ lb. cranberries
2 ½ tsp. baking powder
⅓ cup chopped walnuts

Combine the two mixtures.

Grease your pans and pour in batter.

Bake for 45-60 minutes at 350° (until a toothpick comes out clean).

Ding Wall's Delectable
Old Country Date Bars

Oil one 9 x 13 pan.   Pre-heat oven to 350°

Make crust of: 4 cups rolled oats
                  2 cups whole wheat pastry flour
                  1 cup light oil (safflower or sunflower)
                  ½ cup honey

Break up the oats with a rolling pin or in a blender. Add flour. Slowly pour in oil while mixing. Add honey and stir just a little more. Press firmly into oiled pan.

Make filling of: 4 cups of dates, packed firmly
                  1½ cups of hot water

Soak for 1-2 hours, then mash or blend into a paste. Spread on the crust.

Make topping of: ¼ cup crushed walnuts
                  ¼ cup honey
                  1½ cups coconut
                  1 cup egg whites (about 5)

Mix together lightly and spread over filling. Bake at 350° for 20-30 minutes.

Julia's Favorite
Raisin Oatmeal Cookies

Yielding about 40

Mix together:

> 1 cup light oil (like safflower or sunflower oil)
> 2/3 cup barley malt syrup
> 1/2 cup honey
> 2 tsp. vanilla
> 2 large eggs
> 1 tsp. almond extract

Combine in another bowl:

> 1/2 cup chopped walnuts
> 1/2 cup sunflower seeds
> 1 1/4 cups raisins
> 1 cup wheat germ
> 1/2 cup non-instant powdered milk
> 1 1/4 cups whole wheat pastry flour
> 2 cups rolled oats

Combine both mixtures. Add a little water if necessary to allow the batter to drop off your spoon.

Drop onto oiled cookie sheets. They will spread some so leave room for them to grow.

Bake for 25 minutes at 350°.

Yeast West Bakery

Buffalo, New York

Buffalo's only whole-grain bakery. 100% food. Everything on the ingredients label can be understood by any grade-school graduate. Real food. Real life. The folks in Buffalo just waking up might not know it yet — but if they eat our food, they're eating the best baked goods to be found here.

We are stable-grounded. We've got our own space near the Wonder Bread in all the major supermarkets. Wonder what makes those Wonder Breads tick?

This bakery is a home. There's someone doing something almost always. Alan even sleeps here if he gets too tired to bike home.

Meet the crew. Six men to five women.

Barry is the cave man. The technologically advanced kind. He does the numbers on the new computer. It's working. Barry's pushed a lot of good buttons since he's been here.

So-ten on the production crew — sexes balanced.

Kari + David are at the bakery convention in Washington. They call David "Mr. Science" because he reads a lot of facts. His spirit is super. Things run smoothly when he's in. I'm frozen in the middle of laughter until Kari comes back. She's a smile.

Tracy is amazing. 5'2" redhead. Does the work of an army in half the time. She streams out the coolest logic I've ever heard. Mary Ann comes in to whip us into shape. It's perfect because she's right, you know, and she smells good - patchouli. Johnny Felix - the marathon man. Everybody goes to Johnny with their questions. He fixes things. He has wisdom. Johnny puts on classical music on Fridays - he says it helps the sourdough magic.

Karen is an artist from New York. I don't know what she's doing here. She lives everywhere, really. All the time. But you're never sure where she is exactly. She's probably sitting next to you right now. She's doing space, man.

Rick makes the pizza sauce. He comes in even if he's not scheduled, just so he can make the sauce. He needs that sauce. It mellows him out. He's a clown. Kari + Rick perform for us. He's a smile, too.

Ethan Axelrod. Winner of the Most Suitable Last Name Award. He carries everything. His house is full of stuff, and I think twelve cats now. One intense dude. Laughs insanely, like you might worry. He thinks about kinship a lot.

Josh told me not to call her mom. We went swimming during the lunar eclipse and she hugged me until I stopped shivering. Sometimes she forgets she knows what she's doing, but she does.

They used to call me the Sheik of Sour. That's when I baked the sourdough bread. David calls me McGee. I am Michael and I love these people.

We get up at 5:00 a.m. because we live here. We sweat all morning, working hard because we bake the best bread in Buffalo. Real food for the sustenance of a healthy community.

We sell honesty in a loaf of bread, so this community (people) eats honesty for breakfast out of their toasters. We sleep well at night because we do a good deed daily, and it's tiring. But in these circumstances it feels good to be tired. This is our job, our gift. We must be here.

Hallelujah whole-grains and Happy Birthday
from Yeast West Bakery

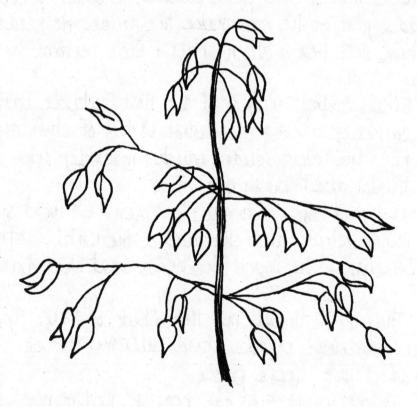

Sprouted 7-Grain Bread

Makes 2 loaves

Two days ahead, begin wheat sprouts by covering ½ cup hard wheat-berries in cold water. Drain that night. Rinse in the morning + again the next night. Let sit in a cool area until the following morning.

Blend in a blender: ½ cup water
 (til smooth and gooey)   2 Tbl. flax seed

Pour into a bowl and add: 1¼ cups warm water
                2 Tbl. barley malt
                ½ Tbl. yeast
Then add: 2 cups hard whole wheat flour
Whip with a spoon or whisk 100 times. Let rest 50 minutes.

Add to the sponge :   2 Tbl. oil
               1 Tbl. vinegar
               1 tsp. salt
Mix together, then knead in: 1½ cups hard whole wheat flour
                1 Tbl. soy flour
                2 Tbl. quick oats
                2 Tbl. rye flakes
                2 Tbl. cornmeal

Knead until dough is firm. Then mix in wheat sprouts. Let rise 1 hour. Divide in two; shape and place in oiled bread pans. Let rise to double. Bake at 375° for 35 minutes.

Buttermilk Dinner Rolls

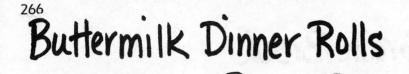

2 dozen rolls

These are light, delicious rolls – perfect for an elegant dinner or special company. For different shapes, see Rolls in How to Bake.

4 Tbl. honey 1½ cups buttermilk ½ cup butter	Combine buttermilk, butter and 4 Tbl. honey in saucepan. Heat gently until butter melts.
3/8 cup warm water 1 Tbl. yeast 1 Tbl. honey	Stir water and 1 Tbl. honey in bowl. Add yeast and let sit a few minutes to proof.
3 cups hard ww flour 2 cups ww pastry flour ½ tsp. salt 1 tsp. baking soda	Sift together the flours, salt + soda. Using large bowl, combine buttermilk mixture, foamy yeast water, and ½ of flour mixture. Beat well and let rise 30 minutes.

Add rest of flour mixture and knead until smooth. Let rise in oiled, covered bowl 30 minutes; punch down and shape the rolls. Allow to rise in oiled pan (covered) for 15 minutes, then bake at 400° for 20 min.

Vegetable Swirls

<u>DOUGH</u>   Mix: 2 Tbl. honey
                   1/2 cup water
                   1 tsp. yeast
             Let rest 5 minutes.

Mix: 1 egg
3 Tbl. oil
(your choice—
even olive oil)
Add to the yeast mixture.

Mix together: 1 tsp. salt
                 3 Tbl. milk powder
                 2 cups hard ww flour

Mix <u>all</u> together, adding: 1 small onion, diced
                             1 Tbl. poppy seeds
                             1/2 tsp. ground rosemary

This should be a soft bread dough.
Let rise one hour. Then roll into a rectangle about 12" x 4".

<u>FILLING</u>   Prepare 1 1/2 cups finely chopped veggies
(we use a combination of zucchini, carrots, onions, peppers
and celery, with a little garlic, marjoram, rosemary + black
                                     pepper)

Cover the dough rectangle with this veggie mixture. Roll into a log; pinch
ends together. Cut into 12 pieces; let rise on an oiled tray til puffy. (1 hour).
Bake at 350° for 35-45 min. Brush with melted garlic butter while warm.

Banana Rice Cupcakes
(wheat-free)

Makes 12 cupcakes

Cream: ½ cup butter
        ⅓ cup honey

Add: 1½ cups mashed bananas
     2 eggs, whipped   (the fluffier the eggs,
                       the fluffier the cake)

In another bowl, combine: 1¼ cups rice flour
                            ¼ tsp. salt
                            ½ Tbl. baking powder
                            ¼ cup chopped walnuts

Gently mix the flour + walnut mixture
with the creamed ingredients and bananas.
Spoon into oiled or papered muffin tins.
Bake at 350° for 35-45 minutes.

Apple Cake

2 - 9" round pans

Fruity, moist and fragrant, this cake was a big favorite with the recipe testers. Dot the top with a few pecans, walnuts or almonds, before baking, for a beautiful coffeecake.

½ lb. butter
1½ cups honey
5 eggs, beaten
3 Tbl. vanilla
1 cup yoghurt (or buttermilk)

Cream butter + honey together. Add beaten eggs, vanilla + yoghurt.

4½ cups whole wheat
        pastry flour
2 tsp. baking powder
2 tsp. baking soda
1 tsp. nutmeg
4 tsp. cinnamon
3½ cups chopped apples

Combine flour, powder, soda and spices in a separate, large bowl. Add the wet ingredients and the apples and stir in. Pour into greased pans at 350° for about 45 minutes or until a knife comes out clean.

Carrot Date Muffins

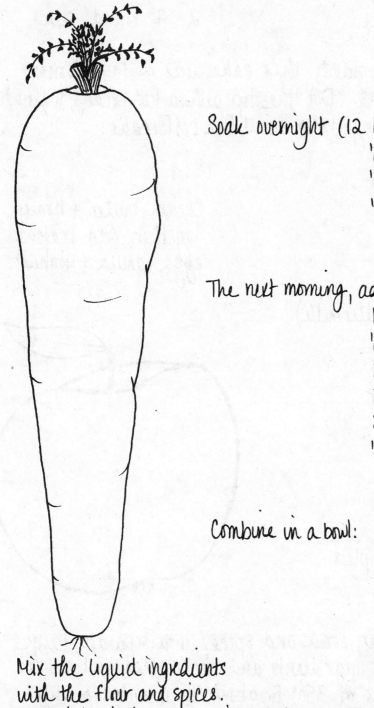

Makes 12 muffins

Soak overnight (12 hours):

- 1/3 cup water
- 1/4 cup chopped dates
- 1/4 cup rolled oats

The next morning, add:

- 1 cup grated carrots
- 1/3 cup safflower oil
- 2 Tbl. honey
- 2 Tbl. molasses
- 2 eggs, beaten
- 1/2 cup chopped walnuts

Combine in a bowl:

- 1 1/2 cups pastry flour
- 1 Tbl. baking powder
- 1 tsp. salt
- 1/4 tsp. nutmeg
- 1/2 Tbl. cinnamon
- 2 Tbl. powdered milk

Mix the liquid ingredients with the flour and spices.
Spoon into oiled muffin tins. Bake at 350° for 20 minutes.

Pecan Pie

Makes 1 - 8" pie

For the holiday season — sweet and chewy.

Filling   Mix until completely combined:
2/3 cup barley malt
1/3 cup molasses
2 eggs, whipped
1/2 tsp. vanilla
1/4 tsp. salt

Crust   Combine: 1 cup whole wheat pastry flour
pinch of salt

Cut in: 1/3 cup chilled butter
until lumps are quite small

Work in: about 1/4 cup chilled water
quickly and lightly

Roll out pie dough, place in pie tin, and flute edges.
Sprinkle 1 cup chopped p‑   nto shell. Pour the
filling over the nuts. P   for 45 minutes.
Top will be sticky

For a wonderful variation, subst‑   es for
1/2 cup pecans.

Ginger Cookies

about 3 dozen 3" cookies

ginger root

Just like Grandma used to make -- even better if you use freshly grated ginger. These cookies are quite sweet, however, and the amount of honey can be adjusted to suit individual tastes.

½ cup oil
½ cup molasses
1 egg, beaten
½ cup honey

1 tsp. cinnamon
1½ Tbl. dry ginger or
        3 Tbl. freshly grated ginger
2 tsp. baking soda
½ cup dry milk
¼ cup wheat germ
2 cups whole wheat flour

Combine wet ingredients in a medium bowl and mix well. In a separate, large bowl combine all dry ingredients and mix well. Pour the wet ingredients into the dry, and combine thoroughly -- but do not overmix. The resulting batter will be quite thick.

Drop by the spoonful onto a greased cookie sheet and bake at 350° for 15-20 minutes.

Oatmeal Sunflower Cookies

3 dozen 2"- 2½" cookies

Yeast West's trademark— one of our very first recipes

Mix together: ½ cup tahini
 ¼ cup water

Add, and mix well: ¾ cup safflower oil
 1 cup honey
 1 Tbl. lecithin
 2 tsp. vanilla
 ¼ tsp. almond extract

Mix together, and add
 to wet ingredients: 7 cups oats
 1½ cups sunflower seeds
 1 cup whole wheat flour
 ¾ tsp. nutmeg
 ¾ tsp. cinnamon
 ¼ tsp. allspice

Scoop or spoon cookies onto oiled cookie sheet and press with cookie press, jar lid or fingers. Bake at 350° for 20-25 minutes until brown. Let cool before taking off sheet.

Yeast West Familia

Makes about 10 cups or 2½ lbs.

A tasty mix. Vary the fruits and nuts as you like.
Good with milk, juice, or even water, say Yeast West.

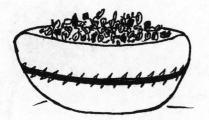

Heat oven to 350°.
Toast ①, ② and ③ on separate
cookie sheets until lightly browned
and smelling tasty.

①: 5 cups rolled oats
1 cup rye flakes
1 cup sunflower seeds
2 tsp. cinnamon

②: 1¼ cups wheatgerm

③: ¼ cup almonds
¼ cup cashews

When cooled mix all three together and add ④.

④: ¼ cup date pieces
½ cup raisins

Starting a Bakery

"The spiritual high is great. The conference has recharged my collective spirit and reaffirmed the purpose of continuing that spirit. The conference reaffirms the unity we have as one family to help, share, and give guidance to one another. We are a positive force in the struggle for unity of all peoples. A seed is planted each year at these conferences. Let us nourish these thoughts in a fertile collective environment so that existing collective bakeries may continue to exist and new ones may sprout."

(Thoughts on the 1981 CWGEA conference by a participating baker.)

One of the goals in writing **Uprisings** was to contribute to the growing consciousness about good food and self-reliance by encouraging people to bake for themselves at home. Another effect we hope for is that by conveying the unique satisfaction we get from being cooperative whole grain bakers, we may promote the establishment of more production collectives.

Every bakery in **Uprisings** has a different history. Many of the earlier ones grew out of the cooperative baking efforts of a few people, often involved with the local food coop. People who enjoyed baking their own whole grain bread at home found themselves being asked to bake for friends or coop members unable to obtain freshly-made natural baked goods anywhere else. From there on the scale of operations grew until a whole grain collective bakery evolved into being. Some of the more recent bakeries, on the other hand, have been founded specifically by people wishing to create a collective work environment and meet the growing demand for fresh, wholesome food. There are now many areas where the demand would easily support a locally-based baking collective. Instead, bread is shipped in from outside, usually from the larger companies in the "natural foods business."

Should the dream of starting a bakery be or become yours, we offer the following very basic suggestions, gleaned from our collective experience.

Contact or visit an existing whole grain collective bakery. We invite you to write to the Cooperative Whole Grain Educational Association with questions and requests for help. Attending a CWGEA conference will give you a wealth of information and inspiration.

Use cheap space to start with. If local codes about kitchen certification permit, bake at home. A common arrangement is to use the kitchen of a local restaurant, pizza place, or bakery during the hours when they are closed.

Develop a reliable, small selection of products at first. You may start by supplying the food coop and then be able to expand production. A few good wholesale accounts can keep a bakery going—for example, natural food stores, or a local restaurant with a steady order for rolls. You may also be able to sell directly to the public, for instance at farmers' markets. Getting your own storefront can be a goal reserved for the future.

You'll need some equipment. Bakeries have started production with not much more than bread pans and an oven, hand-mixing and kneading ten- or twenty-loaf batches. Pretty soon, though, a mixer becomes desirable. Most bakeries have a proof box, too, though you can manage without one, especially in a humid climate. You can build a proof box fairly easily. Good sources of used equipment are close-out sales of restaurants, pizza places, and bakeries. There are also some regional suppliers who accumulate such stock; check with the CWGEA or nearest bakery.

The operating details—everything from pricing to group process—won't be so important at first, but ultimately they can be crucial to your bakery's success or failure. Some basic guidelines can be obtained from the CWGEA or existing bakeries, and are quite simple to initiate. Meanwhile, common sense and respect for others will get you far. **Good luck and stay in touch!**

References

Ballentine, Rupert, M.D.: **Diet and Nutrition** (Himilayan International Institute, PA; 1979)

Blauer, Stephen: **Rejuvenation** (Green Grown Publications, P.O. Box 661, Santa Monica, CA 90406; 1980)

Brewster, Letitia & Michael Jacobson, Ph.D: **The Changing American Diet** (Center for Science in the Public Interest—see CSPI for address; 1978)

Brown, Edward Espe; **The Tassajara Bread Book** (Shambala Publications, Berkeley; 1970)

Center for Science in the Public Interest; **Midget Encyclopedia of Food and Nutrition**, and other publications, posters, etc. (1755 S Street NW, Washington, D.C. 20009)

Co-op Food Fact Sheets (Food Learning Center, [ACA Food Research Committee], 114½ East Second Street, Winona, MN 55987; and ICC Education Project, 953 Jenifer Street, Madison, WI 53703)

Dufty, William: **Sugar Blues** (Warner Books, NY; 1976)

East West Journal, Vol. 10, No. 4 (April 1979); (P.O. Box 970, Farmingdale, NY 11937)

Erewhon: **The Salt Story** and other informational leaflets (Erewhon, 8454 Stellar Drive, Culver City, CA 92030)

Essene Gospel of Peace of Jesus Christ, Book I, (International Biogenic Society, Apartado 372, Cartago, Costa Rica; 1978)

Gabel, Medard, with the World Game Laboratory: **Ho-Ping: Food for Everyone—Strategies to Eliminate Hunger of Spaceship Earth** (Anchor Press / Doubleday, NY; 1979)

Hightower, Jim: **Eat Your Heart Out: How Food Profiteers Victimize the Consumer** (Vintage Press, NY; 1976)

Hunter, Beatrice Trum: **Consumer Beware**, and other publications (Simon & Schuster, NY; 1971)

Institute for Food and Development Policy: several publications (see Lappe) and resource center on agriculture, world hunger, and social justice (IFDP, 2588 Mission St., San Fransisco, CA 94110)

Inter-Cooperative Council Education Project: see **Co-op Food Fact Sheets**

Jacobson, Michael, Ph.D: **Eater's Digest: The Consumer's Factbook of Food Additives** (Doubleday, NY; 1976)—available from CSPI.

Kervran, Louis C., Ph.D.: **Bread's Biological Transmutations** (Happiness Press, P.O. Box D.D., Magalia, CA 95954; 1978)

Kulvinskas, Viktoras, M.Sc: **Sprout for the Love of Everybody: Nutritional Evaluation of Sprouts and Grasses** (1978), **Survival into the 21st Century** (1981), and other publications (21st Century Publications, 401 N. Fourth St., P.O. Box 702, Fairfield, IA 52556)

Lappe, Frances Moore: **Diet for a Small Planet** (Ballantine Books, NY; 1982)

Lappe, Frances Moore & Joseph Collins: **Food First** (Ballantine Books, NY; 1978)

Leon County Food Coop: **Leon County Food Coop Cookbook** (Leon County Food Coop, 649 W. Gaines St., Tallahassee, FL 32304; 1979)

Lyons, Gracie: **Constructive Criticism** (Issues in Radical Therapy, P.O. Box 5039, Berkeley, CA 94705; 1976)

Morgan, Dan: **The Merchants of Grain** (Penguin; 1980)

National Nutritional Food Association: leaflets, information and movie for loan on School Lunches and Nutritional Education in Schools, including details of the pioneering Fulton County, Georgia's, Nutra School Lunch Program (NNFA, 7727 South Painter Ave., Whittier, CA 90602)

Organic Gardening Magazine (Rodale Press, Inc., 33 E. Minor St., Emmaus, PA 18049)

Phillips, David A.: **From Soil to Psyche** (Woodbridge Press, CA; 1977)

Robertson, Laurel, Carol Flinders, & Brian Ruppenthal: **The New Laurel's Kitchen** (Ten Speed Press, CA; 1986)

Robertson, Laurel: **Laurel's Kitchen Bread Book** (1984)

Saratoga Community Garden: **Newsletter No. 19** (Summer 1982) on amaranth (Saratoga, CA 95070)

Sekules, Veronica: **Friends of the Earth Cook Book** (Penguin; 1980)

9780913990704

Senate Select Committee on Nutrition and Human Needs: *Dietary Goals for the United States* (Government Printing Office, Washington, D.C.; 1977)

Simon, Arthur: *Bread for the World* (Paulist Press, 400 Sette Drive, Paramus, NJ 07652; 1975)

Sproutletter, The (P.O. Box 10985, Eugene, OR 97440)

U.S.D.A: *Agricultural Handbook No.8: Composition of Foods* (US Dept of Agriculture, D.C.; 1975)

Wigmore, Ann, D.D.: Why Suffer?, Naturama Living Textbook, and other publications (Rising Sun Publications, Boston; 1976)

Yudkin, John, M.D.: *Sweet and Dangerous* (Bantam Books, NY; 1973) 1978)

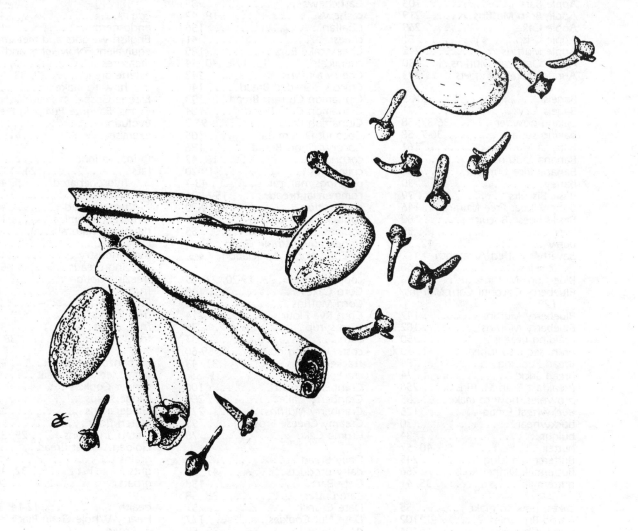

Index

Recipes by Type of Baked Good

Recipes by Special Dietary Characteristic

No Eggs or Dairy

(Since most bread, rolls, and granolas contain no eggs or dairy, they are not listed here.)

Almond Muffins.......... 117
Alternate Oatmeal Cookies. 107
Apple Muffins 242
Banana Muffins 161
Blueberry Muffins 147
Carrot Cake 145
Fruit Bars.............. 246-7
Jam Rolls 165
Maple Oatmeal Cookies ... 250
Non-Dairy Basic Bran Muffins 116
Non-dairy Frosting........ 119
Oat Cookies 153
Oatmeal Sunflower Cookies 273
Parsnip Cake 144
Peanut Butter Crunchies ... 167
Pumpcorn Muffins 114
Pumpkin Bars 118
Sunnyseed Cookies 166

No Eggs
(but contains Dairy)

Almond Muffins.......... 117
Almond Yogurt Coffeecake. 185
Alternate Oatmeal Cookies. 107
Apple Bars 103
Apple Crisp 81
Apple Muffins 242
Banana Muffins 218
Beverly's Puffed Amaranth Cookies
.... 168
Blueberry Muffins 147
Blueberry Muffins 182
Carob Nut Brownies 195
Carrot Cake 145
Coconut Short Bread 186
Crumb Cake 78
Eggless Whole Wheat Bagels 112
Fruit Bars.............. 246-7
Gingersnaps 221
Jam Rolls 165
Jammies 87
Maple Almond Jewels 248
Maple Oatmeal Cookies ... 250
Non-Dairy Basic Bran Muffins 116
Non-dairy Frosting........ 119
Oat Bran Muffins......... 257
Oat Cookies 153
Oaties 86

Oatmeal Sunflower Cookies 273
Parsnip Cake 144
Peachy Keen Pie 83
Peanut Butter Crunchies ... 167
Peanut Butter Raisin Cookies 249
Pecan Sandies 190
Pumpcorn Muffins 114
Pumpkin Bars 118
Rice Poppy Seed Cake 217
Rugelach................ 108
Sunnyseed Cookies 166
Veggie Cheese Stuffed Bagels...
110-1

No Dairy Products
(but contains Eggs)

Almond Muffins.......... 117
Alternate Oatmeal Cookies. 107
Apple Muffins 242
Apple Oat-Bran Muffins ... 130
Banana Muffins 161
Blue Corn Muffins 93
Blueberry Muffins 147
Carrot Cake 145
Carrot Muffins 175
Carrot Muffins 95
Cranberry Muffins 222
Dingwall's Delectable Old Country
Date Bars............. 260
Fruit Bars.............. 246-7
Gingersnaps 131
Jam Rolls 165
Maple Oatmeal Cookies ... 250
Non-Dairy Basic Bran Muffins 116
Non-dairy Frosting........ 119
Oat Bran Muffins......... 187
Oat Cookies 153
Oatmeal Sunflower Cookies 273
Parsnip Cake 144
Peanut Butter Crunchies ... 167
Pumpcorn Muffins 114
Pumpkin Bars 118
Sunnyseed Cookies 166
Tofu-Carob Frosting....... 197

No Wheat

Almond Rice Cookies...... 225
Banana Rice Cupcakes..... 268
Basic Wheat Free Muffins .. 146
Carrot Muffins 95
Corn Cakes 148
Date Bars 188

Date Crunch 251
Honey-Rye Cakes......... 149
Just Rye Bread 233
Krunch Bars 179
Maple Nut Granola 180
100% Rye Bread 143
Peanut Butter Cookies..... 152
Peanut Minus Cookies..... 135
Rice Poppy Seed Cake 217

No Sweetener, or
Fruit-sweetened

Buckwheat Bread......... 125
Cashchews 85
Crumb Cake 78
Date Crunch 251
Honey-less Cake 241
Pecan Raisin Essene Rolls .. 235
Pita 157
Potato Buttermilk Bread 90
Sourdough Bread......... 126
Sourdough Pumpernickel . 202-3
Whole Wheat Bread 122
Yeast West Familia 275

Low- or No-Fat

Bagels 71
Bread Pudding 84
Bread Sticks 74
Buckwheat Bread......... 125
Eggless Whole Wheat Bagels 112
Golden Wheat Bread 70
Just Rye Bread 233
Oat Bran Muffins......... 187
Potato Buttermilk Bread 90
Russian Rye Bread 174
Sour Dough Rye 232
Sprouted 7-Grain Bread.... 265

No Baking

(May involve pre-heating or toasting)

Carob Nut Bars 134
Cashchews 85
Peanut Butter No-Bakes.... 169

No Salt, or Optional Salt

(Salt is in fact optional in all recipes; "goodie" recipes contain no salt, and are not listed here.)

Recipes by Major Ingredients

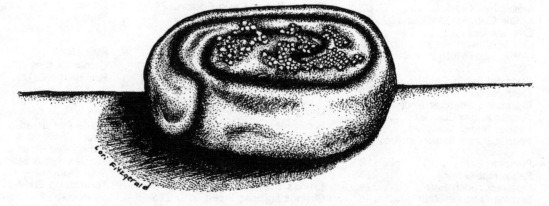